D1231052

Kiss the Blood
Off My Hands

Kiss the Blood Off My Hands

On Classic Film Noir

Edited By
ROBERT MIKLITSCH

UNIVERSITY OF ILLINOIS PRESS
Urbana, Chicago, and Springfield

Library of Congress Cataloging-in-Publication Data
Kiss the blood off my hands : on classic film noir /
edited by Robert Miklitsch.
p.   cm.
Includes bibliographical references and index.
ISBN 978-0-252-03859-4 (cloth : alk. paper) —
ISBN 978-0-252-08018-0 (pbk. : alk. paper) —
ISBN 978-0-252-09651-8
1. Film noir—History and criticism. I. Miklitsch,
Robert, 1953- editor of compilation.
PN1995.9.F54K58   2014
791.43'61—dc23   2014004931

publication supported by
Figure Foundation
black & white & gray:
night & day & take

In memory of the populist spirit of Roger Ebert, who was born and bred in Urbana and graduated from the Department of English at the University of Illinois at Urbana-Champaign

Contents

Acknowledgments

To begin the beguine, I want to acknowledge Danny Nasset, who's been a model of forbearance and good cheer. I count myself lucky to have such a genial editor. Special thanks to the following people at Illinois for their help: Dawn Durante with digital illustrations, Kevin Cunningham with the marketing copy, Matt Mitchell with copyediting, Dustin Hubbart with the cover design, and, in particular, Tad Ringo with production. Since the peregrination of this book has been—like, I imagine, a lot of collections—a "long strange trip," I'm grateful to all the contributors for staying the course, especially Julie Grossman, who's been a steadying correspondent, and Mark Osteen, who, among his many talents, plays the saxophone and composes noir-spiked jazz. I also want to hail Ann Douglas, a fellow traveler whose ethos and writing on classic noir have been a real inspiration. I remain very appreciative of Sherrie Gradin, the chair of the English Department at Ohio University, as well as Dr. Brian McCarthy in the College of Arts and Sciences and the Office for Research and Sponsored Programs for partial funding for this project. Grazie to Daryl Malarry Davidson, a real film buff, for reading my contributions to the volume. Most of all, I owe an unpayable debt of gratitude to my partner, Jessica "Jayne" Burchard, who not only shares my passion for "true crime" TV—not *X*- but *Forensic Files*, a.k.a. *Mystery Detectives*!—but who has been incredibly solicitous about my obsession, sometimes magnificent, sometimes mundane, about this thing called noir.

Preface

Noir Futures

"It's a Bright Guilty World"

Despite the rapidly growing body of literature on film noir, there is no state-of-the-art collection on the classical period. The last collection devoted strictly to classic noir—*Perspectives on Film Noir,* edited by R. Barton Palmer—appeared well over a decade ago. Moreover, even though the canon continues to evolve and the genre as a whole now spans a period of more than seventy years, recent anthologies tend to address both classic *and* neo-noir—a well-nigh impossible task.

Kiss the Blood Off My Hands—the lurid, B-movie title of which is borrowed from Norman Foster's 1948 film starring Burt Lancaster and Joan Fontaine—argues that it's past time for a collection that confines itself to the extraordinary scope and depth, the embarrassment of riches, of classic noir. These riches suggest that film noir is an altogether different and stranger creature than has heretofore been imagined. The "classic" take on the genre has been that it's composed of "gritty," black-and-white pictures set in dark alleys and on neon-splashed streets frequented by dangerous dames and tough-talking men. While this stereotypical scenario is not without resonance, what recent critics have discovered through rescreening the films, revisiting the archive, and reconsidering such issues as the role of women or Jewish directors, sound design or "blackout" production practices, is that film noir is other than itself—which is to say, not so classic.

Just as the meaning of classic noir continues to change, its audience continues to expand, becoming more global as well as more diverse. As the recent spate of books on "women in noir" indicates, more women are teaching and writing about the genre than ever before, and young people are being targeted by the video industry. For instance, in March 2012 *L.A. Noire,* designed by Team Bondi in consultation with Rockstar Games and released on Xbox 360 and PlayStation3, became the first video game to premiere at the Tribeca Film Festival. Set in a scrupulously re-created Los Angeles circa 1947 courtesy of Depth Analysis's cutting-edge MotionScan and Lightsprint's "realtime global illumination" technology, *L.A. Noire,* not unlike Robert Montgomery's audacious experiment in first-person point of view, *Lady in the Lake* (1947), invites us to play along with World War II hero Cole Phelps ("search for clues, chase down suspects, and interrogate witnesses") as he rises through the ranks from beat cop to arson detective in the City of Angels.

The world of video games is not the only place where classic noir can be found. Other noir-inflected venues include music (for example, Noir Music, "one of the most successful, credible, and forward thinking imprints on the market" [www.noir-music.com]), fashion (Bottega Veneta's noir-inspired fall/winter 2013 menswear collection), television (TNT's *Mob City* [2013], HBO's *True Detective* [2014]), and DVD boxed sets (*Best of Film Noir,* vols. 1 and 2 [2013], *Columbia Pictures Film Noir Classics,* vol. 4 [2013]). Classic noir is also alive and well on the Web in the form of sites like Noir Nation, All Things Noir, and Film Noir of the Week. (See the annotated list of online noir sites at the back of this book.) In sum, if the above evidence is any indication (corpus delicti?), the future of classic noir is very bright indeed.

Preview

The body of *Kiss the Blood Off My Hands* is composed of ten chapters, a chronologically sequenced "bibliography" of the critical literature on the subject, and an appendix on "Classic Noir on the Net."

The first set of chapters examines the representation of gender, genre, and race in classic noir.

The problem of femininity and film noir has intrigued critics since the publication of E. Ann Kaplan's *Women in Film Noir* in 1978. In the past, the emphasis in feminist criticism has been, as in Kaplan's collection, on the traditional construction of women in classic noir, but scholars have begun to reinspect the representation of female characters in the genre. Philippa Gates's *Detecting Women* (2011) focuses on the female detective in classical Hollywood cinema from the 1930s to the present. At the heart of this history is the transition from the '30s "girl reporter" to the '40s female sleuth. In her contribution to this book, "Independence Unpunished: The Female Detective in Classic Film Noir," Gates returns to this contested terrain to investigate the way in which the 1940s female "private eye" complicates the conventional, dualistic representation of women in classic noir as either—according to Janey Place in her now canonical article—homemaker or femme fatale, "redeemer" or "destroyer."

If, as Gates contends, a number of '40s Hollywood films can be viewed as noirs and melodramas, in "Women and Film Noir: Pulp Fiction and the Woman's Picture" Julie Grossman, whose *Rethinking the Femme Fatale in Film Noir* (2009) offers an in-depth study of the figure of the femme fatale, pursues a different tack, exploring the affiliation between classic noir and female-authored pulp fiction. Whereas Gates entertains the merits of what she calls the "maritorious" melodrama, in which the female protagonist is excessively devoted to her husband (rather than, as in the "maternal" melo-drama, her daughter), Grossman elucidates how canonical noirs such as Otto Preminger's *Laura* (1944) and Nicholas Ray's *In a Lonely Place* (1950) drama-tize the oppressive character of the dominant masculine culture of the time, rearticulating the female-centered concerns of the original source material, Vera Caspary's *Laura* (1942) and Dorothy Hughes's *In a Lonely Place* (1947).

Just as the issue of gender has generated new, provocative interpreta-tions of film noir, the issue of race has provided a unique lens with which to review its classical legacy. In "The Whiteness of Film Noir" (1997), Eric Lott persuasively makes the case that the marginalization of African Ameri-can characters in "white" noir narratives exposes the racial unconscious of the genre understood as "black film." In "The Vanishing Love Song in Film Noir," Krin Gabbard draws on his own earlier work in *Black Magic* (2004) to meditate on the sort of racial contradictions engendered by the presence of African American musicians in Jacques Tourneur's *Out of the Past* and Fritz Lang's *The Blue Gardenia* (1953). For Gabbard, the title song in *The Blue Gardenia* sheds light on a problem common to Tourneur's and Lang's film: the subtextual association of black musical performance with the dark side of the human psyche. In other words, if the Harlem jazz scene in *Out of the Past* presages the materialization of the "black widow," Kathie Moffat (Jane Greer), Nat King Cole's rendition of "Blue Gardenia" musically implicates the "wrong woman," Norah Larkin (Anne Baxter), and, by extension, the real culprit, Rose Miller (Ruth Storey). As a result, diegetic black music in both films acts as the c(l)ue to the "mystery," a stereotypical one that speaks volumes about the intimate, fraught connection between classic noir and black popular-musical performance.

Music in classic noir has been a topic of interest for some time (see, for example, Robert Porfirio's "Dark Jazz" [1979]), but with the efflorescence of film-sound studies, attention to the genre's sonic or acoustic dimension has waxed accordingly. Neil Verma's "Radio, Film Noir, and the Aesthetics of Auditory Spectacle" makes a substantial contribution to this emergent field, bringing history and theory to bear on its topic: the elective affinity between

1940s radio and cinema. For Verma, the act of audition is crucial to understanding how 1940s audiences experienced film noir, attuned as they were to the "picturesque" modes of listening activated by the medium of radio. In this "golden age," which Verma traces in his *Theatre of the Mind* (2012), offscreen space possesses a determinate dramaturgical valence, instituting an aural "theater" that dynamically interacts with the black-and-white images on the "big screen."

The locution "Disney noir" is, on the face of it, an oxymoron. Although there are notable examples of noir animation (see, for instance, the animated black panthers in the dream sequence in Jacques Tourneur's *Cat People* [1943]), the "wonderful world" of Disney appears to be diametrically opposed to the disenchanted, down-and-out world of film noir. Yet as J. P. Telotte details in "Disney Noir: 'Just Drawn That Way,'" the impact of the noir aesthetic—say, the fantastically intricate plotting that he analyzes in *Voices in the Dark* (1998)—is conspicuous in a series of Donald Duck cartoons produced by the Disney studio in the 1940s. In these surprisingly dark cartoons, Donald Duck becomes an animated double of the doomed antihero of classic noir, a characterization that effectively skewers Uncle Walt's vaunted All-American vision of the postwar period.

While critics have regularly remarked upon the economic rationale for expressionist devices such as canted compositions and low-key, chiaroscuro cinematography, the recourse to other cost-saving techniques such as rear-screen projection has been consistently glossed over, despite their obvious indispensability to the B movie. In "*Detour*: Driving in a Back Projection, or Forestalled by Film Noir," Vivian Sobchack contends that rear-screen projection in Edgar Ulmer's *Detour* (1945) is just as critical to the film's audiovisual economy as voiceover and flashback. Not unlike the radiophonic "theater of the mind" projected, according to Verma, by the 1940s noir sound track, rear-screen projection acts as a secondary screen for the protagonist's psyche. In *Detour*, this oneiric screen, in addition to mobilizing two of the dominant affective modalities of classic noir—claustrophobia and phantasmagoria—operates as a temporal signpost. The result is that even as Al Roberts (Tom Neal), driven by the romance of the open road, strikes out for California, the back-screen projection is a constant reminder that the past can rear up at any moment and dash his dreams.

It's widely recognized that film noir is a function, as in *Detour*, of budgetary restrictions associated with "Poverty Row" studios, but it's now clear that individual producers also played an important role in the formation of the so-called noir style. For example, Fritz Lang made *Scarlet Street* (1945) for Diana Productions, which was formed by Lang, the independent producer Walter Wanger, and his wife, Joan Bennett, and Louis de Rochemont collaborated with Henry Hathaway at Twentieth Century-Fox on a number of seminal semidocumentary noirs such as *The House on 92nd Street* (1945), *Kiss of Death* (1947), and *Call Northside 777* (1948). In "Producing Noir," Andrew Spicer concentrates on three prominent noir figures, Jerry Wald, Adrian Scott, and Mark Hellinger—the "pragmatist," the "ideologue," and the "realist," respectively—each of whom, as these capsule characterizations index, significantly impacted the development of classic noir as a creative and commercial production cycle.

The critical consensus has been that film noir as a creative and commercial cycle began to enter its final, "decadent" phase in the late 1940s or early 1950s. For example, in *A Panorama of American Film Noir*, Raymond Borde and Étienne Chaumeton assert that "from 1949 on, the career of the noir genre, properly called, comes to an end." A serious reconsideration of 1950s noir suggests, however, that the authors may have been too close to their subject to be objective about its historical termination. (*A Panorama of American Film Noir* appeared in 1955.)

The impact of McCarthyism and the House Un-American Activities Committee on Hollywood has been well documented. Less publicized has been the afterlife of certain blacklisted American directors. In "Refuge England," Robert Murphy traces the contributions of four directors to 1950s British noir: Edward Dmytryk, Jules Dassin, Cy Endfield, and Joseph Losey. While Dmytryk and Dassin found success in the United States in the 1940s with a series of classic noirs, after being blacklisted, both directors were forced to expatriate to Great Britain where they helmed pictures inspired by specifically British elements—the serial killer John George Haigh in Dmytryk's *Obsession/The Hidden Room* (1949) and postwar, bombed-out London in Dassin's *Night and the City* (1950). Unlike Dmytryk, who eventually recanted, and Dassin, who proceeded to France to make *Rififi* (1955), Endfield and Losey sought political refuge in England for an extended period in the 1950s, during which "scoundrel time" they made a number of "noir-inflected melodramas" such as *The Limping Man* (1953) and *Time without Pity* (1957) that, in retrospect, brilliantly capture the haunted psyches of these exiled American filmmakers.

The impact of expatriate blacklisted American directors on British film noir is a heretofore hidden facet of the second phase of the genre. Another occluded aspect of 1950s noir is the noir-gangster film. The '50s heist picture, itself a subgenre of '50s gangster noir, can be said to have been kicked off by John Huston's *Asphalt Jungle* (1950) which, as Mark Osteen argues in "A Little Larceny: Labor, Leisure, and Loyalty in the '50s Noir Heist Film," is symptomatic of the sea change that classic noir was undergoing at the time. In Huston's film, the criminal gang resembles nothing so much as a corporation that mimics the increasing organization and alienation of the "age of anxiety."

Subsequent noir heist films elaborate on this topic, dramatizing the conflict between the individual and the crime syndicate. In these "capers," the "foot soldier" frequently finds himself caught between the police and the boss, the Law and "Murder, Inc.," a dire predicament where, as always seems to be the case in the overdetermined universe of classic noir, there's no way out.

No Way Out is the title of a 1950 film noir directed by Joseph Mankiewicz starring Sidney Poitier and Richard Widmark. (It's also the title of a 1987 neo-noir based not on the 1950 film but *The Big Clock* [1947].) Mankiewicz's *No Way Out* is noteworthy not simply because it illustrates the explicit influence of new, explosive elements like race on the evolution of the genre, but because, like Robert Wise's *Odds against Tomorrow* (1959), it revises the received, rise-and-fall narrative of the classical period.

In "Periodizing Classic Noir: From *Stranger on the Third Floor* to the 'Thrillers of Tomorrow,'" I essay to map the history of classic noir by reflecting on the way in which the genre has been discursively constituted via its beginnings and endings, an act of periodization that typically entails nominating particular films as the first and last noir in order to differentiate the intervening films from, respectively, proto- and neo-noir. While the recent critical interest in *Stranger on the Third Floor* (1940) is one sign that Boris Ingster's film has supplanted *The Maltese Falcon* (1941) as the first, titular American noir, recent transnational readings of the genre have problematized the reflexive determination of classic noir as a strictly American phenomenon. In fact, the impact of *Odds against Tomorrow* on transnational neo-noir indicates that the end or terminus of the classical era is just as provisional—just as open to interpretation and, therefore, revision—as its origin.

Kiss the Blood
Off My Hands

Introduction

Back to Black

"Crime Melodrama," Docu-Melo-Noir, and the "Red Menace" Film

Player 4 (draws film noir)
Cut to rundown part of city where
detective Beaugars and his sultry secretary
are solicited to find Gilbert and the hollow
statue in which he hides his cash.
    —Rick Altman, "The Genre-Mixing
        Game"

Black, black, black, black, black, black,
black
I go back to
I go back to
    —Amy Winehouse, "Back to Black"

Film noir is, as Marx says of the commodity, a queer thing. As daunting as it is to define its generic essence, it is almost equally daunting, as I argue in the concluding essay in this volume, to determine its origins. The critical consensus has been that whether one dates its advent from 1940 (*Stranger on the Third Floor*) or 1941 (*The Maltese Falcon*), the classical period begins to flower in 1944 with *Laura, Double Indemnity, Murder, My Sweet,* and *The Woman in the Window,* reaching its full "evil" bloom in 1947 with Jacques Tourneur's *Out of the Past.*

I echo Charles Baudelaire's *Les Fleurs du mal* here for two reasons. First, because film noir has a French provenance. As James Naremore writes in his introduction to the English translation of Raymond Borde and Étienne Chaumeton's *Panorama du film noir américain*, "[T]he first book ever written about a type of film for which Hollywood itself had no name, *Panorama* influenced cineastes of the late twentieth century in almost the same way as Charles Baudelaire's essays on Edgar Allen Poe influenced the literary world of the late nineteenth century."[1] The second reason for the allusion to Baudelaire's book of poems is that *Kiss the Blood Off My Hands* is an anthology. While it is a "collection" of essays, not poems or flowers, "anthology" is the right word (*le mot juste*?) insofar as this volume is not organized around a central idea or topic. In this sense, *Kiss the Blood Off My Hands* is part of the recent trend in noir studies toward decentralization and "decolonization"—toward, in other words, the outskirts and borders, margins and periphery of the noir empire.[2]

This centrifugal trend is arguably an aftereffect of the unusually indeterminate, Minotaur-like nature of the beast, this "genre without a name"[3] that tends to reflect the films themselves, which are often about seduction and mystery, Sphinx-like secrets and labyrinthine riddles. One response to this mystique has been a determined demystification on the part of certain super-skeptical critics, the doom-and-gloom school, as a way to counter the "seductive power of film noir."[4] The result has been a series of grim pronouncements about the nothingness of film noir: to wit, film noir is a "black hole" that "never existed" and "can only be found in books."[5]

Reading such criticism, bracing as it is, one has the vertiginous sense that the subject in question has vanished into thin air. In this hallucinatory scenario, which recalls Alfred Hitchcock's *Vertigo* (1958), the critic is Scottie Ferguson (James Stewart), film noir is Madeleine Elster (Kim Novak), and the "object of beauty" with which you have fallen truly, madly, deeply in love turns out to have been a bloodless simulacrum.[6] Hence the somewhat sadistic, puritanical zeal with which noir skeptics attack the fetish, film noir, and the "seduced," "those critics under the spell of the 'noir mystique,' and desiring to remain so."[7] Lesson: woe be to the critic who errs on the side of desire or pleasure, for he or she shall be condemned to the lowest circle of hell (which, of course, is other critics).

In this infernal state of affairs, it's refreshing to read someone who has a more immediate, less tortured relation to film noir. In *The Noir Forties* (2012), Richard Lingeman, writing about his experience in Japan as a special agent with the army Counterintelligence Corps from 1954 to 1956, recalls that "working in the shadow world, [he] developed a taste for the night city, with its louche back-alley bars and hot-bed hotels, the exhilarating dangers, the sense of living on the edge."[8] Later, Lingeman came upon some "dark crime films" that spoke to his experience in Japan: "Whenever the Film Forum, that temple of cinema on West Houston Street in Greenwich Village, offered a program of films noirs, I would sit through them daily, alone in the dark, watching double and triple features. . . . I have never talked about my rather unremarkable adventures in Japan, since everything we did, down to eating at the PX, was classified, strictly speaking. The films served as divining rods for subterranean memories."[9] In the author's note, Lingeman states that a "large chunk" of his book is devoted to what he dubs "noir culture" after the "body of crime films known as film noir."[10]

In another note—a note within a note (even Lingeman, a journalist and historian, cannot completely escape noir's epistemological tentacles)—he acknowledges that "definitions of film noir differ" and that these "dark crime films have also been called 'crime melodramas.'"[11] The advantage of thinking of film noirs as "crime melodramas" is that this description jibes with the way Hollywood understood these pictures at the time. As Elizabeth Cowie points out, "In the trade papers from the 1910s onwards, the term 'melodrama' referred to 'thrills and spills' films, to adventure, suspense, and action and even—in the 1940s—to prison films. . . . [I]t was in this sense too, that films later considered *films noirs* were described as 'crime melodramas.'"[12]

The disadvantage of thinking of film noirs as "crime melodramas" is that the word "melodrama" has become almost completely pejorative for contemporary audiences, if not film scholars.[13] Melodrama, moreover, is almost as elusive a genre as film noir. For instance, it's no accident that the only genres that receive a separate chapter in Steve Neale's exacting *Genre and Hollywood* (2000) are film noir and "melodrama and the woman's film." But perhaps by returning to what Neale calls "Hollywood's inter-textual relay system,"[14] it's possible to be slightly more specific about what sort of "crime melodrama" film noir is.

In this generic context, it's striking that when the Production Code Administration finally approved the script for *The Maltese Falcon*, it was referred to as a "melodrama-detective mystery."[15] This descriptive twist highlights one of the constitutive components of the "dark crime film," the figure of the detective or, from a less character-driven perspective, the investigative narrative. What, in addition to the investigative figure or narrative, are some of the other elements of this "genre that wasn't there"?[16] In the undergraduate course on film noir titled Kiss Me Deadly that I've been teaching for the past two decades at Ohio University, I usually begin the first day of class by writing a version of the following list on the blackboard. A baker's dozen, then:

- investigative figure or detective
- la femme fatale, or: Cherchez la femme?[17]
- "the dark city"
- low-key, high contrast (chiaroscuro) lighting
- voiceover
- flashback

- canted or "Dutch" angles
- "closed," restricted compositions
- dream or nightmare logic
- "structure of feeling" (paranoia, anomie, alienation, etc.)
- romantic and/or sexual obsession
- "cash nexus" ($)
- fatalism

This list, mixing as it does "grammar" and "rhetoric," "syntax" and "semantics," moves from stock characters and setting to formal features and themes. About almost every term I have to make qualifications, sometimes elaborate, extended ones. For example, not every detective is a private detective (see *Double Indemnity*) or, for that matter, male (see *Phantom Lady*).[18] Not every woman is a femme fatale. (There are, inter alia, *femmes vital, femmes moderne,* and *femmes attrapée*.[19]) Not every femme is, as it were, a femme (see Laurel Gray's [Gloria Grahame] masseuse Martha [Ruth Gillette] in *In a Lonely Place* [1950]). Not every noir is set in the city (see *Out of the Past*).

All of this said, the above list offers a working definition of what, at least practically speaking and despite my own deconstructive inclinations, I think of as the genre of film noir. In *What Is Film Noir?* (2010), William Park advances a more concise definition in terms of its subject matter ("crime, almost always a murder, sometimes a theft"), locale ("the contemporary world, usually a city at night"), and character ("a fallible or tarnished man or woman").[20] In the book's appendices, Park uses this definition to divide the more than five hundred putative film noirs he's seen into three parts: "Within the Genre," "Borderline," and "Period Films." As a critic who feels compelled to "make some value judgments," Park also rates the films according to the Michelin Guide System, which offers additional food for thought. (No stars for *Decoy* [1947]? "One step above Ed Wood"?)

One doesn't have to agree with Park's definition of film noir nor his taxonomy to appreciate the critical gesture. In fact, I want to conclude this introduction by reflecting on some of the categories in *What Is Film Noir?* because they constitute an instance of canon making and, equally importantly, because they shed light on the generic complexity or hybridity of the "dark crime film." The most provocative part of Park's study is the third appendix, "Period Pieces," which designates those categories of films from the classical era that the author has, on the basis of his definition, *excluded* from the corpus: "crime films often identified as film noir" and "melodramas."[21]

Although the first type—"crime films of the noir period which . . . have radiated from the center to other genres"—is subdivided into familiar subgenres such as "cloak and dagger" (*Ministry of Fear* [1944]), "prison films" (*Brute Force* [1947]), and "the boxing racket" (*The Set-Up* [1949]), the first subdivision, "police work—law and order," is the largest and is affiliated with the "semi-documentary," the most famous "model" of which is *The Naked City* (1948).[22] These semi-documentaries or police procedurals are not "generic film noirs," according to Park, because the "police or government officials opposed to the criminals are Dudley Do-Right characters, old-fashioned G-men, upright and flawless, professional crime fighters" and because "many of the films, rather than having the noir style, look just the opposite."[23]

Park's argument explicitly cites Borde and Chaumeton's critique of the "police procedural" in *A Panorama of American Film Noir*[24] and has become the standard criticism of the "pseudo-documentary noir" which, for many critics, is a double oxymoron: neither a documentary nor a "real" noir. But let's take a closer look at one of these "law and order" period pieces.

Elaborating on his second observation about the anti-noir style of the semi-documentary, Park argues that the "look" of *The Naked City* "owes much more to Italian Neo-Realism than to Weegee."[25] The implication is that Italian neorealism, unlike Weegee from whose 1945 book of crime photos *The Naked City* takes its name,[26] is peripheral to classic noir. However, it's entirely possible to imagine a history of the genre that recognizes the impact of both Weegee and Italian neorealism. As for the influence of the latter movement on *The Naked City*, Jules Dassin has recalled in an interview: "When I saw *Rome: Open City*, I said 'that's the way we have to go.' To use the documentary form to bring a city to life."[27]

The content of Weegee's photos aside for the moment, what about the film's lighting? Unlike, say, *The Maltese Falcon*, whose "night scenes were shot during banking hours," those in *The Naked City*, such as the Third Avenue El "chase" sequence, were "shot night for night."[28] "Night for night" shooting represented a "complete about-face" for William H. Daniels, the director of photography of *The Naked City*, who won an Academy Award for his work on the film but who had previously been associated with, as a surprised Herb A. Lightman noticed in the May 1948 issue of the *American Cinematographer*, "the softly-lighted, glossily diffuse type of approach" he favored as "Garbo's cameraman" from *Flesh and the Devil* (1926) to *Ninotchka* (1939).[29]

In fact, *The Naked City* is distinguished by a number of noir set pieces. Consider, for example, the swift track-in through the blinds of an apartment window at night to Garzah (Ted de Corsia) and Backalis (Walter Burke) manhandling Jean Dexter's body before drowning her in a tub (note the knocked-over lamp on the floor that throws Garzah's shadow on the wall before he turns it off); the shaded, high overhead shot of Dexter's blanket-draped body at the Bellevue Hospital Mortuary (catch the dark cross on the blanket); and the extended sequence in which Jimmy Halloran (Don Taylor) and Det. Lt. Daniel Muldoon (Barry Fitzgerald) interrupt Garzah trying to kill Frank Niles (Howard Duff). In this action sequence, which opens with

The Amazing Colossal
Man: Garzah (Ted de
Corsia) dominates the
skyline of New York City
in the Spanish herald for
The Naked City (1948).
Note the white-outlined
figure of Jimmy Halloran
(Don Taylor) shooting
from the fire escape.

a dynamic, slatted shot of the detectives searching for the perpetrator, the
camera rapidly alternates between extreme high and low angles as Halloran
chases Garzah down an exterior fire escape, the windows of the apartment
building lighting up like blank movie screens as the two exchange fire.

Although no one I think would mistake Det. Lt. Muldoon in *The Naked
City* for Sam Spade in John Huston's *The Maltese Falcon*,[30] the "real star"
of *The Naked City* is not Barry Fitzgerald but the city.[31] Park's reference
to Dudley Do-Right, the clueless Canadian Mountie who appeared in the
Rocky and Bullwinkle Show, is presumably satiric, but it represents a real
misprision of the semi-documentary noir. For instance, in Henry Hathaway's
Call Northside 777 (1948), which is "centrally concerned with the plight of
ethnic minorities and their 'voice,'" Tillie Wiecek (Kasia Orzazewski) and her
falsely imprisoned son, Frank (Richard Conte), the *Chicago Times* reporter
Jim McNeal as played by James Stewart anticipates Scottie Ferguson and
his "obsessive quest" in *Vertigo*.[32]

More generally, if it's true that the "semi-documentaries have often been regarded as antithetical to the subversive existentialism of film noir," it's also true that "their politics were more ambivalent than is usually recognized,"[33] as evidenced by the contemporary response to *The Naked City. Cue* recorded that Dassin's film "begins with a plane over the city and ends in the gutter," and the *Denver Post* reported that it pictured New York in all its nakedness: "ratty rooms, dark streets, smelly wharves . . . and cold mortuaries."[34] Just as Nino Frank and Jean-Pierre Chartier intuited that there was something different about *The Maltese Falcon, Double Indemnity,* and *Murder, My Sweet,* a number of contemporary reviewers of *The Naked City* managed to discern the filmmakers' radical intent. In his production notes for the film's producer, Mark Hellinger,[35] the co-screenwriter Albert Maltz insisted, referencing the Soviet documentary filmmaker Dziga Vertov, that the "CAMERA EYE, whenever possible, [should] reflect . . . the architectural beauty and squalor that exist side by side."[36]

Alas, the film that Maltz envisioned and Dassin directed—including a slice-of-life shot of a Bowery derelict sleeping in the doorway of the Hotel Progress[37]—died a quick death in the screening room. Because Maltz and Dassin were suspected of being "reds" (Dassin later emigrated to Europe, and Maltz went to prison as one of the Hollywood Ten),[38] Universal not only refused to give Dassin final cut of *The Naked City* (he was said to have wept when he saw the release print), but the film was "scrutinized to weed out 'subversiveness' and, ultimately, butchered."[39] Edward Dimendberg's epitaph in *Film Noir and the Spaces of Modernity* (2004) suggests what might have been: "Had Maltz's advice and Dassin's direction been heeded, *The Naked City* might have more closely resembled the work of Weegee."[40]

Park's second subdivision, "period films" that do not "belong to the *genre*" of film noir, pertains to "psychological or social dramas"—that is to say, "melo-dramas." Here, I want to consider a film that Park does not cite but which has recently received quite a bit of attention: Ida Lupino's *The Bigamist* (1953). While *The Bigamist* is an odd picture by almost any reckoning, it was primarily viewed as a melodrama when it was first released. The *New York Times,* for example, called the story the "perfect format for the soap opera of them all."[41]

However, due to Lupino's other directorial efforts such as *Outrage* (1950), *Hard, Fast, and Beautiful* (1951), and *The Hitch-Hiker* (1953) as well as her "tough" persona in such proto- and classic noirs as *They Drive by Night* (1940), *High Sierra* (1941), *Road House* (1948), *On Dangerous Ground* (1951), *The Big Knife* (1955), and *While the City Sleeps* (1956), *The Bigamist* has also been categorized as a film noir. Not so incidentally, Lupino's film fulfils Park's three-fold criteria for a film noir: crime (bigamy), the "contemporary world" (San Francisco and Los Angeles circa 1953), and a "fallible or tarnished man or woman" (Harry Graham [Edmond O'Brien], "the bigamist" who finds himself married to two women, Eve [Joan Fontaine] and Phyllis Martin [Lupino]).

In addition to these "situational" elements, the film's extended flashback, investigative narrative, and expressionist, "dark city" lighting are redolent of the "noir style." In terms of *The Bigamist*'s visual rhetoric, George Diskant has been credited as the director of photography, but Lupino reportedly used two different cinematographers for the film, one for San Francisco (which, like Harry and Eve's upscale life there, is shot in a relatively high key) and one for Los Angeles (which, as the location of Harry's illicit affair, is lensed in a duskier light).[42] Similarly, *The Bigamist*'s dual generic focus as a melo-noir is conveyed via mise-en-scène.

Thus, when Harry initially drops Phyllis off at her boarding house after meeting her on a bus tour of the movie stars' homes, he remains at the bottom of the stairs. The second time, after a romantic montage, Harry kisses Phyllis at the base of the stairs, then—as the camera pulls back and tracks to the left for a wider shot—he walks around the staircase, all the while holding on to her white-gloved hand as she ascends the stairs. The scene closes with a long shot of Harry at the bottom and Phyllis at the top of the frame, the staircase between them casting an enormous shadow on the second-story wall to the right. This shadow, which darkly mirrors the double guard-railed staircase, simultaneously comments on Harry's "double life" (this is how Phyllis, the "other half," lives) and reflects his entrapment in a "bi-gamous" arrangement that later makes him feel, as he laments in voiceover after being recognized in Los Angeles with Eve, positively "criminal."

If the "staircase" shadow bespeaks the way in which *The Bigamist* recodes melodrama as noir, the noir aspect of *The Bigamist* is perhaps most apparent in a "classic" shot set in Los Angeles in which "Harry stands at the window of his motel room" (he's a traveling salesman like Walter Neff [Fred MacMurray] in *Double Indemnity*), "the partially open Venetian blinds revealing the blinking neon sign outside."[43] As the visual schema and Harry's character intimate, *The Bigamist* is reminiscent of any number of classic noirs.[44] For instance, the film is retrospectively narrated by Harry, who tells his tragically ironic story to Mr. Jordan (Edmund Gwenn), an adoption agent whom we see at one point talking into a Dictaphone. Instead of Edward G. Robinson playing Barton Keyes as a "dedicated and indigestion-plagued insurance investigator," Gwenn plays—in another self-conscious allusion—a Santa Claus–like figure (see *Miracle on 34th Street* [1947]) who drinks milk for his bad stomach as he diligently investigates "every detail" of his prospective clients' private lives.[45]

But if *The Bigamist* recalls *Double Indemnity* in particular and film noir in general, in its sensitive portrayal of the Canton Café waitress Phyllis, whose name seems to be yet another nod to *Double Indemnity*, it also references more

Not/Wanted: U.S. lobby card of Phyllis Martin (Ida Lupino) alone in bed in *The Bigamist* (1953).

hybrid films such as *Mildred Pierce* (1946), so that *The Bigamist* can be said to invert Michael Curtiz's film, "replacing the noir world with melodrama, and translating Harry's account of his crime into a discourse on feelings."[46] In this sense, *The Bigamist* appears to fuse "two divergent genres: the film noir and melodrama"[47]—with the proviso that these genres may not be quite so divergent as they at first appear. Indeed, since beds are a distinctive feature of the mise-en-scène of *The Bigamist,* the "shared or divided space of the bed—like the shared or divided space echoed in the film frame"—can be said to provide a "rudimentary representation" of the differential relation between film noir and melodrama.[48] Put another way, while separate beds in the master bedroom (and the master's house?) are a convention of classical Hollywood cinema, it may be time to begin "unlocking gender from specific genre types."[49]

For Julie Grossman, the films that Lupino directed remain an "important model" for rethinking the stereotypical notion of film noir as a "male," hard-boiled "fantasy" and melodrama as code for the soft-boiled "woman's film." With this "ungendering of genre" in mind, it's noteworthy that *The Bigamist*'s hybridity is not limited to film noir and melodrama. On August 7, 1949, Lupino and her husband Collier Young announced in the *New York Times* that the Filmakers, the company the couple had formed with Malvin Wald (who, together with Paul Jarrico, penned the original story for Lupino's first directorial feature, *Not Wanted* [1949]),[50] would make "documentary movies."[51] In February 1950, Collier and Lupino proceeded to publish a "Declaration of Independents" in which they praised "fellow independent producers" like Louis de Rochemont, whose *The House on 92nd Street* (1945)—another film on Park's "law-and-order" list—originated the semi-documentary noir in the United States.[52]

Lupino had previously met Roberto Rossellini, the director of *Roma, città aperta* (1945), at a Hollywood party, and he had pointedly asked her, "When are you going to make movies about ordinary people, in ordinary situations?"[53] Almost sixty years later, writing about American neorealism, Thom Andersen observed that Lupino's films "depict the journeys and struggles of ordinary, vulnerable people patiently and observantly, with an open sense of life naturally unfolding."[54] And Amelie Hastie, registering what Ronnie Scheib calls *The Bigamist's* "full-frame documentary realism," has classified Lupino's picture as "part melodrama," "part detective or crime film," and "part social film."[55]

Needless to say, not all films identified by fans or critics as noirs exhibit these particular generic markers, just as not all noirs possess all the elements or ingredients on my blackboard list. Still, the following Venn diagram arguably proffers a more productive model for thinking about the "crime melodrama" or "dark crime film" than those that consign limit cases to the unstarred wilderness beyond the borders of the genre:

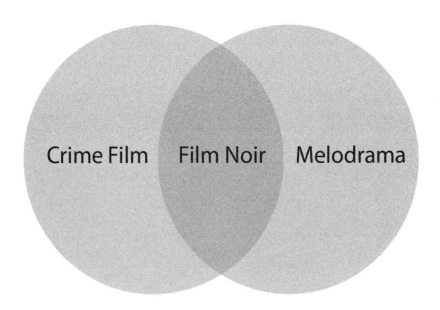

Crime Film   Film Noir   Melodrama

Another benefit of this more fluid, less rigid model is that it affords an entrée to perhaps the most refractory subgenre associated with classic noir, the "anticommunist noir." These "red menace" films are, for many critics, verboten because they are politically suspect and aesthetically bankrupt or aesthetically bankrupt because politically suspect. It's therefore no surprise that a much-maligned film such as Gordon Douglas's *I Was a Communist for the FBI* (1951) does not appear on any of Park's lists.[56] However, given its volatile mix of inky noir graphics, semi-documentary technique, and melodramatic plotting, this docu-melo-noir exposes the genre at the very moment when film gris was dying and with it (or so the story goes) classic noir itself.

The fact that *I Was a Communist for the FBI* engages not only the fear of a red but a black planet also signals that the film is channeling cultural tensions and contradictions that will later materialize in more concentrated thematic form in *The Crimson Kimono* (1959) and *Odds against Tomorrow* (1959).[57] A "red scare" film like *I Was a Communist for the FBI* may not be the sort of picture critics or even fans want to re-screen, let alone consider admitting to the canon, but as "bad objects," these films tell us more about the exclusionary logic that subtends the law of the genre than more highly esteemed, canonical noirs.

In "Red Hollywood" Andersen modestly proposes that film gris, like film noir, "can't be defined so that any film can be definitely placed inside or outside its borders."[58] I'm reminded here of the penultimate sequence in *The Bigamist,* in which Eve Graham stands on the balcony of her apartment building watching her husband as he walks across a parking lot to the waiting police. The reverse high-angle shot, which reprises an earlier one from Harry's point of view, shows a black police car parked aslant spaces marked "in" and "out."

This classic noir shot eloquently mirrors Harry's equivocal, in-between position as a bigamist, neither "in" nor "out" or, maybe, "in" *and* "out." It also neatly illustrates the predicament of the critic faced with having to adjudge whether any given film is a noir or not. The famously ambiguous ending of *The Bigamist,* in which Phyllis and Eve exit the courtroom before Harry is led away by an officer of the law,[59] suggests that sometimes the wisest thing to do, as Lupino resolved, is not to decide and leave it up to the viewer—to, in other words, you, *mon lecteur, mon semblable.*

Notes

1. James Naremore, "A Season in Hell or the Snows of Yesteryear," in *A Panorama of American Film Noir,* by Raymond Borde and Étienne Chaumeton, trans. Paul Hammond (San Francisco: City Lights, 2002), ix.

2. In addition to the texts I discuss in chapter 10, see Stanley Orr, *Darkly Perfect World: Colonial Adventure, Postmodernism, and American Noir* (Columbus: Ohio State University Press, 2010).

3. Thomas Doherty, "The Genre without a Name," in *Hollywood Censorship: Joseph Breen and the Production Code Administration* (New York: Columbia University Press, 2007), 241–53.

4. Frank Krutnik, *In a Lonely Street: Film Noir, Genre, Masculinity* (London: Routledge, 1991), 28.

5. On film noir as a "black hole," see Thomas Elsaesser, *Weimar Cinema and After: Germany's Historical Imaginary* (London: Routledge, 2000), 424. For the phrase "noir . . . doesn't exist," see Steve Neale, *Genre and Hollywood* (London: Routledge, 2000), 173. And on noir as a genre that "can only be found in books," see Marc Vernet, "*Film Noir* on the Edge of Doom," trans. J. Swenson, in *Shades of Noir*, ed. Joan Copjec (London: Verso, 1993), 26.

6. Vernet, "*Film Noir* on the Edge of Doom," 4.

7. Krutnik, *In a Lonely Street*, 28.

8. Richard Lingeman, *The Noir Forties* (New York: Nation Books, 2012), 12.

9. Ibid., 13.

10. Ibid., ix.

11. Ibid., x.

12. Elizabeth Cowie, "*Film Noir* and Women," in *Shades of Noir*, ed. Joan Copjec (London: Verso, 1993), 129. See also Joel Greenberg and Charles Higham, *Hollywood in the Forties* (New York: Paperback Library, 1970), 39–40. Greenberg and Higham categorize *The Maltese Falcon* as a melodrama. Although they also cite Huston's film in the chapter on "Black Film," their recourse to the term "melodrama" suggests how the early generic sense of the word persisted into the late 1960s. See also their description of *The Naked City* as a "sociological melodrama" (54).

13. On the difference between the "industrial" and academic conception of melodrama, see Neale, *Genre and Hollywood*, 179–204.

14. Ibid., 8.

15. Sheri Chinen Biesen, *Blackout: World War II and the Origins of Film Noir* (Baltimore: Johns Hopkins University Press, 2005), 45.

16. My list is indebted to Alexander Ballinger and Danny Graydon's summary of noir characteristics at the beginning of "The Genre That Wasn't There," in *The Rough Guide to Film Noir* (London: Rough Guides, 2007), 4.

17. I'm reappropriating Jacques Lacan's notorious formulation that "the woman does not exist" ("La femme n'existe pas"). See Lacan, "Seminar of 21 January 1975," in *Feminine Sexuality: Jacques Lacan and the école freudienne*, ed. Juliet Mitchell and Jacqueline Rose and trans. Jacqueline Rose (New York: Norton, 1982), 167. In this context, consider Evelyn Mulwray's (Faye Dunaway) interrogative response—"Cherchez la femme?"—to Jake Gittes's postcoital narration of his traumatic past in *Chinatown* (1974). Since Jake doesn't understand Evelyn's question, she translates it as, "Was a woman involved?" The phrase—loosely speaking, "Look for the woman!"—has been associated since Alexandre Dumas's *The Mohicans of Paris* (1854–59) with women as the root cause of men's troubles. (See "Put the Blame on Mame" in *Gilda* [1946].) The beauty, as it were, of the English usage ("Look for the woman!") is that it points up the specular stakes associated with the femme fatale, stakes foregrounded in the optical tropes in Roman Polanski's *Chinatown*, which underline Jake's inability to see until it's too late that Evelyn is not, in fact, a femme fatale.

18. For a succinct list of noir protagonists who are not private detectives, see William Park, *What Is Film Noir?* (Lewisburg, Pa.: Bucknell University Press, 2011), 23–24. On female detectives, see Philippa Gates's essay in this volume.

19. On *femmes vital,* see Mark Osteen, *Nightmare Alley: Film Noir and the American Dream* (Baltimore: Johns Hopkins University Press, 2013), 185–219. On *femmes moderne,* see Julie Grossman, *Rethinking the Femme Fatale in Film Noir: Ready for Her Close-Up* (London: Palgrave Macmillan, 2009), 95–99. On *femmes attrapée,* see Jans Wager, *Dames in the Driver's Seat: Rereading Film Noir* (Austin: University of Texas Press, 2005), 4.

20. Park, *What Is Film Noir?* 25.

21. Ibid., 136.

22. Ibid., 60.

23. Ibid.

24. Borde and Chaumeton distinguish between film noir and "police documentaries" on the basis of the "angle of vision" (internal, "criminal" versus external, "official") and "morality" (the police in the semi-documentary are "edifying" rather than "dubious" or "corrupt" like the criminals in film noir). See Raymond Borde and Étienne Chaumeton, *A Panorama of American Film Noir,* trans. Paul Hammond (San Francisco: City Lights, 2002), 6–7.

25. Park, *What Is Film Noir?* 60.

26. Arthur Fellig, a.k.a. Weegee (a "cross between 'Ouija' and 'Squeegee'") was paid "$3,000 for the movie rights to *Naked City."* Jeffrey Deitch, "Weegee in the Dream Factory," in *Naked Hollywood: Weegee in Hollywood,* ed. Richard Meyer (New York: Skira Rizzoli, 2011), 7. Weegee also "photographed the film sets and camera crew." MacKenzie Stevens, "Chronology," in *Naked Hollywood,* 123.

27. Rebecca Prime, "Cloaked in Compromise: Jules Dassin's 'Naked' City," in *"Un-American" Hollywood: Politics and Film in the Blacklist Era,* ed. Peter Stanfield, Frank Krutnik, Brian Neve, and Steve Neale (New Brunswick, N.J.: Rutgers University Press, 2007), 147. Prime adds that Maltz's "interest in on-location sound and casting non-actors echoes Dassin's desire to bring the tenets of Italian Neo-Realism to bear upon the film" (148).

28. Carl Richardson, *Autopsy: An Element of Realism in Film Noir* (Metuchen, N.J.: Scarecrow, 1992), 88.

29. Herb A. Lightman, *"The Naked City:* Tribute in Celluloid," *American Cinematographer* 29. 5 (May 1948), 178, qtd. in ibid., 93. Daniels's work with Garbo is not, of course, without variety. For Daniels's own take on the issue ("Even my lighting of Garbo varied from picture to picture"), see Charles Higham, "William Daniels," in *Hollywood Cameramen: Sources of Light* (Bloomington: Indiana University Press, 1970), 57–74.

30. Malvin Wald recounts that Mark Hellinger wanted the role of Muldoon to be played by James Stewart, but as Wald wrote the treatment, the "leading character turned out to be a sixty-five-year-old veteran with an Irish brogue." Malvin Wald, Afterword to *The Naked City: A Screenplay,* ed. Matthew Bruccoli (Carbondale: Southern Illinois University Press, 1979), 140. Ironically, Barry Fitzgerald "initially turned down the part because he thought it was better suited to someone like Humphrey Bogart." Peter Shelley, *Jules Dassin: The Life and the Films* (Jefferson, N.C.: McFarland, 2011), 120.

31. In *The Three Faces of the Film* (1960), Parker Tyler describes *The Naked City* as a "crime melodrama without star actors." Qtd. in Wald, Afterword, 148.

32. Andrew Spicer, *Film Noir* (London: Longman, 2002), 28. In the most nuanced reading of the cultural politics of the semi-documentary noir, Will Straw, citing Siegfried Kracauer's "Those Movies with a Message" (1948), argues that in films such as *The Naked City* and *Call Northside 777* the "institutional frame was one from which characters departed. As narratives got under way and characters followed their investigative

paths into Kracauer's 'social textures,' the richness and diversity of those textures were always at odds with the solemn flatness of the institutional point of view." Will Straw, "Documentary Realism and the Postwar Left," in *"Un-American" Hollywood: Politics and Film in the Blacklist Era,* ed. Peter Stanfield, Frank Krutnik, Brian Neve and Steve Neale (New Brunswick, N.J.: Rutgers University Press, 2007), 141.

33. Spicer, *Film Noir,* 58.

34. "New York Is the Star of 'Naked City,'" *Cue,* February 14, 1948, 15, and Harry Lowery, *Denver Post,* April 14, 1948, qtd. in Richardson, *Autopsy,* 78 and 81.

35. See Andrew Spicer's discussion of Mark Hellinger and *The Naked City* in this volume.

36. Albert Maltz qtd. in Richardson, *Autopsy,* 107.

37. Richardson, *Autopsy,* 109.

38. See Robert Murphy's overview of Dassin's post-blacklist career in this volume.

39. Richardson, *Autopsy,* 8. Rebecca Prime is only the most recent critic to recount that Universal executives "threatened to use the exteriors [of *The Naked City*] for stock footage and throw away the rest" ("Cloaked in Compromise," 150).

40. Edward Dimendberg, *Film Noir and the Spaces of Modernity* (Cambridge, Mass.: Harvard University Press, 2004), 73.

41. *New York Times,* December 26, 1953, 10:4, qtd. in Ellen Seiter, "*The Bigamist,*" in *Queen of the B's: Ida Lupino behind the Camera,* ed. Annette Kuhn (Westport, Conn.: Greenwood Press, 1995), 115.

42. Ronnie Scheib, "Ida Lupino: Auteuress," *Film Comment* 16.1 (1980): 64.

43. Amelie Hastie, *The Bigamist* (London: British Film Institute, 2009), 41.

44. It is also useful to compare *The Bigamist* to *D.O.A.* (1950) and *The Prowler* (1951). Rudolph Maté's *D.O.A.* not only stars Edmond O'Brien but features a t(r)opological divide between Banning (the well-lit location of Frank Bigelow's bourgeois life and secretary/girlfriend) and San Francisco/Los Angeles (the dark metropolises associated with sex, death, and jazz). As for Joseph Losey's *Prowler,* the plot turns, like *The Bigamist's,* on a baby. The difference is that in *The Prowler* it threatens Webb Garwood's (Van Heflin) desperate bid to realize his big, dollar-sign version of the American dream.

45. Jans Wager, "Ida Lupino," in *Film Noir: The Directors,* ed. Alain Silver and James Ursini (Milwaukee: Limelight, 2012), 238–39.

46. Seiter, "*The Bigamist,*" 110.

47. Ibid., 105.

48. See Hastie's trenchant analysis of this filmic trope in *The Bigamist,* 55–61.

49. Julie Grossman, "Mothers, Daughters, and Melonoir: Female Ambition in *Hard, Fast, and Beautiful*," in Therese Grisham and Julie Grossman, "Women's Place in Men's Space: Ida Lupino's Melonoirs," *Desistfilm* 4 (July 2013), accessed December 7, 2013, http://desistfilm.com/womens-place-in-mens-space-ida-lupinos-melonoirs.

50. Lupino is not credited as the director of *Not Wanted,* although she assumed directorial duties for Elmer Clifton after he suffered a heart attack a "few days before cameras were to roll." William Donati, *Ida Lupino: A Biography* (Lexington: University of Kentucky Press, 1996), 150.

51. Donati, *Ida Lupino,* 156.

52. Ibid., 173–74.

53. Roberto Rossellini, qtd. in ibid., 146.

54. Thom Andersen, Afterword to *"Un-American" Hollywood: Politics and Film in the Blacklist Era,* ed. Peter Stanfield, Frank Krutnik, Brian Neve, and Steve Neale (New Brunswick, N.J.: Rutgers University Press, 2007), 275.

55. Scheib, "Ida Lupino," 58; Hastie, *The Bigamist*, 29. Given my discussion of *The Naked City*, it should be noted that the screenplay for *The Bigamist* was written by Malvin Wald, based on an original story by Larry Marcus and Lou Schor.

56. To his credit, Park places *I Married a Communist* (1949), a.k.a. *The Woman on Pier 13* (1950), "within the genre"; he also gives it two stars, noting that it "is one of the most underrated noirs" with "parallel and interlocking subplots [that] give the film more than usual depth" (Park, *What Is Film Noir?* 151). See my "The Red and the Black: Gender, Genre, and the Romance of (Anti-) Communism in *The Woman on Pier 13*," *Camera Obscura* (forthcoming).

57. See Robert Miklitsch, "Fear of a Red Planet: *I Was a Communist for the FBI* as 'Black Film,'" *Journal of Popular Film and Television* 41.1 (Spring 2013): 43–54.

58. Andersen, Afterword, 267. See also Osteen's discussion and renomination of film gris as "red noir" in *Nightmare Alley*, 224–25.

59. I wonder whether this "open" ending is partly a function of Lupino's own identification with Harry. I'm thinking here of Lupino's off-screen life at the time—in particular, her complicated relationships with Collier Young and Joan Fontaine (see Donati, *Ida Lupino*, 201–4)—as well as her ambivalence about being both the director and one of the stars of *The Bigamist*. See, for example, Patrick McGilligan and Debra Weiner's interview with Lupino in *Film Crazy: Interviews with Hollywood Legends* (New York: St. Martin's, 2000), 226.

1

Independence Unpunished

The Female Detective in Classic Film Noir

PHILIPPA GATES

Film noir arose in concert with U.S. involvement in World War II. As the war came to a close, noir narratives were often centered on the problems facing returning servicemen, from unemployment to broken homes—problems often regarded as the result of increased female independence. During the war, women had supported the men fighting overseas and the war effort back at home by going to work; when the war was over and the men returned, how-ever, women were encouraged to return back to the home. In the immediate postwar years, women were needed to nurture the physically and mentally wounded veterans—not to compete with them in the workplace—and this led to a bifurcation of roles for women in film noir. In reality, many women had left the home to take up employment and pursued sexual gratification in the absence of their husbands; in noir, these women were branded as evil and punished or restored to a subordinate place in the home.

As Sylvia Harvey explains, "The two most common types of women in film noir are the exciting, childless whores, or the boring, potentially childbear-ing sweethearts"—in other words, "the femme fatale" and what Janey Place refers to as "the woman as redeemer."[1] Julie Grossman argues that, in film criticism, "film noir has been understood in a feminist context in two central ways: first, as a body of texts that give rise to feminist critique; and second, as a celebration of unchecked female power."[2] Certainly, feminist film critics have tended to critique noir's representation of the "good girl" (the redeemer) as boring and unappealing and to celebrate that of the femme fatale as empowered—despite her vilification and punishment within noir narratives. In the world of the male-centered noir film, women represent oppositional choices for the male hero—safe versus tempting, good versus evil. For example, Robert Porfirio describes the femme fatale as "the worst of male sexual fantasies."[3] Mary Ann Doane suggests that she is a "symptom of male fears about feminism."[4] Janey Place proposes that the femme fatale is, for the noir hero, "the psychological expression of his own internal fears of sexuality, and his need to control and repress it."[5] Elizabeth Cowie confirms that the "'femme fatale' is simply a catchphrase for the danger of sexual difference and the demands and risks desire poses for the man."[6] Lastly, Tania Modleski argues that film noir "possesses the greatest sociological importance (in addition to its aesthetic importance) because it reveals male paranoid fears, developed during the war years, about the independence of women on the homefront."[7]

Noir scholars have discussed at length the figure of the femme fatale as the epitome of dangerous femininity and the good girl as the noir hero's positive, but bland, choice. Many noir films, however, presented alternative roles for women—especially those films centered on a female protagonist. Although overshadowed by the critical focus on noir as a male genre, women have been the central driving force of many noir narratives, even some of the most memorable and critically praised ones, notably Michael Curtiz's *Mildred Pierce* (1945). More recently, attention has been paid to noir's gothic thrillers with female protagonists, including Alfred Hitchcock's *Rebecca* (1940) and George Cukor's *Gaslight* (1944), but noir's female investigative protagonists have been relatively underexamined. This is an oversight in noir scholarship, especially in light of the fact that the male investigative thriller is one of the most significant types of noir narrative—according to Frank Krutnik's classification—and those protagonists have been identified by critics as hard-boiled reactions to America's wartime and postwar social shifts.

The aim of Julie Grossman's work has been to expose "the misreadings of women in *noir*, first by the men whom they encounter within the films, and second by film viewers and critics who then perpetuate, and eventually institutionalize, these misreadings."[8] Similarly, the aim of this essay is to contribute to the growing body of scholarship dedicated to revising our erroneous assumptions about the role of women in the classic phase of film noir by examining one of the significant roles available to women: the detective. Women in classic noir are never detectives by profession, whether working for the police or as private investigators, but a number of them serve as amateur investigators (in the footsteps of Miss Marple and Nancy Drew), seeking out the truth about a crime most often to clear the name of a man they love. The sex of the female detective complicates the traditionally male noir detective narrative as the narrative is driven forward as much by the female protagonist's personal desires (as in the woman's film) as by her investigation (as in the detective film), and the heroine's independence as a detective and exploration of her sexuality pose undesirable challenges to the masculinity of her husband—just like the femme fatale. Unlike the femme fatale, however, the female detective is allowed to enjoy her foray into masculinity and conclude the film unpunished.

Investigating the Genre

Film noir, beginning in the early 1940s and concluding in the late 1950s, was initially a film style or film movement (rather than necessarily a genre) defined by themes, characters, and visual style that were darker than the typical classical Hollywood film. The label "film noir" was applied retrospectively by French critics (as opposed to a category identified by producers) to describe a group of Hollywood films that, at the time, were released as detective films, crime melodramas, or thrillers. With the return of noir in the 1970s with films like Roman Polanski's *Chinatown* (1974), noir style and narrative were solidified into what many critics regard as a genre. Consequently, I prefer the term "noir films" to "film noir," referring to individual films with noir elements rather than a genre.

Krutnik argues that there are three types of protagonist in three types of noir film: the victim hero in "the male suspense thriller," the criminal hero in "the criminal-adventure thriller," and the detective hero in "the investigative thriller."[9] As Cowie confirms, Krutnik's argument assumes that noir is "a male preserve," and, as Deborah Thomas suggests, film noir is regarded by most as a "male-centred" genre.[10] Out of the frontier and onto America's twentieth-century city streets came the myths of rugged individualism and the American dream, both of which embodied the idea that if a man worked hard and lived a moral life then he would be successful. Servicemen returning from World War II, however, came back to a changed society and significant obstacles: unemployment, alienation, degradation, disablement, broken homes, and new gender roles. The expectation to conform—to embrace the role of the "grey flannel suit" (i.e., working for someone else rather than being one's own man)—contradicted the idea of being a rugged individual. Noir's hard-boiled private eye offered a fantasy of the rugged individual during the immediate postwar years: he worked for himself, by himself, and brought the villains to justice without having to work within the bureaucratic machinery of law enforcement. This identifiably American hero solved the mystery of the crime not through contemplative ratiocination, as would the British sleuth Sherlock Holmes, but through streets smarts, quick wit, and the ability to commit violence. The noir hero was not a secure, stable, and content man but jaded, troubled, and lonely. While the noir film introduced a mystery for the hero to solve, ultimately the mystery he investigated was that of his own masculinity and his place in postwar society. What then of the female investigator in noir films?

Richard Maltby defines the noir detective as "the man assigned the task of making sense of the web of coincidence, flashback, and unexplained circumstance that comprised the plot." Maltby also notes that, importantly, the detective "was not always the central protagonist," despite his role as investigator.[11] Women in noir films are also sometimes assigned this same task, and they did not always complete the task alone. While detective fiction of the 1930s began to focus on the tough, hard-boiled, male heroes that would populate film noir a decade later, Hollywood—in the wake of the Depression—presented a range of female detectives that could be young or old, spinsters or lovers, feminine or masculine, hard-boiled or soft. Alongside the popular B-series male detectives, including Philo Vance, Perry Mason, and Charlie Chan, appeared the female amateur detective, including Torchy Blane, Nancy Drew, and Hildegarde Withers, who were all popular enough to sustain their own film series. Hollywood's female detectives defied their socially prescribed, "proper" roles by stepping out of the domestic sphere and taking on the presumed male pursuit of detecting. Because the Depression had made working women a reality, they were common Hollywood protagonists, and the female detective often rejects a proposal of marriage at the end of the film to continue with her career. With the United States joining World War II, gender roles—in Hollywood film and reality—experienced a repolarization, and the female investigator changed her mind. The wartime and postwar heroine sees the two "ambitions" of marriage and a career combined: the solution of the mystery will make the love interest available to the heroine to marry.[12]

While William Covey states that "[t]here were very few female investigators and no female detective in classic *film noirs*," Krutnik acknowledges that two films—Boris Ingster's *Stranger on the Third Floor* (1940) and Robert Siodmak's *Phantom Lady* (1944)—foreground the investigations of female protagonists.[13] Krutnik, though, is critical of the female detective, arguing that that her "detective activity" is "compromised by her femininity," and he dismisses her agency because "the woman's placement in the conventional masculine role as detective is motivated by, and ultimately bound within, her love for the wrongly-convicted hero."[14] I disagree that such a motivation should negate the agency that such female detectives demonstrate, since several male detectives in noir films—most famously Dana Andrews in Otto Preminger's *Laura* (1944)—are also motivated to investigate out of love/desire. Indeed, Krutnik himself explains, "When, from 1944, the Hollywood studios began to produce 'hard-boiled' thrillers in a concerted manner, they tended either to introduce or to increase the prominence of a heterosexual love-story, a factor which in many cases shifted the emphasis from the story of a crime or investigation to a story of erotic obsession. The love story complicates the linear trajectory of the hero's quest."[15] I would argue that, in the case of the female investigator, there is *not* a shift in emphasis away from the investigation *despite* the foregrounding of a heterosexual romance, and that the linear trajectory of the heroine's quest is not necessarily complicated by it, especially in films such as *Phantom Lady* and Norman Foster's *Woman on the Run* (1950), in which the love interests are absent for the majority of the story. In response to Krutnik's assertions, Helen Hanson suggests that the romantic strand is as necessary to the female detective narrative as the crime strand: "The 'woman's angle' and her investigative quest, with the question of her male counterpart's innocence at its centre, allows her to 'test' her male counterpart before the film closes in marriage."[16]

In her article on victims/redeemers and working girls, Sheri Chinen Biesen mentions that two of the latter are detectives.[17] In his discussion of homefront detectives, Dennis Broe argues that the noir adaptations of three Cornell Woolrich stories centered on female detectives are part of a broader trend of narratives featuring "outside-the-law" detectives.[18] Angela Martin identifies nine noir films with women in investigative roles, and Cowie five, but both discuss them only briefly as one of several types of central female protagonists in film noir.[19] As William Park notes, "[S]uch films deserve a book of their own, which should do much to dispel the false notion that noir is confined to a boy's game."[20] Hanson offers an analysis of the female detective in four films but regards them as an extension of the female detective tradition established in the mystery-comedies of the 1930s—such as the Nancy Drew, Hildegarde Withers, and Torchy Blaine series—which I argue they are a deviation from.[21]

The noir films with an investigating heroine tend to fall into two distinct categories: the gothic melodrama in a rural setting in which the heroine investigates the mysterious past of the male love interest to determine if, or to ensure that, they can have a happy future together, including James V. Kern's *The Second Woman* (1950) and Vincente Minnelli's *Undercurrent* (1946); and the detective film in an urban setting in which the heroine investigates a crime that the male love interest has been accused of committing, including H. Bruce Humberstone's *I Wake up Screaming* (a.k.a. *Hotspot,* 1941) and Harold Clurman's *Deadline at Dawn* (1946). The former type often sees its heroine's investigation abandoned or short-circuited by a man and places the romance as the primary narrative focus; the latter typically provides the heroine a significant role as detective and places the investigation, rather than the romance, as the primary focus of the narrative. My research has uncovered at least twenty noir films with women in various roles as detectives: "minor," possessing only some investigative agency in relation to a male detective, including *Stranger on the Third Floor,* Jacques Tourneur's *The Leopard Man* (1943), Henry Hathaway's *The Dark Corner* (1946), John Reinhardt's *Open Secret* (1948), and Harry Horner's *Vicki* (1953); "significant," often assisting a male investigator, including *I Wake up Screaming,* Mark Robson's *The Seventh Victim* (1943), William Castle's *When Strangers Marry* (a.k.a. *Betrayed,* 1944), Sam Newfield's *The Lady Confesses* (1945), *Deadline at Dawn, Undercurrent,* Joseph M. Newman's *Abandoned* (1949), *The Second Woman,* and Vincent Sherman's *Backfire* (1950); and "major," as the primary investigator, including Alfred Hitchcock's *Shadow of a Doubt* (1943), *Phantom Lady,* Roy William Neill's *Black Angel* (1946), Edward L. Cahn's *Destination Murder* (1950), *Woman on the Run,* and Roy Rowland's *Witness to Murder* (1954).[22] Elsewhere I have discussed some of the last group of films as generic hybrids—part melodrama and part noir, or "melo-noir."[23] In this essay, however, I will explore how the female detective represents a third type of female role in the film noir—one that combines aspects of the femme fatale and the redeemer figure into a compelling, driven, sexualized, yet unpunished female figure. I consider the female detective in terms of her degree of investigative ability (Are her detective abilities comparable to a man's?), the kinds of skills she possesses (Are her skills specific to her sex, such as "female intuition"?), her degree of autonomy (Does she depend on a man for assistance?), her degree of agency (Is she forced to bow to male authority?), and her degree of access to knowledge (Does she have access to all aspects of the mystery surrounding the crime?).

Investigating Female Knowledge

Krutnik argues that in the gothic noir films, "Female experience, female vision, and female knowledge tend to be negated or invalidated."[24] In contrast, I argue that the gothic noir films with a female investigator, such as *Undercurrent* and *The Second Woman,* suggest that female experience, vision, and knowledge are key to seeing justice served. There was some debate among early noir scholars as to whether gothic films should even be considered noir because of their female protagonists,[25] and the sex of the protagonist appears to have been the main point of contention in terms of allocating noir status to a particular film and/or giving it adequate scholarly attention. Catherine Ross Nickerson cites the "female gothic" tradition established by Ann Radcliffe's *The Mysteries of Udolpho* (1794) as the progenitor of female detective fiction.[26] Similarly, Diane Waldman argues that the gothic romance films of the 1940s, including *Undercurrent,* follow the "female gothic" plot in which a female protagonist is faced with a secret or mystery around her (potential) husband's past.[27] Certainly this is the mystery that the heroines must solve in *Undercurrent* and *The Second Woman,* but, unlike the heroines of the other gothic romances that Waldman discusses—including *Rebecca,* Hitchcock's *Suspicion* (1941), *Gaslight* (1944), and Douglas Sirk's *Sleep, My Love* (1948)—these women actively investigate their love interest's pasts and do so using the skills they have learned in their employment in male work.

In *Undercurrent*, after a brief romance, the tomboyish and spinsterly daughter of a famous professor, Ann Hamilton (Katharine Hepburn), marries the handsome industrialist Alan Garroway (Robert Taylor). For the first half of the film, not unlike *Rebecca*'s heroine (Joan Fontaine), Ann attempts to adapt to her husband's sophisticated world. About halfway into the film, however, Ann realizes that her husband is psychologically troubled and that, in order to secure a happy future with him, she must play detective, investigating his past and especially the rumor that he may have killed his brother, Michael. Michael haunts their marriage, and every reminder of him—whether his old horse or a song that Ann plays on the piano—incites Alan to anger. When Ann accompanies Alan on a business trip to California, she takes the opportunity to question his former girlfriend, his office assistant, and the caretaker of his ranch in the hopes of finding out the truth about Michael's disappearance—not realizing that the caretaker she speaks to is actually Michael himself (Robert Mitchum). Whereas Alan is most comfortable (read: in control) in the urban environments of Washington, D.C. and San Francisco, Michael feels more at home at the ranch in California or the family farm in Virginia. As he explains to Ann, his "oak-paneled office" is a cluster of oak trees overlooking the ocean on the ranch. When he speaks critically of the corporate rat race and high society that Alan craves, Ann shares Michael's view. Alan is furious when he finds out that Ann has been asking questions and exploring the ranch; he expects her to be a dutiful wife, not a detective investigating his past—even though she explains that she has done so only to save their marriage. While out for the evening in San Francisco, Ann overhears some socialites gossiping about how Alan has enacted a "reconversion" of Ann. She subsequently confronts Alan, accusing him of marrying her only to receive credit for transforming her from a small-town spinster into a society wife; in other words, he values her as his "invention," not his wife. Upon their return home to the farm in Virginia, the mystery of Alan's past is seemingly solved when Michael appears alive and well, and Ann gratefully gives up her investigation and ignores the evidence she has discovered against her husband. It is Michael, then—not Ann—who reveals that Alan killed a German engineer in order to claim his invention as his own, gaining his social status and wealth from it.

In terms of her investigative skills and ability, Ann is presented as "masculine" in the sense that she uses deductive reasoning and ratiocination to investigate the mystery, no doubt because her years of assisting her father in his chemistry research have sharpened her mind and honed her research skills. Ann's success as a detective, however, is undermined by the fact that, in terms of agency and determination, she abandons her investigation and puts her marriage ahead of her quest for the truth—although she is still rewarded for her efforts to uncover the truth with the replacement of her selfish husband with his kinder brother. Michael's reappearance provokes Alan

"Why couldn't you have kept out of it?!": newlywed bliss takes a noirish turn in *Undercurrent* (1946) when Ann's (Katharine Hepburn) husband discovers that she has been investigating his past.

to act on his paranoid delusions. Alan lost his former girlfriend to Michael and now fears that he will lose his wife to him as well, even though, as far as Alan and Ann are concerned, she has not met Michael yet. To prevent this, Alan attempts to kill Ann by pushing her off her horse by the edge of a cliff. In melodramatic fashion, Alan receives his comeuppance as a victim of his own vice: Michael's horse, which Alan has continuously mistreated, exacts its revenge by trampling Alan to death. In the final scene, Ann meets Michael officially as she plays the piano; as a widow, she is free to fall in love with him. Nevertheless, a noir tone hangs over the seemingly happy ending as Ann is bound to a wheelchair, suggesting that her sexuality may be in check even though she has met a good man.

While *Undercurrent* follows the "female gothic" tradition with a heroine investigating her husband's past in a gothic, rural setting, the majority of noir films with female detectives are mysteries in keeping with the male "investigative thriller" in distinctly modern, urban settings. In *I Wake up Screaming, Phantom Lady, The Lady Confesses, Deadline at Dawn, The Dark Corner,* and *Black Angel,* women come to the rescue of their love-interests-in-distress by investigating a murder to prove their men innocent of the crime. For example, in *I Wake up Screaming,* the promoter Frankie Christopher (Victor Mature) is suspected of murdering Vicky Lynn (Carole Landis), a "hash slinger" that he has transformed into a celebrity. Vicky's sister, Jill (Betty Grable), remains unconvinced that the police are pursuing the right man, and she starts to investigate on her own. Surprisingly, Jill is given equal narrative authority as Frankie: the first half hour of the film alternates between their flashbacks (accompanied by their respective voiceovers) of the events leading up to Vicky's murder. Initially, Jill is unsure whether Frankie killed her sister but finds herself falling in love with him and then tries to protect him from a police frame-up. She displays an unusual degree of coolness and strength of character when Inspector Cornell (Laird Cregar) arrests Frankie at Jill's apartment. While Frankie stands helpless and handcuffed as Cornell punches him, Jill cracks Cornell over the head, knocking him unconscious, then traps the other officer in a Murphy bed. Frankie confesses to Jill that he in fact never loved her glamorous and more feminine sister, and it is Jill's displays of masculine heroism that attract Frankie, as the following exchange suggests:

> **Frankie:** You're a great sport, Jill. . . . Why did you do it?
> **Jill:** I don't know. But when I saw you standing there so helpless and that big fat-head bullying you, I just had to hit something.

She then takes a saw to Frankie's handcuffs. Like many of the heroines in these noir films, Jill feels the need to protect and save the male hero—and, in 1940s noir films, he always needs saving.

When Good Girls Turn Fatal: in *I Wake up Screaming* (1941), Jill (Betty Grable) is transformed by noirish lighting when she decides to take action against a corrupt detective.

In terms of her degree of investigative ability, Jill is very competent. In terms of her skills, some are specific to her sex, in that she can date the prime suspect, while others are more typically male skills, such as deductive reasoning, physical action, and ditching her police tail. (She attributes the last skill to her days as a "campfire girl.") She initially works autonomously but then enlists the assistance of her love interest, and he takes over for the last ten minutes of the film to confront Vicky's killer and then Cornell, who is branded as the real villain for framing Frankie for her murder. *I Wake up Screaming* is interesting as an early film noir with a heroine functioning as a significant investigator with equal narrative and investigative power as the man (at least until the last ten minutes). Similarly, what is now regarded by many film scholars as the first film noir, *Stranger on the Third Floor,* also features a heroine (Margaret Tallichet) who takes on the role of criminal investigator (even though it is only for the last ten minutes of the film) when her fiancé (John McGuire) is charged with the murder of his neighbor.

A distinction is drawn in these films between "male" skills—observing, deducing, and pursuing leads—and "female" skills—female intuition and "female knowledge" (specifically the things that women learn about being feminine, such as make-up and fashion). For example, in *Open Secret,* female intuition is identified as one of the skills possessed by newlywed Nancy Lester (Jane Randolph), who investigates alongside her husband when his army buddy disappears. As Nancy explains to her husband, "Paul, I'm worried about Ed. There's something wrong, I feel it." He is dismissive of her feelings and replies, "Now, honey, don't go jumping to conclusions," yet she backs up her concerns with evidence. Or, as Gary Giddins remarks about the young heroine of *When Strangers Marry,* "She has nothing to rely on but her instinct."[28] June Goffe[29] (Susan Hayward) may not be the sole investigator in *Deadline at Dawn,* as she is accompanied by a group of men, but it is her female knowledge that helps her uncover key clues, including that the lipstick found is the right shade for a blonde. Also, it is she who comes up with a plan to expose the killer by using the scent of the victim's perfume to provoke a reaction. Lastly, the female detective can often gain access to certain witnesses or suspects because of her sex. In *Abandoned,* Paula Considine (Gale Storm) accepts the assistance of the reporter Mark Sitko (Dennis O'Keefe) to investigate the death of her sister and the disappearance of her niece born out of wedlock. Mark completes the majority of the active investigation, but it is Paula who is able to investigate the home for unwed mothers to expose the illegal adoption racket. Importantly, the female investigator is able to possess either set of skills ("male" or "female") and often both—unlike noir's male detectives. The one key problem with the sex of the female detective is that—also unlike noir's male detectives—it puts her in danger of being the next victim of the killer they seek (see Jane in *Stranger on the Third Floor,* Nancy in *Open Secret,* Carol in *Phantom Lady,* and Vicki in *The Lady Confesses*)—and she often needs to be rescued by a more physically capable man.

Investigating Female Sexuality

Erich Kuersten highlights the lesser-known 1943 noir films *The Leopard Man* and *The Seventh Victim*—both produced by Val Lewton—for their subversive undertones that outshine the noirs that we uphold as classics today:

> For all the praise heaped on *Double Indemnity* (1944) or *The Postman Always Rings Twice* (1946) for their sly critiques of sexual and familial crises, such films at best offer catharsis via expression of social issues in the form of a "good story." Lewton on the other hand manages to address all the pertinent issues of noir—the threat of feminine sexuality, the rise of corporate culture, the dehumanization of the big city, the whole phallic fallacy family—and not just cathartically mythologize via pulp fiction trappings, but actually find solutions to the problems. [30]

In general, the noir films with a female detective bring many of these issues to the fore because of their female protagonists and the kinds of narratives and themes that the presence of a woman at the center of the film encourages. These films explore the dehumanizing effect of the big city on the struggling working girl, the impact of corporate culture as it feminizes (and often unhinges) the male, and the problem with exclusive patriarchal control over a nuclear family. Rather than being seen as a threat, as it is in the figure of the femme fatale, female sexuality is reimagined in these noir films as a way to transform the nurturing good (white, middle-class, virginal, often small-town) girl into an independent, self-confident, and self-fulfilled (sexualized, modern, urban) woman. [31]

The need to become sexually mature is deemed necessary, especially for the teenaged heroines of *The Seventh Victim,* *When Strangers Marry,* and *Shadow of a Doubt.* In *The Seventh Victim,* a schoolgirl, Mary Gibson (Kim Hunter), investigates the disappearance of her sister in New York City alongside her brother-in-law, Gregory Ward (Hugh Beaumont), while falling in love with him. When her sister commits suicide, Mary and Gregory are free to marry, and Gregory's femme-fatale wife is replaced with a more appropriate "good girl." Hunter also plays the heroine of *When Strangers Marry,* a small-town girl who marries a man she has only met three times. When she comes to the big city and discovers that her husband, Paul (Dean Jagger), is suspected of murder, she decides to seek evidence to prove him innocent. As she says to her former suitor, Fred Graham (Robert Mitchum), "You think he's the man they're looking for, don't you? . . . I'm going to find out." The film implies that Paul is guilty and that Fred makes a better match for Millie as a dashing and exciting man, but in the end it is revealed that Fred committed the murder and framed Paul in the hopes of having Millie for himself. At the beginning of the film, Millie is presented as impossibly naïve and in danger of becoming a victim of the big city. Her foray into detective work and her clearing of a stranger's name of murder forces her to mature into an adult woman—ready for marriage (and sex).

The Second Woman is one of the most daring noir films in terms of presenting its good girl (read: virgin) heroine, Ellen Foster (Betsy Drake).[32] Although the film belongs to the gothic tradition, Ellen is very different from *Rebecca*'s meek second Mrs. de Winter or *Undercurrent*'s blindly devoted Ann. In contrast, Ellen is an intelligent woman with a successful career, demonstrably sexual, and a successful detective. Significantly, she is not punished for her masculine behavior nor required to become more feminine (other than to marry her love interest at the end). In terms of a career, she is a certified public accountant who compiles actuarial tables for an insurance company (similar to Keyes [Edward G. Robinson] in *Double Indemnity*), and her knowledge regarding accidents is necessary to convince architect Jeff Cohalan (Robert Young) that he is not unlucky—or, worse, insane—but the victim of sabotage. In terms of her skills as a detective, Ellen's observations and

Not Your Typical Gothic Heroine: although *The Second Woman* (1950) echoes *Rebecca* (1940), Ellen Foster (Betsy Drake) is a capable detective, and it is the hero's (Robert Young) sanity that is in question.

deductions prove that he is the victim rather than the paranoiac perpetrator that a local doctor suspects he is, but she also uses science, sending out soil samples for chemical analysis. Although her investigation grinds to a halt for the final fifteen minutes of the film when Jeff takes over, in terms of agency and autonomy, Ellen is the primary investigator with no assistance from her love interest or the official authorities for the majority of the film.

What makes Ellen remarkable, however, is that, more so than any noir female detective mentioned above, she has a demonstrably healthy sexual appetite and makes advances on the film's traumatized hero. Early on, Jeff tries to warn her, saying, "You're not safe with me." He means that he is unlucky that something might happen to her if she gets close to him, since his previous fiancée tragically died in a car accident. Ellen thinks he means that she will not be safe because he will try to seduce her, and she responds suggestively, "Suppose I don't want to be safe?" Similarly, later in the film, after she is almost run over by a car that was the same color and make as his, Jeff warns her again, "You're asking for trouble." She replies, "Am I? Then I'll really ask for it!" She then kisses him fervently. Such sexually aggressive behavior was punished in the case of the femme fatale, yet here the heroine's desire for the victim-hero is used to justify her need to investigate. As she confesses to her Aunt Amelia, "I love him. I've got to help him, if I can . . . whether he likes it or not." In the end, she is rewarded for her devotion with Jeff's declaration of love.

While *The Second Woman* is bold in that it offers a self-determined heroine, the film contains her empowerment as a detective by having her hand over her investigation to male authorities. As early as 1949, noir's female detectives were losing their guts—in terms of their desire and drive to investigate—and their glory—in terms of being the one who uncovers the truth and/or brings the criminals to justice. In fact, noir films with female detectives became less socially critical and more conservative in general: while noir films of the 1940s regarded bureaucratic law enforcers as ineffectual and crime-solvers as operating necessarily outside the law, those of the 1950s lauded the efforts of the agents of law enforcement and promoted official detectives as key to seeing justice served. For example, in *Woman on the Run,* the mystery that Eleanor Johnson (Ann Sheridan) must solve is not the murder that her husband witnessed but rather who killed their marriage. The film identifies Eleanor as the culprit, and she must submit to male authority—her husband and the police—by the end of the film. In *Destination Murder,* Laura Mansfield (Joyce MacKenzie) is forced to investigate her father's murder on her own when the police run out of leads. Despite the fact that she correctly identifies her father's shooter, she falls in love with the man who ordered the hit and, in terms of autonomy and agency as a detective, ends up having to apologize to the detective in charge of the investigation for ever doubting his superior abilities. *Vicki* is a remake of *I Wake up Screaming*, and, although it follows the original film very closely, there

Female Detectives in Classic Noir

Title (Director, Date) [in order of release]	Actor (Character)	Type of detective - Official, amateur - Reason for investigating	Autonomy and Agency - Primary, secondary, minor - Alone, shared, assists	Detective Skills [possessed by female lead] - Masculine/ Feminine (the skills aligned with each sex in the crime genre at this time: e.g., questioning witnesses and actively pursuing leads are regarded as male skills, while relying on intuition is regarded as female)
Stranger on the Third Floor (Ingster 1940)	Margaret Tallichet (Jane)	- Amateur - clears fiancé of murder	Primary; but only briefly, as film focuses on paranoid male	Masculine: active investigation / Feminine: female intuition
I Wake up Screaming (Humberstone 1941)	Betty Grable (Jill)	- Amateur (stenographer) - clears love interest of murder	Secondary; shared, and man takes over investigation from her	Masculine: observant and follows leads / Feminine: nurturer for the male lead
Shadow of a Doubt (Hitchcock 1943)	Teresa Wright (Charlie)	- Amateur (teenager) - suspects uncle is a serial killer	Primary; continues to pursue murderer after official investigators leave	Masculine: observant and active investigation
The Leopard Man (Tourneur 1943)	Jean Brooks (Kiki)	- Amateur (club performer) - inadvertently causes first death	Minor; encourages her love interest to pursue the case	Feminine: "softens" male and instigates investigation
The Seventh Victim (Robson 1943)	Kim Hunter (Mary)	- Amateur (teenager) - her sister disappears	Shared; requires assistance and encouragement of man to continue	Masculine: initially active / Feminine: bows to male authority
Phantom Lady (Siodmak 1944)	Ella Raines (Kansas)	- Amateur (secretary) - clears boss's name	Primary; but assisted by the real killer	Masculine: active investigation / Feminine: undercover work
When Strangers Marry (Castle 1944)	Kim Hunter (Millie)	- Amateur (newlywed) - clears husband's name	Primary; assisted by former suitor but ends up working alone	Masculine: active investigation / Feminine: nurturer for the male lead
The Lady Confesses (Newfield 1945)	Mary Beth Hughes (Vicki)	- Amateur (undercover) - clears fiancé's name	Primary; but assisting the real killer	Masculine: questions club workers / Feminine: goes undercover
Deadline at Dawn (Clurman 1946)	Susan Hayward (June)	- Amateur (taxi dancer) - helps sailor clear his name	Primary; but assisted by the real killer and works with up to four other people	Masculine: uncovers the key clues

Film	Actress (Character)	Role	Investigation	Gender coding
The Dark Corner (Hathaway 1946)	Lucille Ball (Kathleen)	- Amateur (secretary) - works for private eye	Minor; assists man and is mainly support but figures out key clue	Masculine: observant and follows leads / Feminine: nurturer for the male lead
The Black Angel (Neill 1946)	June Vincent (Cathy)	- Amateur (housewife) - clears husband's name	Primary; shared; assisted by the real killer	Masculine: active investigation / Feminine: undercover work
Undercurrent (Minnelli 1946)	Katharine Hepburn (Ann)	- Amateur (newlywed) - investigates husband's past	Primary; competent but believes husband's lies and abandons investigation	Masculine: active investigation (30 mins.) / Feminine: bows to male authority
Open Secret (Reinhardt 1948)	Jane Randolph (Nancy)	- Amateur (newlywed) - husband's friend is murdered	Secondary; assists husband but responsible for key clue	Masculine: some key clues / Feminine: feminine intuition
I Wouldn't Be in Your Shoes (Nigh 1948)	Elyse Knox (Ann)	- Amateur (dance instructor) - clears husband of murder	Minor; mainly inspires detective to reopen case but does investigate at end	Feminine: uses the detective's love
Abandoned (Newman 1949)	Gale Storm (Paula)	- Amateur (sister) - investigates sister's death	Shared; assists male reporter to expose a baby-selling racket and sister's murder	Feminine: active but only on the "female" aspects
Backfire (Sherman 1950)	Virginia Mayo (Julie)	- Amateur (nurse) - helps love interest find friend	Secondary; assists love interest in clearing army buddy's name	Masculine: some active investigation (10 mins.) / Feminine: "female" knowledge
Destination Murder (Cahn 1950)	Joyce MacKenzie (Laura)	- Amateur (undercover at club) - her father is murdered	Primary; works for authorities; competent but falls for the mastermind	Feminine: dates the gunman to entrap him
The Second Woman (Kern 1950)	Betsy Drake (Ellen)	- Amateur (accountant) - assists a paranoid man	Primary; does all key work, but man takes over for climax	Masculine: research/tests, observation, deduction / Feminine: nurturer for the male lead
Woman on the Run (Foster 1950)	Ann Sheridan (Eleanor)	- Amateur (housewife) - helps husband clear his name	Primary; but assisted by the real killer	Masculine: active investigation
The Blue Gardenia (Lang 1953)	Anne Baxter (Norah)	- Amateur (phone operator) - she may have killed a man	Passive; she gives up trying to uncover the truth and man takes over	Feminine: damsel-in-distress who requires assistance
Vicki (Horner 1953)	Jeanne Crain (Jill)	- Amateur (stenographer) - clears love interest of murder	Secondary; shared, and man takes over investigation from her	Masculine: observant, leads / Feminine: nurturer for the male lead
Witness to Murder (Rowland 1954)	Barbara Stanwyck (Cheryl)	- Amateur (artist) - witnesses a murder	Primary; competent but her sanity is questioned by the police	Masculine: active investigation / Feminine: bows to male authority

is something different about its heroine. The first Vicky Lynn (Carole Landis) was presented as hard-boiled, ambitious, and cutthroat—looking for her big break at any cost. Her decade-later incarnation (Jean Peters), by contrast, is more innocent and honest—a Cinderella type. Similarly, while the original sister was played by a more gutsy Betty Grable as a working girl, in the remake she is played by a more feminine and refined Jeanne Crain as a middle-class woman and is less involved in investigating her sister's murder. Within a couple of years, it would be not only the female detective's ability that was questioned but her very sanity—notably, Barbara Stanwyck's heroine in *Witness to Murder.* After 1954, the female detective disappears from the screen for decades.

Conclusion: Black and White and Gray

The aim of this essay has been to demonstrate that, rather than women being reduced to two types—"the boring, potentially childbearing sweethearts" (nurturing redeemers) and the "exciting, childless whores" (femmes fatales)—noir films offered women a third type of role: the detective. These women rarely begin the narrative already in this role but rather adopt it in order to see justice served when the authorities fail. They often embody aspects of the traditionally identified two types or, more accurately, move from the first (the good girl) through the second (the femme fatale) as the third (the investigator) to find a new middle ground. It was this kind of woman who was upheld as the ideal for the immediate postwar years—the one needed to soothe and impassion returning servicemen in the years of readjustment. As Michael Renov suggests, the ideal woman presented in postwar dramas like William Wyler's *The Best Years of Our Lives* (1946) was "a sexy mother figure, for the twin attributes of the rehabilitating female are seduction and nurture—the former to revitalize the sexual identity, the latter to soothe the traumas to mind and body."[33] The noir female detective is similarly a sexualized figure for the hero who, although often absent for the duration of the film, will return needing her comfort from his ordeal of being falsely accused. These noir films with a female detective reveal that noir presented a range and variety of psychologically complex women rather than just a Madonna/whore division. In *Phantom Lady,* Scott Henderson (Alan Curtis) blames his failed marriage on the fact that his wife was "too spoiled and too beautiful"—in other words, a femme fatale; his secretary Carol, as the girl-next-door-turned-vamp (along with the other female detectives of noir), represents a more positive alternative in the wartime and postwar years.

A question thus arises from these noir films of the 1940s: Why is the female investigator allowed to be sexualized and independent, whereas the femme fatale is punished? The answer would appear to be dependent on the woman's motivation. While the war meant that real-life women could pursue opportunities beyond the traditional and socially sanctioned roles of wife and mother, especially in terms of employment, Susan Hartmann notes that popular discourse at the time set limits on the possibility of social change: first, that women were replacing men in the workforce only for the duration of the war; second, that women would retain their femininity even as they performed masculine labor; and, third, that there were feminine motivations behind women's willingness to work—they did so to support their men.[34] Similarly, in these noir films, the heroine's foray into detective work and the resulting independence and sexualization that she experiences are contained or excused by the fact that she is investigating to save her love interest, a man who can offer her the socially prescribed role of wife—that is, once she is done playing detective.

In relation to the femme fatale, Grossman argues, "It is the leading female's commitment to fulfilling her own desires, whatever they may be (sexual, capitalist, maternal), at any cost, that makes her the cynosure, the compelling point of interest for men and women."[35] Noir's female detective proves just as compelling with her commitment to fulfilling her own desire to uncover the truth and to save her man. Although this may make her less subversive, in that she is aligned with the law rather than defying it, as many femmes fatales did, she represents a subversion of the male-dominated noir detective film as a successful investigator possessing both male and female skills. As E. Ann Kaplan suggests in relation to Fritz Lang's *The Blue Gardenia* (1953), the male discourse of the noir narrative represented by Casey's (Richard Conte) investigation is undercut in two ways: because Norah (Anne Baxter) possesses more knowledge than the male investigators, and because the film presents a woman's perspective and an acknowledgment of female sexuality through the alignment of the audience with Norah rather than Casey.[36] This is true as well of the majority of the noir films I have discussed. As Broe argues in relation to the Woolrich adaptations featuring a female detective, "[I]n a refusal to displace the crimes of power onto the woman, the detective film sheds its archaic patriarchal past."[37]

One of the key differences between male- and female-centered noir is that, when a man is at the center of the noir narrative, he is the tough guy—hardboiled by his experiences in the war and disillusioned about postwar society; conversely, the female detective brings with her an idealism—a faith in other people and America's future. In terms of the films produced by Lewton (*The Leopard Man* and *The Seventh Victim*), Kuersten argues, "Standing unobtrusively amidst the murder and noir shadows, Lewton's deep faith in humanity quietly waits for the smoke to settle so it can step in and start patching up the wounds."[38] Similarly, Donald Phelps contends that the noir films based on Woolrich stories, in particular *Black Angel*, "express something virtually alien to *noir* mood and *noir* ethos: a lingering, faintly nostalgic sensitivity, a persistent albeit wistful humanism."[39] Most significantly, the noir female detectives do not seem to be tainted, as noir's male detectives are, from their brush with evil. Indeed, for the adolescent (in *The Seventh Victim* and *Shadow of a Doubt*) and naïve adult detectives (in *Black Angel* and *Phantom Lady*), the price of exploring America's darker side and confronting villainy is to become tougher and discover their sexuality; for women hardened by their urban experiences (in *Deadline at Dawn* and *Woman on the Run*), it is to become softer and rediscover their nurturing side. In contrast, the male detective, by becoming as violent as the criminals he seeks, is distanced from "good" society and the benefits of that society, including community, marriage, and family. Like the hero of the Western, the noir hero remains alone. While the male detective is punished for his desire to investigate, the female is altered, improved, and rewarded (at least by Hollywood's standards) with marriage to the man she loves. Perhaps it is for this reason that her reward is also her containment: marriage will bring to a close her yearning to investigate, and the female detective—like the redeemer figure—is safely returned to a more desirable social role. However, for the audience, like the heroine, her journey into the dark side of American society resonates well beyond the tacked-on "happy endings" prescribed by Hollywood's Production Code, and that makes these female detectives exciting and satisfying noir heroines.

Notes

1. Sylvia Harvey, "Woman's Place: The Absent Family of Film Noir," in *Women in Film Noir*, new ed., ed. E. Ann Kaplan (London: British Film Institute, 2001), 38; Janey Place, "Women in Film Noir," in *Women in Film Noir*, 60.

2. Julie Grossman, *Rethinking the Femme Fatale in Film Noir: Ready for Her Close-Up* (Basingstoke, U.K.: Palgrave Macmillan, 2009), 1.

3. Robert Porfirio, "No Way Out: Existential Motifs in the Film Noir," *Sight and Sound* 45.4 (1976): 216.

4. Mary Ann Doane, *Femmes Fatales: Feminism, Film Theory, Psychoanalysis* (New York: Routledge, 1991), 2–3.

5. Place, "Women in Film Noir," 53.

6. Elizabeth Cowie, "*Film Noir* and Women," in *Shades of Noir: A Reader*, ed. Joan Copjec (London: Verso, 1993), 125.

7. Tania Modleski, *Feminism without Women: Culture and Criticism in a "Post-Feminist" Age* (New York: Routledge, 1991), 21.

8. Julie Grossman, "'Well, Aren't We Ambitious,' or 'You've Made up Your Mind I'm Guilty': Reading Women as Wicked in American Film Noir," in *The Femme Fatale: Images, Histories, Contexts*, ed. Helen Hanson and Catherie O'Rawe (Basingstoke, U.K.: Palgrave Macmillan, 2010), 199.

9. Frank Krutnik, *In a Lonely Street: Film Noir, Genre, Masculinity* (London: Routledge, 1991), 86.

10. Cowie, "*Film Noir* and Women," 125; Deborah Thomas, "How Hollywood Deals with the Deviant Male," in *The Book of Film Noir*, ed. Ian Cameron (London: Studio Vista, 1992), 59.

11. Richard Maltby, "Film Noir: The Politics of the Maladjusted Text," *Journal of American Studies* 18.1 (1984): 53.

12. America's involvement in World War II also sparked a desire for introspection, resulting in the phasing out of comedy with a shift to more socially critical noir, preoccupied with a society that was at best flawed and at worst corrupt.

13. William Covey, "Girl Power: Female-Centered Neo-*Noir*," in *Film Noir Reader 2*, 2d ed., ed. Alain Silver and James Ursini (New York: Limelight Editions, 2003), 311.

14. Krutnik, *In a Lonely Street*, 194.

15. Ibid., 97.

16. Helen Hanson, *Hollywood Heroines: Women in Film Noir and the Female Gothic Film* (London: I. B. Tauris, 2007), 30.

17. Sheri Chinen Biesen, "Manufacturing Heroines: Gothic Victims and Working Women in Classic Noir Films," in *Film Noir Reader 4: The Crucial Films and Themes*, ed. Alain Silver and James Ursini (Pompton Plains, N.J.: Limelight Editions, 2004), 166. The films she mentions are *Stranger on the Third Floor* and *Phantom Lady*.

18. Dennis Broe, *Film Noir, American Workers, and Postwar Hollywood* (Gainesville: University Press of Florida, 2009), 29. He mentions William Nigh's *I Wouldn't Be in Your Shoes* (1948), *Phantom Lady*, and Roy William Neill's *Black Angel* (1946). Other films based on short stories or novels written by Woolrich (sometimes as William Irish) include Jacques Tourneur's *The Leopard Man* (1943) and Harold Clurman's *Deadline at Dawn* (1946).

19. Angela Martin, "'Gilda Didn't Do Any of Those Things You've Been Losing Sleep Over!': The Central Women of '40s Films Noirs," in *Women in Film Noir*, new ed., ed. E. Ann Kaplan (London: British Film Institute, 2001), 218–19; Cowie, "Film Noir and Women," 133.

20. William Park, *What Is Film Noir?* (Lewisburg, Pa.: Bucknell University Press, 2011), 120.

21. Hanson, *Hollywood Heroines*, 27. In terms of the deviation of the noir female detective from the mystery-comedy detective, see Philippa Gates, *Detecting Women: Gender and the Hollywood Detective Film* (Albany: State University of New York Press, 2011).

22. There are other films that offer a female protagonist who functions as an instigator, inspiring a male detective to investigate, including *I Wouldn't Be in Your Shoes* and Fritz Lang's *The Blue Gardenia* (1953).

23. Philippa Gates, "The Maritorious Melodrama: *Film Noir* with a Female Detective," *Journal of Film and Video* 61.3 (Fall 2009): 24–39; and Gates, *Detecting Women*.

24. Krutnik, *In a Lonely Street*, 195.

25. See Steve Neale, *Genre and Hollywood* (London: Routledge, 2000), 163.

26. Catherine Ross Nickerson, *The Web of Iniquity: Early Detective Fictions by American Women* (Durham, N.C.: Duke University Press, 1998), xiii.

27. Diane Waldman, "'At Last I Can Tell It to Someone!': Feminine Point of View and Subjectivity in the Gothic Romance Film of the 1940s," *Cinema Journal* 23.2 (1984): 29–30.

28. Gary Giddins, "Hitched," *Film Comment* (March–April 2007): 21.

29. Some sources cite the heroine's name as "Goffe" (e.g., the American Film Institute catalog) and others as "Goth" (e.g., the Internet Movie Database).

30. Erich Kuersten, "What It Takes to Make a Softie: Breaking with Noir Tradition in *The Leopard Man*," *Bright Lights* 50 (November 2005), accessed July 16, 2012 http://www.brightlightsfilm.com/50/leopard.php.

31. A couple of films offer the opposite—that is, a woman whose experiences in urban America have made her hard-boiled, and the film suggests that she needs to soften up—including the nightclub performer Kiki Walker (Jean Brooks) in *The Leopard Man* and the taxi dancer June Goffe (Susan Hayward) in *Deadline at Dawn*. The reviews of the latter particularly noted this: the reviewer for the *New York Herald Tribune* describes her as "a harsh, plain-speaking but essentially soft-hearted type" (April 4, 1946); and the reviewer for *Variety* as "a disillusioned but warm-hearted taxi dancer . . . sympathizing with his helplessness and drawn to him despite her outwardly hardboiled attitude towards men" (February 12, 1946). In the former, Kiki tells her boyfriend/manager, "I'm tired of pretending that nothing bothers me, that all I care about is myself. . . . We've been so busy trying to play tough guys. Confession? I'm a complete softie. I've been conscience-stricken and worried sick ever since that leopard got loose."

32. The gothic-set noir, *The Second Woman*, also borrows from *Rebecca*, this time with its opening shot of a destroyed house and the voiceover of the heroine, which promises to recall the events that led from happier times at the home to its destruction and abandonment.

33. Michael Renov, *Hollywood's Wartime Women: Representation and Ideology* (Ann Arbor, Mich.: UMI Research Press, 1988), 132.

34. Susan M. Hartmann, *The Home Front and Beyond: American Women in the 1940s* (Boston: Twayne Publishers, 1982), 23.

35. Grossman, *Rethinking the Femme Fatale*, 3.

36. E. Ann Kaplan, "The Place of Women in Fritz Lang's *The Blue Gardenia*," in *Women in Film Noir*, new ed., ed. E. Ann Kaplan (London: British Film Institute, 2001), 81, 85.

37. Broe, *Film Noir, American Workers, and Postwar Hollywood*, 29.

38. Kuersten, "What It Takes to Make a Softie."

39. Donald Phelps, "Cinema Gris: Woolrich/Neill's *Black Angel*," *Film Comment* 30.1 (January–February 2000): 64, 66.

2

Women and Film Noir

Pulp Fiction and the Woman's Picture

JULIE GROSSMAN

Many discussions of film noir are dominated by the categories of the hard-boiled detective and the femme fatale. While these character patterns tend to govern our thinking about the genre, classification of films *as* noir itself poses problems because of the term's cultural pervasiveness. This essay reconsiders the categories conventionally associated with film noir, not only because these labels tend to overshadow discussion of narrative, but also because focusing on such stock characters excludes consideration of other generic associations that can shed light on some of the most intriguing films from the classic period. The most compelling film-noir movies, finally, are blends of male and female stories that don't reinforce patriarchy; they feature both good and bad kinds of agency (rather than being mere primers in moralistic thinking). Lastly, film-noir movies cross genres to include what we conventionally refer to as melodrama, as is certainly the case in all three versions of *Mildred Pierce* (the novel, film, and HBO miniseries).[1]

Far from providing a pat repetition of familiar character patterns and narrative clichés, the best film-noir movies, like much of the fiction that these films adapt, have had an important role in depicting gender distress in modern culture. This essay explores the conversations that take place between classic noir films about love, violence, and gender and the female-authored fiction that served as their sources.[2] Looking at 1940s novels written by women that were brought to the screen as "film noirs" underscores the problems inherent in limiting discussion of film noir to the "classic" character patterns—specifically, the "femme fatale" and the "hard-boiled" male protagonist.[3]

Linking noir with its female-authored source material will, I hope, help to reorient (and reorder) gender associations with film noir so that male experience is not its exclusive focus. Rather, such linkage renders the shared concerns of film noir and melodrama (and its often-discussed subgenre, the "woman's picture") more evident and interprets the relationship between gender and genre more as a dialogue, less as an opportunity to rank texts in terms of an evaluation-laden hierarchy.[4] Seeing women as the literal source of film noir will, I hope, advance a discussion of the centrality of women *in* noir, but my hope is also that in connecting several film noirs to their female-authored sources, this analysis will promote broader ways of thinking about adaptation spearheaded by Linda Hutcheon, Thomas Leitch, Robert Stam, and other postfidelity adaptation theorists. The dialogical, performative, nonhierarchical models for adaptation articulated by these critics offer more fruitful and creative ways of talking about film and literature than are available in the context of dyadic or heavily evaluative models that borrow the language of origins and fidelity.[5] A relational model of reading film and literature can recognize how different media, as well as cultural contexts, transpose form and content. More important, this approach also focuses on the meanings that emerge when we think of texts as being discrete, while still being in some sense connected: texts in dialogue *with,* rather than in opposition *to,* one another. Looking at classic film noir in proximity to feminist sources is one example of how relational models of adaptation can enrich our understanding of culture, society, and textual production.

In what follows, I look first at Dorothy Hughes's novel *In a Lonely Place* (1947) and Nicholas Ray's film *In a Lonely Place* (1950); second, at Vicki Baum's novel *Mortgage on Life* (1946) and Ray's film *A Woman's Secret* (1949); and, finally, at Vera Caspary's novel *Laura* (1942) in relation to Otto Preminger's film *Laura* (1944). These works, all made within an eight-year period, exemplify the nonschematic presence of gender issues in noir and the continuities between the treatment of gender in the genre and the exploration of gender in the source novels. While the feminist force of film noir generally comes from a variety of factors that can include writing, acting, and mise-en-scène, the fascination with gender in these particular films derives in large part from the female-authored source material.

Feminist film critique has begun to dissociate film noir from the masculinist perspective that dominated earlier discussions of the genre. Critical work by feminist scholars such as E. Ann Kaplan, Elizabeth Cowie, Helen Hanson, Philippa Gates, Jans Wager, and others has shown the centrality of women to film noir.[6] While popular associations with film noir still seem strongly connected to conventional gender stereotypes (the tough though often righteous male protagonist, the evil seductress), these works on gender and noir, dating from the first publication in 1978 of Kaplan's *Women in Film Noir,* have significantly changed scholarly views of the genre. Whether these critics focus on female protagonists, the subversive nature of the femme fatale, or a feminist critique of the male position in the genre, the revised focus on women in noir has rendered the assumption of noir as an *exclusively* male sphere obsolete.

Alongside this feminist upsurge in noir studies has been an increasing concomitant interest in revising strict genre definitions, with some critics suggesting that there are important continuities among the genres of noir, melodrama, and its subset, the woman's picture, that challenge conventional gender/genre associations. For example, Elizabeth Cowie has observed that film noir addresses the psychic worlds of women and rehearses an idea of melodrama that has been rooted in the genre from its beginning in 1940s classical cinema. While critics have recognized that certain noir films may be called "crime melodramas," that a number of noir films are also "gothic melodramas," and that some noir films take on a female perspective, ostensibly constituting them as "women's pictures,"[7] these observations haven't had a huge impact on the fixity of film noir as a category, perhaps because the term has become such a cultural touchstone. However, the many films talked about in relation to film noir offer stories and stylistic approaches to narrative that run the gamut across conventional genre boundaries, and, as Cowie has noted, such hybridization was in fact part of the early history of film noir, when studios tried to merge genres in order to tap into as wide an audience as possible: "[W]hat has come to be called *film noir,* whilst it does not constitute a genre itself, does name a particular set of elements that were used to produce 'the different' and the new in a film; hence the term *film noir* names a set of possibilities for making existing genres 'different.' With this view of genre and of *film noir,* it is no longer possible to speak of 'the' *film noir,* as so many writers seek to do."[8] Cowie's reminder that film noir as a category grew to some extent out of a commercial interest in overlapping genres spurs a reconsideration of the relationships among noir and other classic film genres.

Reevaluation of standard genre associations will hopefully continue to loosen the grip of noir enthusiasts on "fatal" character patterns. Helen Hanson has, for example, explored the subjectivity of women in the female gothic and film noir in *Hollywood Heroines,* and Thomas Schatz has discussed the "family resemblance" between the female gothic and the hard-boiled detective film,[9] coining the phrase "femmes noires" to refer to postwar thrillers in which women are central: "The female viewpoint, meanwhile, was privileged in films like *The Strange Love of Martha Ivers* and *Temptation* . . . thus effectively melding the woman's picture with the *noir* thriller."[10] Attempts to nuance an understanding of film noir are, however, often thwarted by the figure of the femme fatale, who dominates discussions of gender and noir, certainly in popular consciousness but also in critical studies. Jon Lewis, for instance, subscribes to the feminist reading of the "fatal women" in noir as a reflection of postwar anxiety about female independence but asserts that the "castrating woman" is at the heart of film noir: "At the center of many noir films is a devouring woman, a femme fatale."[11] As I've argued elsewhere, the presence of an unambiguous evil woman in the genre is wildly overstated.[12] In fact, the most interesting noir films construct a sliding scale of narrative types—from malevolent seductress, to intrepid and victimized female characters, to ambitious yet helpless females—in suggestive and intriguing ways.

Close examination of film noirs reveals a systematic representation of female characters who cannot express their desire or attain satisfaction within conventional social roles. Examples of such characters who are given subjectivity in film noir while still often being tagged as simply femme fatales abound. Lizabeth Scott's Mona Stevens in *Pitfall* (1948) directly criticizes Dick Powell's John Forbes ("You're a little man with a briefcase"); her insight casts her as the controlling voice of the narrative. Gloria Grahame's Vicki Buckley in *Human Desire* (1954) is also a tragic figure mislabeled as a "femme fatale."[13] Like Mona, Vicki conveys feminist insight in her comments about women's experience: "Most women are unhappy. They just pretend they aren't." Barbara Stanwyck's Mae Doyle in *Clash by Night* (1952) also draws viewer sympathy. She's hard-boiled herself, which may lead viewers to categorize her as a femme fatale, but her story is one of privation, like the situation of many women in film noir; Mae had, on her own report, "big dreams, small results." Debby Marsh in *The Big Heat* (1953) parodies thug Vince Stone's (Lee Marvin) pandering to his boss Lagana in her imitation of Stone's "circus jumping" at Lagana's bidding. Debby's wry commentary establishes her as a sympathetic voice of critique. So, too, in *Notorious* (1946), Alicia Huberman (Ingrid Bergman) perceives and articulates Devlin's (Cary Grant) limitations as a lover. Alicia repeatedly calls attention to his lack of trust in her ("What a little pal you are"; "Not a word of faith. Just down the drain with Alicia").

These characters, like many others, critique male privilege and men's obsessiveness, lack of trust in women, and will to power. The well-known characters whose noir films are named after them—Laura, Mildred Pierce, and Gilda—are certainly not malevolent. Many other female characters (such as Norma Desmond in *Sunset Boulevard* [1950] and Cora Smith in *The Postman Always Rings Twice* [1946]) may behave criminally, but their stories, as in a good Victorian novel, contextualize their behavior in ways that make these characters sympathetic. And yet, our long-standing assumption in discussions of film noir is that such women have no subjectivity. In his interesting discussion of Dorothy Hughes's subversive representation of gender in *In a Lonely Place*, Stanley Orr claims, for example, that the film "stands out as one of the few films noir that permits a female figure to transgress the

"You're a little man with a briefcase": Mona Stevens (Lizabeth Scott) to John Forbes (Dick Powell) in *Pitfall* (1948).

boundaries of the angel/femme fatale binary in favor of the lonely centrality of authenticating alienation."[14] Orr is certainly right that *In a Lonely Place* doesn't portray women in schematic ways. He's wrong, however, to assume that the character construction in the movie is rare. The portraits that emerge from so many noir films are of men and women brutalized by class and gender roles. Looking at the female-authored sources of several classic film-noir movies helps us to see one way in which the genre shows persistent gender disharmony in American culture.

In her essay "Why Film Noir? Hollywood, Adaptation, and Women's Writing in the 1940s and 1950s," Esther Sonnet takes Richard T. Jameson to task for what she sees as his recuperation of Otto Preminger's *Daisy Kenyon* (1947) by virtue of its noir affiliation. In other words, the film was formerly labeled as a "woman's picture" but should, for Jameson, be instead newly appreciated for its status as a "kissing cousin to film noir." Having "rescued" the film based on its now-recognizable noir elements, Jameson demonstrates for Sonnet the genre's hierarchical privileging of *"masculine affiliation."*[15] Sonnet's claim "that categorization as a film noir will secure for the film some critical value that it might not otherwise deserve" is based on her concern that the feminist source material in Elizabeth Janeway's novel will be obscured. To make her point that *Daisy Kenyon* does not fall easily into the category of film noir represented by *Double Indemnity* (1944), *The Postman Always Rings Twice, Gilda* (1946), and *The Big Heat,* Sonnet unfortunately contends that all of these films are "predicated on the function of the femme fatale"—an assumption, certainly for *Gilda* and *The Big Heat* and arguably for *The Postman Always Rings Twice,* that is deeply problematic, as I have claimed elsewhere.[16] Sonnet's questioning of the genre assumptions we bring to our viewing of adaptations is important, especially as it foregrounds the centrality of the female voice and social critique that underlies the source material for classic Hollywood films. However, the assumption that noir is "predicated on the function of the femme fatale" is based on a conventional view of noir derived from a troubling focus on only a few mainstream films, such as *Double Indemnity.* This critical stance fails to take into account the strength of many independent-minded women in noir and their struggle for empowerment, which is sometimes intriguingly connected to the women involved in either the source material or its adaptation.

Although Nicholas Ray's *In a Lonely Place* contains neither a femme fatale nor a hard-boiled detective, it was recently called "one of the finest of all films noir."[17] It is also an example of a film whose noirness derives from a woman's work. As many have noted, *In a Lonely Place* departs significantly from its source novel of the same name. Dorothy Hughes portrays Dix Steele as a hack novelist; in Ray's film, Dix (Humphrey Bogart) is a besieged yet "authentic" artist/writer who must ward off the efforts of the Hollywood machinery to turn his "art" into slavish Hollywood "popcorn" scripts. The trajectory of the narrative is altered, too, since in the novel Dix is in fact the serial murderer the characters in the film only suspect him to be.

While both novel and film address gender psychosis, the tone of the works is also different. Ray's *In a Lonely Place* adds romantic melodrama to Hughes's crime story. In the film, while Laurel (Gloria Grahame) grows increasingly fearful of Dix, the lovers' heightened emotion grounds the film. Their exceptional yet ill-fated romance is captured in the lines Dix writes for a script he's been working on: "I was born when you kissed me. I died when you left me. I lived a few weeks while you loved me." These lines are repeated by Dix and Laurel throughout the film, establishing them as the subject of the narrative and exemplifying Jonathan Rosenbaum's description of a "passionately symmetrical relationship" in *In a Lonely Place* and Ray's other films. In contrast, Dorothy Hughes focuses in her novel on Dix's pathology as she charts his actual serial killing. Though Dix's status as a serial killer seems a crucial plot distinction in both novel and film, the presence of the male serial murderer

An Ambiguous Embrace: Dix Steele (Humphrey Bogart) and Laurel Gray (Gloria Grahame) in *In a Lonely Place* (1950).

is this story's feminist MacGuffin,[18] the seeming central question of the story that is finally irrelevant to the real interest of these works, which is, in the case of the novel, the inevitable violence of conventional gender roles, and in the case of both the novel and the film, the nearness of trauma to everyday American experience. The film's tragedy is that though Dix is cleared of suspicion for the murder at the end of the story, his temper and quickness to violence have so upended his relationship with Laurel that it doesn't matter that he isn't the murderer.

While Dana Polan's reference to *In a Lonely Place* as a "woman's film"[19] depends on its exploration of a female (gothic) perspective on male violence, the film's interest in gender trauma can be directly linked to Dorothy Hughes's exploration of deviant masculinity. Polan contrasts the film's assumption of a female perspective with the novel's point of view: "Significantly, in light of the serious recognition that the film of *In a Lonely Place* gives to a woman's point of view, Hughes does not seem a writer much concerned to give women power in a narrative."[20] While the novel limits perspective to the psychotic point of view of Dix, however, Polan's comparison doesn't acknowledge the extent to which the film's interest in gender and masculinity is derived from the novel's analysis of postwar gender roles. In other words, the film's treatment of masculinity as a form of psychosis adapts the novel's investigation of psychosocial gender disorder. Thus, the distinction Polan draws between Ray's characteristic representation of social milieu and Hughes's psychological portrait of Dix's madness underestimates the extent to which Dix's psychology in the film as well as the novel is a symptom of the impossibility of "normal" human interaction in modern postwar social space.

It is Dix's masculinity that is felt to be under siege in the novel, and Hughes makes a point of delineating the great loss of power associated with men coming home from the war. This is a familiar noir scenario, one nowhere better portrayed than in the first twenty minutes of *The Blue Dahlia*.[21] It is interesting, however, that the most explicit articulations of this motif—violent vets (think Robert Ryan as Montgomery in *Crossfire* [1947]) unable to adapt to "normal" life after the war—can be found in a novel in which the narrator says of the main character, "The war years were the first happy years he'd ever known. . . . You were the Mister"; "The world was yours."[22] There is a radical feminist assumption at work here: for someone who has been constructed psychologically as a killer by the pressures of masculine role-playing, war would be strangely satisfying. A "normal" world where one can't kill people would be the harder environment to be in. This alignment of murder and masculinity is the source of Lisa Maria Hogeland's evaluation of the novel. For Hogeland, the book seems to be a consummate portrait of a dangerous misogynist, but "the vet ruse . . . works two ways: on the one hand, it creates suspicion of Dix in relation to the images circulating in the postwar period of veterans as liable to 'snap,' while on the other, it connects him to a very large number of 'average,' 'normal,' American men who have been capable of killing."[23]

The portrait in film noir of postwar America as a place where repressed violence threatens to seep out in unlikely places is familiar to us from many noir films, including *Out of the Past* (1947), *On Dangerous Ground* (1952), *The Hitch-Hiker* (1953), and *The Night of the Hunter* (1955). The fine line that divides the murderers from the romantic heroes is where noir resides.[24] Both the novel and the film version of *In a Lonely Place* locate this observation about the proximity of psychosis to "normal" behavior in masculinity.

However, not only gender but also class consciousness feeds psychosis in the novel *In a Lonely Place*. Hughes makes a point of Dix's contempt for work and his anger at the vulgar Uncle Fergus, who withholds money from Dix because of his failure to work:

> Dix knew damn well he'd go through hell at the university. He did. He suffered. God how he suffered, that first year. He'd have quit, he'd have flunked out quick but the alternative was far worse: being packed off like a piece of cattle to a farm Uncle Fergus owned. Either he had to be a gentleman, according to Uncle

Fergus' standards, or he could resort to the peasantry. Dix was smart enough
to know he couldn't get a job, stand on his own feet. He didn't want to work
that hard. He took the first year, working in the hardware store after school,
afraid to look anyone in the eye, afraid he'd see the sneers openly, or the pity.[25]

As this passage suggests, class issues help to explain Dix's violence. Unable
to "stand on his own feet," Dix doesn't fit into class-defined categories—
"gentleman" or "peasant"—and is helpless to create a place for himself. He
is radically alienated from class and gender norms, which fuels his anger
and explains his deviance. Hughes's novel reveals noir's submerged feminist
sources that powerfully critique the ways in which class and gender make
freedom, love, and meaningful agency impossible in the modern world.

While Ray's *In a Lonely Place* focuses more on the impossibility of love and
intimacy surviving anxiety about domestic violence, it also adapts the novel's
interest in women as victims of male rage. As Polan says, "One can easily
read the film as a proto-feminist work that argues that men *per se,* not this
or that murderous man, can pose a threat of violence to women."[26] Because
women's roles and behavior are directly linked to threatening male behavior
and identity, the generic conventions of noir are blurred. Not only is Dix an
"homme fatal," but women are neither domestic angels nor femme fatales.
Geoff Andrew comments that the film's Laurel is "freed from the conventions of the *femme fatale* to portray a woman at once strong, intelligent, and
vulnerable."[27] Similarly, Stanley Orr notes that in the novel, Sylvia Nicolai
and Laurel Gray are strong women: Sylvia assumes the role of detective, as
she hones in on Dix's secret life as a serial killer, and Laurel "complicates the
neat binaries of noir."[28] At the same time, female aggressiveness is not treated
as malevolent in these works but instead as feminist rebellion. For example,
the script adapts Sylvia's suspicion about Dix via Freudian slips that reveal a
suppressed hostility. On the beach with Brub, Laurel, and Dix, Sylvia reveals
that Laurel has been to see Detective Lochner (without Dix's knowledge),
which sends Dix into a fury. Sylvia immediately repents: "I don't know why I
said it. Brub especially asked me not to." Here, Sylvia "acts out" her anxiety
about Dix's submerged violence and counters Brub's defense of him as "an
exciting guy" by eliciting proof of Dix's dangerous rage. An even more veiled
rendering of female agency is Martha the masseuse's warning to Laurel about
Dix ("You'll be sorry, Angel"). As Andrew astutely observes, the way the
scene is filmed with the use of back lighting, low-angle shots, and extreme
close-ups[29] suggests Laurel's repressed fear and desire to escape her relationship with Dix. These instances in the film of female rebellion and "the special
solidarity among women"[30] transpose the novel's theme of women under
threat who nevertheless assert their agency (Sylvia, for example, appearing
as a detective figure).[31]

I have been arguing that the ambiguities in the representation of female experience in film noir are obscured by the heavy weight of the character patterns ("hard-boiled detective," "femme fatale") and generic assumptions that swamp readings of noir narrative. The gendered categories of "film noir" and "women's picture"[32] short-circuit sustained attempts to reorient viewers to a more nuanced reading of gender in film noir. Critical attention, too, has mostly been articulated in categorical terms, not only the femme fatale figure and the hard-boiled detective but also "postwar anxiety" and the "mean streets" of the city. All of these categories have historically been organized around the male figures in these films (postwar trauma for men, the threat that bad sexy women pose to men, interrogation about why modern men in the city are cynical or hard-boiled). Moreover, auteurist attention to directors (in the case of the films discussed here, the prominent directors Preminger and Ray) reinforces critical attention on directors' style and vision as opposed to the films' representation of gender violence drawn from the source material. For example, the romantic light Nicholas Ray shines on Dix Steele—Ray's portrait of an angry artist who imagines that redemptive love can ward off opportunistic Hollywood and a brute social world—taps viewer associations not only with disappointed men in noir but also with Ray's characteristic cynicism and idealism. As Rosenbaum observes, "[E]ven within a vision as fundamentally bleak and futile as Ray's, a clear view of paradise is never entirely out of mind or even definitively out of reach."[33] In connection with *In a Lonely Place*, critical focus on Ray's "naked paw prints"[34] has overshadowed the film's dialogue with Hughes's novel and its portrait of violence specifically linked to gender and culture. This may explain an overidentification with Dix that, as Polan points out, causes some viewers and critics such as Jean Wagner "to believe that Dix deserves more sympathy than the murder victim Mildred."[35] Ray's "deep romanticism," combined with a generic expectation of a hard-boiled protagonist, may eclipse the feminist force of the narrative.

In its exploration of Dix Steele as the "homme fatal," Ray's *In a Lonely Place* modifies noir's conventional gender associations, a refashioning of familiar character types presaged by Hughes's novel. Another Nicholas Ray adaptation of female-authored fiction from the classic Hollywood period similarly explores modern gender trauma and also blurs the generic boundaries that separate the woman's picture from film noir. In 1949, Ray directed *A Woman's Secret*, based on Vicki Baum's 1946 novel *Mortgage on Life*. Critics have noted "noir elements" in *A Woman's Secret*[36] and have also compared the film to "Freudian Gothic melodrama."[37] The mixed tone of *A Woman's Secret* and its cynical treatment of celebrity in contemporary America constitute a hybrid generic model of melodramatic and noir elements difficult to separate. Further, the film pursues an analysis of gender and the objectification of women that is deeply related to its fictional source. Both of these points—the film's complicated generic status and its fascination with gender—are clarified when it is juxtaposed with Baum's novel. Indeed, reading all of the films discussed here in relation with their source novels reveals their generic elasticity and their feminist characteristics.[38]

In the novel *Mortgage on Life,* the ambitious and intelligent Bess Poker ("Pokey," as she is nicknamed) takes over the life and career of the naïve, "indolent," and beautiful Mary Lynn, renamed "Marylynn." Bess Poker transforms the "disarmingly young and stupid"[39] Marylynn into a Broadway star who leaves men in her trail, while plain-Jane Pokey writhes ambivalently on the sidelines, watching the love of her life, the composer Luke Jordan, chase after Marylynn, writing songs for her that make the two of them famous and successful. Bess's lack of self-esteem is accompanied by "bitterness and hatred," as she negotiates the cynical landscape of "ruthless" men who fall for Marylynn. One of these is A. W. Huysmans, who "had ruined many of his opponents, politically, socially, financially. He had driven some of them into suicide without batting an eyelash."[40] Another suitor is the narcissistic politician Dale Corbett, who is "all ambition" and empty at the core.

There is a fair amount of melodrama in the novel, including some extremely traumatic episodes: the fire at the nightclub that horrifically burns Marylynn (repaired through a grafting of Pokey's skin!); the storm during which Marylynn meets Huysmans; the World War II battle surrounding the foxhole in France, where the soldier Lee Crenshaw protects and saves Marylynn from German fire; and the shooting of Marylynn by Pokey, when the performer insists on leaving her life as a singer to marry Lee Crenshaw and return to middle America. However, there is also a noir commentary: first, on modern social relations that are viewed as utterly objectifying; second, on the nearness of violence to "normal" everyday life in America; and third, on the desperation of men and women in America who resort to such violence because of their narrow prospects for living a fulfilling life. Driving Pokey to "make Marylynn" is her anxiety about her alternative to success as an agent: "scraping, saving, going back to the small life of small people. There were various prospects, and all of them unbearable."[41] Like the women in noir often mislabeled as "femme fatales," Bess is a hard-boiled protagonist who is ambitious yet also frustrated with the limits of her prospects.

Much attention is paid in the novel to Bess's physical plainness, and her physiognomy becomes a metaphor for her overreaching ambition. Bess has "too much of a nose, too much of a mouth, an awful lot of strong, big teeth that must have somehow got out of control at the time there was not enough money for braces."[42] Bess's physical mien reflects her "unnatural" desire to be a player in society, to be empowered beyond the conventional roles available to women in postwar America. It is fascinating to note that Bess's noir act of attempted murder is cast as a "suicide": "I had no life of my own. My life was—Marylynn. And so I shot her." Bess is seen as only "half a woman": Luke says, "Jesus Christ, if I could only make one girl out of the two of you! If you'd have Mary's figure and her sort of voice—or if she'd have your brains and personality—then we would really go places."[43] Luke's fantasy that he can constitute and market the perfect woman reflects the objectifying social gaze and frantic consumerism that characterize living in the modern world. Such attention to the exploited lives of women and the limits of their experience in culture and society is paramount in film noir, as it is in the so-called woman's picture.

A Woman's Secret, the Nicholas Ray film adapted from Baum's novel, begins, as Mildred Pierce does, with a flashback sequence and an ambiguous murder. The mystery revolves around whether Marian Washburn (Bess/Pokey in the novel) has killed Susan Caldwell, the film's version of Marylynn (here, Susan's stage name is similarly objectifying, the one-word "Estrellita"). Like Mildred Pierce, A Woman's Secret is referred to both as a noir and as a woman's picture. Like many films central to the noir series, it addresses the theme of female ambition and the limited venues for women to express their desires. Ray's A Woman's Secret shares with its source material a melo-noir representation of the underbelly of American consumer culture and women's often despairing role as a commodity within that system. If, as Geoff Andrew says, A Woman's Secret is "Ray's most anonymous work, and he himself felt no affection for it,"[44] perhaps Cullen Gallagher is right to suggest that "it is precisely because of its position as a studio—rather than a personal—project that Secret demands alternative ways of understanding, appreciation, and criticism."[45] I would suggest that a focus on the film's adaptation of Baum's novel rather than an auteurist consideration of its marginal place within the body of Nicholas Ray's work can provide one fruitful "alternative" approach to A Woman's Secret.

There is no doubt that Gloria Grahame's portrayal of Susan/Estrellita is the most appealing aspect of the film. Grahame brings her charisma to the part and carries off the best lines of Herman Mankiewicz's script with utter insouciance. Her description of where she comes from, "Azusa" ("it's a made-up name—everything from A to Z"), is a brilliant noir sendup of the emptiness of American culture—again, a vision of America as a void, its inhabitants on a quest for meaning in a denuded cultural landscape. Susan seems to be looked at by others in the film as malevolent, a response out of keeping with the portrayal by Grahame and a misreading then proliferated by Nicholas Ray's biographer, Patrick McGilligan, who writes that Susan "metamorphoses into the torch singer Estrellita, a bewitching monster. Frankenstein never looked so good."[46] Far from a stereotypical femme fatale, Susan/Estrellita comes across to viewers as a sympathetic naïf, meandering through the American wasteland. The following figure nicely captures Susan's exploitation by her mentors, Marian and Luke.

The Project: from right to left, Marian Washburn (Maureen O'Hara), Susan Caldwell/Estrellita (Gloria Grahame), and Luke Jordan (Melvyn Douglas) in *A Woman's Secret* (1949). The Kobal Collection at Art Resource, N.Y.

McGilligan's misreading of Grahame's character strangely replays the objectification that is already satirized in the narrative. This is evident in the derivation of the name "Estrellita." A popular folk song written by the the Mexican composer Ponce, who died in 1948 (a year before *A Woman's Secret* was released), "Estrellita" means "little star" in Spanish. Susan's objectification in the narrative is thus signaled in her pseudonym, a motif introduced at the very beginning of the film when "Estrellita" sings the song after which she is named.

It is further worth noting that the novel places Mary's "home" as Blythe, California, perhaps a play on the word "blithe," since Mary's life has been anything but carefree. The setting of Blythe is described starkly in the novel as "just a small dump in the desert."[47] Mary/Susan, in the film and novel, is distracted from her rootlessness by the attention of men and the promise of celebrity. The story of both of the women in novel and film repeats a pattern in classic noir of presenting women as trapped, lonely, and either insufficiently armed to protect themselves or extremely ambitious in their attempts to create meaningful lives for themselves. In *Mortgage for Life*, Marylynn has a doll called Emily that (like Mary for Bess) is her other half, a reliable source of comfort and opportunity for emotional expression ("Emily cries at night"[48]). Because she has to be so hard-boiled in her life, Marylynn sublimates her vulnerability in playacting with "Emily." Given the sympathy lent to Mary/Susan in her vulnerability, her dismissive treatment by men, and her objectification by Bess/Marian, the role of the "seductress" is thus complicated in tone. The sympathy for the aggressive yet exploitative Bess/Marian is there too, for she has no self-esteem and is clearly in search of a means for expression of her ambition.

British Film Noir and Portraits of Women in the Two *Bedelia*s

Vera Caspary's 1945 *Bedelia* and the British film noir adapted from Caspary's novel the following year work in dialogue to portray gender psychosis in the modern period.[1] Caspary's novel is set in Connecticut in 1913, at the moment when Victorian culture was giving way to modernism and New Woman gender politics. The 1946 film adaptation, directed by Lance Comfort, cowritten by Caspary, and starring Margaret Lockwood as Bedelia, is set initially in Monte Carlo, where Bedelia and Charles Carrington (Ian Hunter, portraying an Anglicized version of the novel's Charlie Horst) vacation following their wedding. While Monte Carlo may have appealed to a contemporary postwar audience (the setting projected backward, however, to 1938 before the war), the film then shifts its locale to Charles's home in Yorkshire, England, evoking a Bronte-esque atmosphere of romantic isolation and Victorian domestic constraints. This fascinating pair of postwar portraits of female distress gradually shows the lovely Bedelia to be a psychotic serial killer of husbands.

The novel and film both establish a familiar literary setting of Victorian repression. The novel is set in New England, where Charlie Horst's home is haunted by "the ghosts of Puritan ancestors,"[2] and Charlie's dead mother marshals these phantoms through time, as her portrait hangs in Charlie's bedroom. The picture depicts the stalwart matriarch "at seventeen, a righteous girl, her lips tight with disapproval" (30). In stark contrast, Charlie's new wife Bedelia embodies amoral energy run amok. Her crossing of American geography, as she moves from place to place poisoning husbands and trashing the stolid ground of family relations, is thus placed symbolically in opposition to a markedly repressive Puritan view of women.

In the bedroom in which Charlie's mother's portrait radiates her "scorn of weakness," Charlie indulges his desires, glad to have "married a widow" and quietly excited by Bedelia's "careless tresses," which carry "sluttish charm" (26) for him. The contrast between Bedelia and Charlie's mother is drawn distinctly. While the matriarch Harriet Philbrick "never colored her lips and cheeks with rouge," Bedelia's "fervor embarrassed" Charlie (88). Bedelia's presence exposes a Puritan double standard whereby Charlie wishes to maintain the repressive code instilled in him by his mother while unleashing his sexual desire on a woman for whom virginal innocence is no longer a concern. The very beginning of the novel establishes the male fantasy of indulgence and containment, as the fire is stoked and Charlie is pleased with his new mate: "She wore a dark-blue velvet dress whose sheath skirt was slit to show her pretty ankles and high-heeled bronze pumps. The Yule log caught fire. Flames licked the crusty bark. This was a great moment for Charlie" (10). Despite Charlie's "great moment," Bedelia's secret excesses cannot be channeled into acceptable behavior patterns. The "ghosts of Puritan ancestors" are no match for Bedelia, whose "brunette radiance" contrasts with Charlie's "pallid, angular, and restricted" mien. The setting and introduction of the characters as gendered types thus provide an important context for defining Bedelia's psychosis as symbolic, a staged opposition to social norms.

In the film, the theme of trapped women is presented symbolically through repeated scenes of Bedelia being "captured" visually. Recalling Caspary's *Laura,* as well as Otto Preminger's 1944 adaptation of the earlier work, Bedelia is introduced to viewers, first, in a portrait, as Ben Chaney (Barry K. Barnes), the detective pretending to be a painter, describes her in his voiceover as a lethal "femme fatale." Second, she is observed through the window of the French jeweler's shop in Monte Carlo, as Ben and the jeweler watch her. Third, Bedelia is figured as an image when her painting is positioned as the mediating absent "subject" of the conversation between Ben Chaney and Ellen (a possible love interest for Charles). Finally, Bedelia's suicide is captured in a reflection of the mirror. All of these scenes underscore the film's insistence on Bedelia's simultaneous—and paradoxical—power and objectification. The notion of apprehending Bedelia is not only figured in the repeated references to her as a visual object but also thematized in Ben Chaney's repeated taunting of her, as he pretends to be unaware of her past but suggests names and images that subtly convey to Bedelia that he knows her secrets. Ben paints a picture, for example, and signs it "Raoul Burgess," the name of Bedelia's fictional former husband. When Ben suggests to Bedelia and Charles that he has found an "original" "Raoul Burgess" ("Raoul Cochran" in the novel), Bedelia's response repeats the filmic refrain of her wild-eyed desperation, an hysteria that designates her not as an exposed criminal but as Ben Chaney's prey, the object of his predatory detective manipulations.

The repeated images of Bedelia's terror—Bedelia "caught" between Charles and Ben, represented in the camera's slow dolly shots toward Bedelia and the close-ups of her horrified reactions to Ben's subtle accusations—depict a truth

that is counter to the plot of her serial killing: Bedelia's hysteria and desperation are expressions of female energy with no outlet and active resistance to
masculine power.

Bedelia's object status is also dramatized in her submission to Ben's and
Charles's exhortation to "sit" for Chaney's painting sessions. In one scene Ben
Chaney taunts Bedelia with flirtatious comments about the color of her hair.
We later learn in the film that as "Mrs. McKelvey," Bedelia had red hair. As Ben
draws her portrait in Monte Carlo, he says, "You ought to have red hair. Nature
got her colors mixed when she was making you." Ben's ironic suggestion
here that Bedelia is not a "natural" woman echoes his initial voiceover about
Bedelia's "curious innocence" that veils a "poisonous flower." "Watching"
Bedelia try to evade the false painter's capture invites viewers to imagine a
counter-perspective in which Bedelia's actions symbolize a breaking out of
the frame, an "acting out" that is, indeed, outside of the social roles women
are supposed to assume, including a convention of women "sitting pretty."
Ben's comments about Bedelia's red hair thus conflate the "natural" with the
conventional, establishing the idea that the story's portrait of a wild murderess, a "femme fatale" of the first order, is a cover for the story's real interest
in a female rebellion against gender conventions and domestic settings that
entrap women.

Notes

1. This piece is excerpted from a longer version of my essay "The Fervor and Framing
of Bedelia: Gender Psychosis in Vera Caspary's Novel and Film Noir," *La Furia Umana* 15
(Winter 2013).

2. Vera Caspary, *Bedelia* (1945; reprint, New York: Feminist Press at the City University
of New York, 2005), 27 (subsequent references will appear parenthetically in the text).

Vera Caspary's novel *Laura* also works in tandem with its film adaptation
to draw a portrait of a shallow world of possibilities for women. While some
critics contrast the film's fetishizing of Laura as an image to the novel's "giving
voice" to the independent working-woman Laura, the novel and film seem
to me to be in conversation about female independence, about the theme of
watching and "detecting" female malfeasance, and about a contemporary social
milieu that is generally exploitative and specifically hostile to female ambition.
Liahna Babener describes Caspary's novel as a feminist exploration—first, of
the difficulties facing independent women in American culture, and second,
of the detective's coming to love the "real" Laura as opposed to the image of
her with which he has been obsessed. Unlike the novel, the film focuses for
Babener primarily on Laura as an image, not as a subject with her own story
to tell.

However, I think Babener misses the complexity of Laura's role in the film when she says that Laura is "blameworthy and threatening to masculine composure." Preminger's film is in fact about Laura's *eliciting* of male gender psychosis from the men around her. While Preminger was famously dictatorial and may have been misogynist, and Caspary did object to a number of changes made to the novel in the adaptation,[49] the film's relation to viewers is considerably richer than Babener's blanket dismissal of its gender politics suggests. Babener's claim that "the woman's discourse that propels the novel is choked off"[50] leaves out the film's analysis (intentional or not) of the over-reading of Laura that *is* a major focus of the narrative and mise-en-scène: We are not "with" McPherson when he grills Laura at the police station. We are, on the contrary, with her in her rejection of his "testing" of her. Laura may be "refused a voice-over," in Babener's terms,[51] but her presence in the film defies the conventional idea of the femme fatale. Just as Karen Hollinger suggests that Johnny's perverse narration of Gilda in *Gilda* breaks down and undermines Johnny's authority,[52] here, too, Waldo's voiceover is also symptomatic of sex and gender obsession, the bid for control by an homme fatal who fails to possess Laura. Like the Duke in Robert Browning's "My Last Duchess," as I've noted elsewhere,[53] Waldo must resort to killing her. Tierney's "Laura" does not play as a "reproachable temptress," nor do we read her behavior as simply "coy manipulation."[54] The impulse to read her as such may, in the case of a feminist approach, result from disappointment that the film fails to re-present a source text that functions differently, textually and culturally, an attitude that underlines the problems with using fidelity as a central criterion for evaluating adaptations. Alternatively, the impulse to identify simplistically with McPherson—in the case of some viewers and perhaps Preminger himself—registers a failure to acknowledge the film's deconstruction of sex and gender obsessions. That the film "continues to be revered by viewers" may be less a sign of "how difficult it is to tell women's stories in classical forms"[55] (though Babener's observation here is certainly right) and more an indication of the richness of the film from the standpoint of changing views of the representation of sex and gender in film noir. The film *Laura* is not, in short, simply a masculine bastardization of the novel.

In the novel, Laura strongly resists "positions" held by men that are taken for granted, especially in her striking comments about the smallness of detectives: "I don't like people who make their livings out of spying and poking into people's lives. Detectives aren't heroes to me, they're detestable."[56] An interesting expression of resistance to male intrusions into female experience, the comment is given force by McPherson's ambiguous rifling through Laura's personal things in her apartment. On the one hand, an inflated notion of the detective hero is articulated in Caspary's novel by a "girl detective," who says (rather shockingly) to McPherson, "I shouldn't mind being murdered half so much, Mr. McPherson, if you were the detective seeking clues to my private life."[57] On the other hand, Lydecker's bloated body in the novel and feminized penchant for taking baths in the film contrast with McPherson's brawny detective credentials. Further, and perhaps more to the point, the dubiousness of the classic detective figure is surely distilled in the uncanny moment of mis/recognition when Laura believes an intruder has entered her apartment. In the film, Preminger's mise-en-scène visually symbolizes that McPherson's engagement with Laura has been mediated by powerful fantasy (the framed "image" of Laura). McPherson's narration in the novel goes as follows:

> "I spoke with authority. 'You're dead.'"
>   My wild stare and the strange accusation convinced her that she was facing a dangerous lunatic. She edged toward the door.[58]

The novel's and film's riff on the potentially sinister side—again, the theme of impending violence—of detectives' intrusive power calls into question the practices of the "classic" hard-boiled protagonist, an idea embedded in noir from its source in this case and throughout the noir cycle.

(Mis)Recognition: Laura Hunt (Gene Tierney), Mark McPherson (Dana Andrews), and the image of desire in *Laura* (1944).

"What difference does it make what I say? You've made up your mind I'm guilty": Laura Hunt (Gene Tierney) interrogated by Detective McPherson (Dana Andrews) in *Laura* (1944).

In Preminger's film, there are memorable moments of Laura's independence and determination, even as she faces questionable authority figures—when she says, for example, "I will never do anything that is out of keeping with my own free will." More pointedly, Tierney's Laura asserts her subjectivity when she rejects the light literally cast on her at the police station and calls McPherson to task for his investigation and suspiciousness regarding her.

This exchange exemplifies Preminger's "concern with contrasting discourses and gestures,"[59] McPherson sublimating his feelings for Laura in police procedure. The camera angles and lighting (the scene is "steeped in noir shadows"[60]) cast Laura as a murderess, a role she rebelliously then assumes. "What difference does it make what I say," she says coldly. "You've made up your mind I'm guilty." The scene, like the moment of mis/recognition in Laura's apartment, communicates Preminger's visual theme of disorientation, that sense of "terror and loneliness of the secret emptinesses that surround the fora where dialogue and understanding take place."[61] Such trauma, however, is directly concerned with gender: McPherson's unstable masculinity is insecurely masked by his role as detective, just as Laura's anxiety-provoking femininity is masked by her "mysteriousness."

In Caspary's novel, Lydecker makes a comment about the process of objectifying Laura: "By the necromancy of modern journalism, a gracious young woman had been transformed into a dangerous siren who practiced her wiles in that fascinating neighborhood where Park Avenue meets Bohemia. Her generous way of life had become [in the press] an uninterrupted orgy of drunkenness, lust, and deceit, as titivating [*sic*] to the masses as it was profitable to the publishers."[62] Lydecker's analysis could be said to predict the making of the femme fatale as an industry. Caspary describes the process by which popular commentary stokes cultural anxieties about what women do to men. "You never know about women,"[63] says McPherson to Lydecker (when the real question in film noir could be, "You never know about men—what do the men do to the women?"). Lydecker's surprising reply, "Don't tell me you're a misogynist," reveals the novel's interest in the process by which interest in women is so easily adapted into sources of male anger and anxiety. In response to Lydecker's reply, "[McPherson] clamped his teeth hard upon his pipestem and glanced at me with an air of urchin defiance." These scenes from Caspary's novel and Preminger's classic film establish a continuity between pulp fiction and film noir in their investigation of thwarted female power and threatened masculinity.

An often-ignored element in Caspary's novel is the portrait of Diane Redfern, whose presence in the film is limited to her role as the one who is mistaken for Laura and thus killed by Lydecker when he finds her at Laura's apartment. Diane's real story is that of down-and-out "Jennie Swobodo," one in a long line of ambitious young women whose dreams turn into brutal realities in noir narrative: "You could tell that Diane had dreamed of Hollywood. Less beautiful girls had become stars, married stars, and owned swimming pools. There were some of those confessional magazines, too, the sort that told stories of girls who had sinned, suffered, and been reclaimed by the love of good men. Poor Jennie Swobodo."[64] McPherson's narrative about Diane Redfern introduces sympathy for an undistinguished female character: "I sat on the edge of the bed and thought about the poor kid's life. Perhaps those photographs represented a real world to the young girl. All day while she worked, she lived in their expensive settings. And at night she came home to this cell." McPherson's insight into Diane Redfern's domestic prison leads to the striking image of a "suicide staircase": "I felt sorry for the kid, being young and expecting something of her beauty and coming home to this suicide staircase."[65] It is worth noting the lineage from Jennie Swobodo to another divided personality, one of whose selves is also called "Diane": *Mulholland Drive*'s tragic Diane Selwyn in David Lynch's 2001 film. The comparison evokes the gendered machinery of modern American industry as it "patterns" women into images that can't be sustained in real psychosocial terms or experience. These submerged stories, I believe, constitute the cynical and desolate tone of film noir as much as the disappointments of the male protagonists, and these stories have been engaged by films conventionally regarded as noir as well as by melodrama and the woman's picture.

Far from being "the male genre" it is still proclaimed to be (despite recent feminist work), film noir is, more broadly, fundamentally about gender and society. The novels that are sources for the films discussed set the stage for film noir's exploration of troubling gender configurations. Like many melodramas and the so-called woman's pictures now too easily appropriated by Hollywood and by consumers as "chick flicks," film noirs adapt our continual reflection on the failure of conventional social roles to sustain human individuals, forcing a reassessment of the gender assumptions that have transformed over time and those that remain resistant to change. Such reconsideration demands the tight focus required of careful reading as well as broad appreciation for the blended universe of film noir so that the "suicide staircase" of Jennie Swobodo doesn't go unnoticed. My hope is that more sustained emphasis on the submerged stories of women and the sliding scale of concerns shared by melodrama and film noir will more systematically anchor studies of the genre. Further, film adaptations can perhaps more usefully be theorized as being in conversation with their source material rather than in discrete opposition to textual predecessors. The latter approach invokes a model of difference that leads to evaluation and competition between and among texts. The elements of conventionally defined melodrama and noir in each of the works examined here should not only raise questions about the narrow purview of gender and genre labels but also ignite critical discussion about the efficacy of emphasizing textual distinctiveness as opposed to relationships among texts. What, finally, are we talking about when we address the set of texts known as "Laura" or "In a Lonely Place"? Adaptation studies may benefit from a more feminist approach, in which meaning emerges as a by-product of cultural dialogue. A shift in emphasis away from examination of discrete texts and toward investigation of the relations among texts may offer a more productive, culturally relevant, and resonant stream of analyses.

Notes

1. Adaptations of *Mildred Pierce* help to spur considerations of the category of noir and the inflexibility with which so many approach it. Much of the discussion surrounding Todd Haynes's adaptation has centered on its identity as melodrama. However, like James M. Cain's novel and, I would argue, also like the 1945 film with Joan Crawford, the miniseries is largely concerned with the pressures that class and conventional gender roles bring to bear on men and women. Haynes is feminist in a way that Cain is not; through the acting and especially his signature mise-en-scène, the director foregrounds a sympathy for Mildred's desolation that is somewhat different from the more disinterested tone of Cain's novel. Haynes's exploration of the crises that beset individuals in society is much more deeply connected to the cultural work of film noir than has been generally acknowledged.

2. Like Shelley Cobb, I employ the "metaphor of conversation" to talk about adaptation. For Cobb, the language we use to describe the relationship between an adapted

text and its source is deeply gendered (thus, hierarchical) and has implications for cultural ideation surrounding gender as well as adaptation studies. See Shelley Cobb, "Adaptation, Fidelity, and Gendered Discourses," *Adaptation* 4.1 (2010): 28–37.

3. See Daniel Hodges's Web site devoted to interrogating clichés about film noir, "The Film Noir File: A Dossier of Challenges to the Film Noir Hardboiled Paradigm," accessed October 23, 2012, http://www.filmnoirfile.com.

4. Examples of such ranking include director Curtis Hanson's "preferential treatment" of the film *In a Lonely Place* in comparison with Dorothy Hughes's novel of the same name. In the DVD commentary for *In a Lonely Place,* Hanson glosses over the extent to which these texts converge and diverge. Another example, one I will return to later in this essay, is Liahna Babener's diatribe against what she sees as the antifeminist rewriting of Vera Caspary's *Laura* in Otto Preminger's film, while, in my view, the novel and film approach the theme of threatened female independence and survival in equally intriguing ways. See Liahna Babener, "De-Feminizing *Laura*: Novel to Film," in *It's a Print! Detective Fiction from Page to Screen,* ed. William Reynolds and Elizabeth A. Trembley (Bowling Green, Ohio: Bowling Green University Popular Press, 1994), 83–102.

5. For some of the most intriguing work in adaptation studies that develops postfidelity models of discourse, see Kamilla Elliot, *Rethinking the Novel/Film Debate* (New York: Cambridge University Press, 2003); Linda Hutcheon, *A Theory of Adaptation* (New York: Routledge, 2006); Thomas M. Leitch, *Film Adaptation and its Discontents: From* Gone with the Wind *to* The Passion of the Christ (Baltimore, Md.: Johns Hopkins University Press, 2007); Brian McFarlane, *Novel to Film: An Introduction to the Theory of Adaptation* (Oxford: Oxford University Press, 1996); R. Barton Palmer and David Boyd, *Hitchcock at the Source: The Auteur as Adaptor* (Albany: State University of New York Press, 2011); Julie Sanders, *Adaptation and Appropriation* (New York: Routledge, 2007); and Robert Stam, *Literature through Film: Realism, Magic, and the Art of Adaptation* (Malden, Mass.: Blackwell, 2004).

6. See, for example, Elizabeth Cowie, "*Film Noir* and Women," in *Shades of Noir,* ed. Joan Copjec (New York: Verso, 1993); Philippa Gates, *Detecting Women: Gender and the Hollywood Detective Film* (Albany: State University of New York Press, 2011); Julie Grossman, *Rethinking the Femme Fatale in Film Noir: Ready for Her Close-Up* (Basingstoke, U.K.: Palgrave Macmillan, 2012); Helen Hanson, *Hollywood Heroines: Women in Film Noir and the Female Gothic Film* (London: I. B Tauris, 2007); E. Ann Kaplan, *Women in Film Noir* (London: British Film Institute, 1980); and Jans B. Wager, *Dames in the Driver's Seat: Rereading Film Noir* (Austin: University of Texas Press, 2005).

7. Indeed, Pam Cook makes the point that the "the relationship between melodrama and the women's picture has been assumed rather than argued." Pam Cook, "Melodrama and the Woman's Picture," in *Imitation of Life: A Reader on Film and Television Melodrama,* ed. Marcia Landy (Detroit: Wayne State University Press, 1991), 248.

8. Cowie, "*Film Noir* and Women," 131.

9. Thomas Schatz, *Boom and Bust: American Cinema in the 1940s* (Berkeley: University of California Press, 1999), 236.

10. Ibid., 378.

11. Jon Lewis, *American Film: A History* (New York: W. W. Norton, 2008), 204.

12. Grossman, *Rethinking the Femme Fatale in Film Noir.*

13. See Steve Neale, "'I Can't Tell Anymore Whether You're Lying': *Double Indemnity, Human Desire,* and the Narratology of *Femmes Fatales,*" in *The Femme Fatale: Images, Histories, Contexts,* ed. Helen Hanson and Catherine O'Rawe (Basingstoke, U.K.:

Palgrave-Macmillan, 2010), 187–98, in which Neale shows the systematic victimization of Vicki Buckley.

14. Stanley Orr, *Darkly Perfect World: Colonial Adventure, Postmodernism, and American Noir* (Columbus: Ohio State University Press, 2010), 123.

15. Esther Sonnet, "Why Film Noir? Hollywood, Adaptation, and Women's Writing in the 1940s and 1950s," *Adaptation* 4.1 (2011): 1–13 (quotation on 2).

16. Grossman, *Rethinking the Femme Fatale in Film Noir,* 45–48.

17. Anne Hockens, "A Schoolgirl with a Sorceress' Eyes," *Noir City* 7.1 (Summer 2012): 9–22 (quotation on 13).

18. Dana Polan quotes James W. Palmer's original observation: "In Hitchcockian terms, the murder story is simply this film's MacGuffin." Polan, *In a Lonely Place* (London: British Film Institute, 1993), 13.

19. Ibid., 66.

20. Ibid., 27.

21. In this 1946 film, the World War II vet Johnny Morrison (Alan Ladd) "comes home" to his wife Helen's partying household. An inebriated woman opens the door, and Morrison says, "I'm looking for my wife." The response? "The place is full of wives," then to the partygoers, "Hey, everyone, Helen's got a husband!" Later, Helen: "My husband wants you to leave. He probably wants to beat me up"—a scarcely suppressed expression of postwar disillusionment, a heroism that, for some men, has no outlet in postwar domesticity (this scene suggests) except for domestic violence.

22. Dorothy Hughes, *In a Lonely Place* (1947; reprint, New York: Feminist Press at the City University of New York, 2003), 113–14.

23. Lisa Marie Hogeland, Afterword to *In a Lonely Place,* by Dorothy Hughes (1947; reprint, New York: Feminist Press at the City University of New York, 2003), 225–48 (quotation on 237).

24. I have elsewhere coined the term "Victorinoir" to describe Victorian literary sources for the male and female protagonists in film noir, but here, one can similarly see the continuities in gender representation from a Heathcliff or Rochester, the male romantic figures in classic Victorian novels (respectively, *Wuthering Heights* and *Jane Eyre*). These men, like Dix Steele, or countless other passionate men in noir (played, for example, by Humphrey Bogart or Robert Ryan or Orson Welles), are often living at the border of romance and madness, while women in their midst must navigate their own bid for independence within this context.

25. Hughes, *In a Lonely Place,* 112.

26. Polan, *In a Lonely Place,* 46.

27. Geoff Andrew, *The Films of Nicholas Ray* (London: British Film Institute, 2004), 52.

28. Orr, *Darkly Perfect World,* 121.

29. Andrew, *Films of Nicholas Ray,* 48.

30. Polan, *In a Lonely Place,* 40.

31. In *The Celluloid Closet,* Rob Epstein and Jeffrey Freidman's 1995 documentary based on Vito Russo's book about gay subtext in classic Hollywood film, Susie Bright observes that Martha's evocation of lesbian power and female bonds communicates a theme of female desire for freedom from male dominance.

32. While some critics have interestingly merged the nomenclature—"noir melodrama" or "melo-noir"—my target here is the persistence of an idea of noir that is stubbornly grafted to established character patterns and genre categories.

60 Pulp Fiction and the Woman's Picture

33. Jonathan Rosenbaum, "Nicholas Ray," *Senses of Cinema* 21 (2002), accessed November 5, 2013, http://sensesofcinema.com/2002/great-directors/raynick/.

34. Rosenbaum, "Nicholas Ray."

35. Polan, *In a Lonely Place*, 37.

36. Hockens, "A Schoolgirl with a Sorceress' Eyes," 11.

37. See Thomas Elsaesser, "Tales of Sound and Fury: Observations on the Family Melodrama," in *Critical Visions in Film Theory*, ed. Timothy Corrigan, Patricia White, and Meta Mazaj (Boston: Bedford/St. Martins, 2011), 496–511 (quotation on 511, n. 7).

38. In a *USA Today* article on his 2013 film *Trance*, Danny Boyle commented on his sense of film noir as "cold": "I wanted to do an updated noir, give it a contemporary spin in terms of emotion. . . . Noir is usually cold. I wanted it to be more emotionally charged. It's the first time I put a woman at the heart of a movie." While Boyle's assumption may be shared by the culture at large, in fact the genre's grounding in issues of gender and society, as well as its close affiliation with melodrama, belies Boyle's reading of film noir as emotionally cool. See Susan Wloszczyna, "Sneak Peek: Boyle Falls into 'Trance' with Thriller," *USA Today*, accessed December 27, 2012, http://www.usatoday.com/story/life/movies/2012/12/26/danny-boyle -trance-james-mcavoy-movie/1779189/.

39. Vicki Baum, *Mortgage on Life* (New York: Triangle Books, 1946), 28.

40. Ibid., 155.

41. Ibid., 140.

42. Ibid., 13.

43. Ibid., 37.

44. Andrew, *Films of Nicholas Ray*, 32.

45. Cullen Gallagher, rev. of *A Woman's Secret*, Not Coming to a Theater Near You, August 18, 2008, accessed November 8, 2013, http://notcoming.com/reviews/awomans secret.

46. Patrick McGilligan, *Nicholas Ray: The Glorious Failure of an American Director* (New York: HarperCollins, 2011), 146.

47. Baum, *Mortgage on Life*, 29.

48. Ibid., 82.

49. These include Caspary's objection to Preminger's vulgar and bombastic insistence that Laura is "a whore" and the change from novel to film in what was to be the murder weapon. See Eugene McNamara, *Laura as Novel, Film, and Myth* (Lewiston, N.Y.: Edwin Mellen Press, 1992), 34. As McNamara observes, Caspary "was furious when she learned that her device of hiding the murder gun in Waldo's walking stick had been changed into a mundane shotgun. To her, the stick was a symbol of Waldo's impotent, frustrated love for Laura, twisted into destructive rage" (9). In his *Otto Preminger: The Man Who Would Be King* (New York: Knopf, 2007), Foster Hirsch comments on the change: "In this case Caspary was right: the phallic symbolism of the gun concealed in the impotent man's walking stick is revelatory, whereas the ending Preminger proposed is merely a narrative device" (97).

50. Babener, "De-Feminizing *Laura*," 88.

51. Ibid., 93.

52. Karen Hollinger, "Film Noir, Voice-over, and the Femme Fatale," in *Film Noir Reader*, ed. Alain Silver and James Ursini (New York: Limelight Editions, 1996), 243–59.

53. Grossman, *Rethinking the Femme Fatale in Film Noir*, 31.

54. Babener, "De-Feminizing *Laura*," 94, 90.

55. Ibid., 100.

56. Vera Caspary, *Laura* (New York: Dell, 1942), 89.

57. Ibid., 44.

58. Ibid., 82.

59. Chris Fujiwara, "Otto Preminger," *Senses of Cinema* 20 (2002), accessed November 8, 2013, http://sensesofcinema.com/2002/great-directors/preminger/.

60. Hirsch, *Otto Preminger,* 112.

61. Fujiwara, "Otto Preminger."

62. Caspary, *Laura,* 35.

63. Ibid., 39.

64. Ibid., 136.

65. Ibid, 135.

3

The Vanishing Love Song in Film Noir

KRIN GABBARD

This essay is about a musical practice in two canonical noirs. In Jacques Tourneur's *Out of the Past* (1947) and Fritz Lang's *The Blue Gardenia* (1953), a romantic ballad (1) plays over the opening credits, (2) recurs regularly as it becomes associated with the central characters, but (3) is *not* heard at the end of the film. Although the scores for both films are otherwise entirely typical of Classical Hollywood, a vanishing love song is unusual. The phasing out of a love theme nevertheless seems well suited to film noir, if only because so many noirs begin with the promise of romance before descending into negativity. I cannot, however, locate any films besides *Out of the Past* and *The Blue Gardenia* in which a love song is heard at the beginning but not at the end. I could not even locate a resource that charts how songs come and go in Hollywood films. Regardless of whether or not these two films are unique in their use of love songs, it is significant that, in both films, the songs are introduced diegetically by African American musicians. The songs may disappear from the films because they are associated at the outset with otherness.

Even before studios began aggressively bundling the promotion of a film with the promotion of a song, it was not unusual for a film to feature the same song or songs from beginning to end. The practice probably begins with Otto Preminger's *Laura* (1944), in which David Raksin's song "Laura" is first heard over the opening credits.[1] The song is heard throughout the film, both diegetically and nondiegetically, as it becomes associated with Laura (Gene Tierney) and then with the couple, Laura and Mark (Dana Andrews). As the film ends, the same song plays over the closing credits. Mark's love for Laura is presented at first as vaguely necrophiliac, but the film eventually validates the love affair according to the familiar standards of Hollywood heteronor-mativity. Jeff Smith has documented the extent to which producers in the 1950s demanded that films promote a single musical theme.[2] He has coined the term "monotheme score" to describe music that could easily be marketed alongside the film. Smith writes, *"Laura* (1944) is perhaps the paradigmatic example of the monotheme score, but its formula was successfully duplicated in *High Noon* (1952), *Love Is a Many-Splendored Thing* (1955), and *Around the World in Eighty Days* (1956)."[3]

Unlike the romance between Laura and Mark in *Laura,* the love affair be-tween Jeff Markham/Bailey (Robert Mitchum) and Kathie Moffat (Jane Greer) in *Out of the Past* quickly turns murderous and remains so until the end. The love song that plays behind their romance seems at first to genuinely celebrate the affair, but as the film winds down, it is played in a minor key if at all. Similarly, the song that introduces *The Blue Gardenia* is associated first with the flirtation between Norah Larkin (Anne Baxter) and Harry Prebble (Raymond Burr) and later between Norah and Casey Mayo (Richard Conte). The romance with Prebble ends in his death, while the Norah/Casey romance is compromised by Casey's willingness to exploit Norah for the sake of his own newspaper headlines. The conclusion of the film holds out the hope for a rapprochement, but as many critics have pointed out, any real understanding between the two seems unlikely after what has taken place between them. The music is more "realistic" about the possibility of romance than is the script.

Although there are narrative justifications for phasing out the love songs in the two films, there were no compelling economic reasons. Both songs had some success as pop tunes, either before or after the release of the film in which it is heard. The song that begins *Out of the Past* is "The First Time I Saw You," written by Nathaniel Shilkret and Allie Wrubel. The score for *Out of the Past* is by the composer Roy Webb, who worked regularly in Hollywood, frequently for Jacques Tourneur. In his book on movie music, Christopher Palmer holds Webb in great esteem, both for his scores for film noirs such as Norman Foster's *Journey into Fear* (1943), John Brahm's *The Locket* (1946), and Edward Dmytryk's *Crossfire* (1947), and for his composi-tions for horror films. Palmer calls Webb's score for Tourneur's *Cat People* (1943), for example, a marvel of "musical chiaroscuro."[4]

"Blue Gardenia" was written specifically for *The Blue Gardenia* by Bob Russell and Lester Lee. The song was intended for Nat King Cole, who sings it in the film. Raoul Kraushaar, who wrote the score of *The Blue Gardenia,* began his Hollywood career as a music supervisor and conductor and then went on to write the scores for an endless succession of B movies, including *Abbott and Costello Meet Captain Kidd* (1952), *Bomba and the Jungle Girl*

"The First Time I Saw You"

The lyrics to "The First Time I Saw You" are not heard in *Out of the Past,* but both the words and the music were prominently featured in Rowland V. Lee's *The Toast of New York* (1937), where it is played on a harp and sung by Frances Farmer. (The song was also featured in another film noir, Irving Reis's *Crack-Up* [1946].) Before he wrote the melody for "The First Time I Saw You," Nathaniel Shilkret had great success with the song "Jeannine, I Dream of Lilac Time," originally part of the score for the World War I melodrama *Lilac Time* (1928). Shilkret had several other hits, including "The Lonesome Road," first written for Gene Austin and later recorded by numerous artists. After its introduction in *The Toast of New York,* "The First Time I Saw You" was widely recorded by jazz orchestras, including those led by Charlie Barnet, Jimmy Lunceford, and Bunny Berigan, and by the singers Chick Bullock and Seger Ellis. The many credits for the lyricist Allie Wrubel include "Zip-A-Dee-Doo-Dah," a song that won an Academy Award after it was sung by James Baskett in the Disney film *Song of the South* (1946).

(1952), *Island of Lost Women* (1959), and *Billy the Kid versus Dracula* (1966). *The Blue Gardenia* may be one of the few films for which he is remembered.

The Tough Guy and the Femme Fatale

Shilkret-Wrubel's "The First Time I Saw You" would have been ten years old by the time *Out of the Past* was released in 1947, but most of the audience surely recognized it. In Webb's lavishly orchestrated version, the song plays over RKO's signature logo, a radio antenna sitting on a globe, even before the title of the film appears on the screen. Once Webb's score has established the melody of "The First Time I Saw You" in two different keys, the score segues into the more pastoral music associated throughout the film with the great outdoors. *Out of the Past* is typical of film noir in many ways, but not because of its moments of pastoral beauty. Robert Miklitsch observes that in the opening sequence, Webb's music is just as effective as Nicholas Musuraca's lyrical cinematography in creating the illusion of an idyllic paradise. Together, the music and the photography tell us that, in Miklitsch's words, "this is God's country."[5] The film is unusual for its vanishing love song but also for the lovingly photographed lakes and mountains that are so strongly differentiated from the film's conventionally noir urban locations.

After "The First Time I Saw You" is played over the opening credits, the audience does not hear the song again until several minutes into the film.

"Blue Gardenia"

Nat King Cole's 1953 version of "Blue Gardenia" was not a hit. The song was rediscovered by Dinah Washington, who recorded it with more success in 1961 with a jazz orchestra led by Quincy Jones. In my opinion, the song now belongs to Dinah, especially in an earlier 1955 recording she made for the Mercury label with a small group of up-and-coming young jazz artists that included Clark Terry, Paul Quinchette, and Wynton Kelly.

In addition to providing the words for "Blue Gardenia," Bob Russell wrote memorable lyrics for three tunes by Duke Ellington. The most popular were "Do Nothin' till You Hear from Me" and "Don't Get Around Much Anymore." The first song was a hit after the Ellington orchestra recorded it in 1947 with its regular vocalist of that period, Al Hibbler. The tune had been recorded without lyrics a few years earlier as "Concerto for Cootie," one of many three-minute masterpieces by Ellington's Blanton/Webster band of the early 1940s. Two days after Duke recorded "Do Nothin' till You Hear from Me," he went back into the studio and transformed "Never No Lament," a 1940 showcase for the alto saxophonist Johnny Hodges, into "Don't Get Around Much Anymore." Again the vocalist was Al Hibbler, who pointedly concluded his vocal by singing "don't get around much ENTY more." For me, Bob Russell's best work with Ellington was his lyrics for "I Didn't Know about You," recorded in 1944 with a vocal by Joya Sherrill. It was based on "Sentimental Lady," an instrumental from 1942. In 1959, Russell also wrote Peggy Lee's hit "You Came a Long Way from St. Louis," in collaboration with John Benson Brooks. In spite of all these urbane, knowing lyrics, Russell appears to have had a maudlin side, which he revealed in the commodified hippie anthem, "He Ain't Heavy, He's My Brother," recorded by Neil Diamond in 1970.

Lester Lee, who wrote the music for "Blue Gardenia," was a very busy composer for Hollywood and Broadway but left behind little that we remember today, with the possible exception of "The Pennsylvania Polka," heard multiple times in Bill Murray's repeated visits to the park in Harold Ramis's *Groundhog Day* (1993). The choice of the song for this particular scene in *Groundhog Day* was hardly a compliment to the art of Lester Lee, and not only because the film was shot in Woodstock, Illinois, rather than in Pennsylvania.

First, however, the audience sees the arrival of Joe Stefanos (Paul Valentine) in Bridgeport, an actual town in northern California. They then see Jeff with Ann (Virginia Huston), the local woman with whom he has fallen in love, as they enjoy a fishing trip near at a lake. After Jeff meets with Joe and realizes that he must revisit his past, he begins the seventy-eight-mile drive from Bridgeport to Lake Tahoe with Ann in the passenger seat. With Jeff's voiceover driving the flashback, the audience sees his first encounter with Whit Sterling (Kirk Douglas), who hires Jeff and his sleazy partner Fisher (Steve Brodie) to find Kathie and bring her back, along with forty thousand dollars she has taken from him.

Jeff's flashback continues as he enters an African American nightclub, where he hopes to speak with the black woman who worked as a maid for Kathie. At fifteen minutes into the film, the audience hears the first diegetic version of "The First Time I Saw You." The music begins with a tight close-up of the face of an African American trumpeter who plays a bracing, unaccompanied jazz cadenza before the orchestra launches into a swing version of the song. The trumpeter is only on camera for three seconds, so it is not surprising that, especially in a film from the classical era, a black musician is nowhere identified by name. But it is surprising when even the scrupulous completists who fill out the credits pages on www.imdb.com do not seem to know who he is. Mark Cantor, surely the most eminent collector of jazz on film, has identified the trumpeter as Gerald Wilson.[6] As of this writing, Wilson is still alive after a long career as an important if underappreciated arranger and as the leader of several well-regarded jazz orchestras. When Cantor interviewed Wilson in 1998, he confirmed that he was the trumpeter who appears briefly but prominently in *Out of the Past*.

The nightclub scene that begins with Wilson's solo is remarkable on multiple levels. For one thing, Wilson appears to be playing his trumpet in real time. Standard Hollywood practice usually requires the music to be prerecorded and then played back as the musicians mime playing. The scene also features a performance by Theresa Harris as Eunice, Kathie's now-unemployed maid. As Jans Wager has pointed out, Theresa Harris was a very busy actress in the 1930s, '40s, and '50s, usually playing maids but almost always with a bit of glamour and sexiness.[7] A few years earlier she had appeared as Bette Davis's maid Zette in *Jezebel* (1938), in which she gives a performance so spirited that Richard Dyer cited it in an important essay on Hollywood's practice of displacing onto African American characters the emotion that whites are expected to repress.[8] Harris had also worked for Jacques Tourneur, giving what James Naremore has called "a fine, unstereotypical performance" in Tourneur's *I Walked with a Zombie*.[9]

After the camera cuts from the trumpeter, it quickly pans across the club to reveal that Jeff is the only white person in the room. As Jeff interacts with Eunice, her boyfriend (Caleb Peterson), and another couple who politely excuse themselves when Jeff begins asking questions, there is a distinct matter-of-factness to the exchanges between the black patrons and the white interloper. The well-dressed black customers are not so much surprised by

Jeff's presence as they are intrigued by what he wants to find out. To quote Naremore again, "the scene as a whole is played without condescension" (240). Surely one purpose of this scene is to show that Mitchum's private investigator is well schooled in extracting information from people of all "creeds and colors." The scene also reveals that he is hip enough to treat blacks with a degree of respect and solicitude. "The First Time I Saw You," however, is associated at its first diegetic hearing with a milieu that was held in contempt by most Americans in 1947 and that the film itself ultimately disparages.

The scene in the nightclub, during which the band never stops playing "The First Time I Saw You," is the beginning of Jeff's pursuit of Kathie, and it takes him from the exotic underworld of African American culture to the exotic underworld (as in *under* the United States of America) of Acapulco, Mexico. Only after Jeff has passed through this portal does Kathie walk out of the sun and into his life. William Luhr has suggested that Kathie's character is strongly marked by these essentially racist associations with Harlem and Mexico through which Jeff makes his way to find her.[10] Luhr also points to the workings of fate in the film. After his first encounter with Kathie, Jeff goes to the telegraph office to notify Whit. But the office is closed, and he is unable to accomplish what he was being paid to do. By the time the telegraph office has reopened, he has presumably become so besotted with Kathie that he decides to betray his employer. As Luhr suggests, the screenplay implies that Jeff is subject to forces beyond his control, a trope that is common in film noir but is seldom handled as deftly as in this scene in *Out of the Past*.[11]

At twenty-one minutes into the film, "The First Time I Saw You" has its second diegetic appearance. As Jeff greets Kathie in Pablo's, the cantina where she tells him she "sometimes" goes, a violinist begins a version of the tune accompanied by a pianist. At no point during this scene does Jeff acknowledge the coincidence of the same song popping up in two different locales. He does not even appear to be listening. As Claudia Gorbman has suggested in her essential work on film music, the song is essentially "inaudible" (unless, of course, one is an academic trying to develop a thesis about the music in film noir).[12] But by this time, "The First Time I Saw You" has become the official love song for Jeff and Kathie. It plays nondiegetically a few minutes later when they share their first kiss. The song is heard again moments after that when they meet in a lyrical day-for-night shot on the beach that is as impressive as the nature scenes that the cinematographer Nicholas Musuraca shot in the California mountains. Still supplying the voiceover as he narrates the flashback for Ann, Jeff says that Kathie would "come along like school is out" as the song plays on the score.

Then, in a scene that would be incomprehensible to viewers not familiar with the Production Code or with Hollywood's various strategies for circumventing it, the tune moves seamlessly from the diegetic to the non-diegetic register and then back again. For the first time, Kathie has invited Jeff to her bungalow. As they come in from the rain, Kathie walks to her record player and puts the tonearm onto a disc with still another version of "The First Time I Saw You." Kathie briefly resists as Jeff vigorously but playfully applies a towel to her wet hair. As they kiss once again, the camera pans to the front door, which suddenly sweeps open to let in the wind and the rain, a conventional metaphor for sexual intercourse. Like every adult in the audience, the censors at the Hays Office knew what the film was saying, but the Production Code was clear: there could be no explicit acknowledgment that anyone had engaged in premarital sex. So, as the music on the record morphs into another elaborately orchestrated variation of "The First Time I Saw You," the audience sees a fully clothed Jeff, his hair combed and dry, closing the door. The music then becomes diegetic once again as Kathie, also fully put back together, lifts the tonearm off the record, and the music stops. At this moment, the lovers agree to run off together and forget about Whit.

Two minutes later, Jeff is in his hotel room preparing for his trip back north with Kathie. As he puts items into his suitcase, he actually whistles the melody to "The First Time I Saw You." Although he did not appear to be listening when musicians played the tune at the black nightclub or at the cantina in Acupulco, Jeff has apparently picked it up. Or, if we wish to take the film literally, Jeff could be like many in the 1947 audience who had frequently heard the various recordings of the tune on the radio. Jeff's performance of the song, however, is interrupted by the unexpected arrival of Whit and Joe. The song will suffer another significant interruption six minutes later, when the lovers meet at the cabin where they are hoping to avoid Fisher, Jeff's erstwhile partner who correctly believes that he has been cut out of the deal of bringing Kathie back to Whit. Knowing that Fisher is looking for them, Jeff and Kathie have stayed away from each other for several days. When they first reencounter each other at the cabin, they lock eyes as the song once again becomes part of the nondiegetic score. But when Fisher appears out of the darkness, Webb has written a cue directing the musicians to hold a chord in the middle of the tune. Then tympani provide a crescendo. The song essentially stops dead, as it did when Jeff ended his whistling the moment he saw Whit and Joe outside his hotel room.

Kathie reveals herself to be a murderous sociopath when she shoots Fisher and drives off in his car, leaving Jeff to clean up the mess. The film is approximately half over when Jeff's flashback ends. He and Ann arrive at Whit's estate in Lake Tahoe, and the audience never again hears Jeff's voiceover. He

In *Out of the Past* (1947), Jeff
(Robert Mitchum) is surprised
by an unexpected visit from
Whit Sterling (Kirk Douglas).

has even more definitively lost control of the narrative when, to his surprise
as well as to that of the audience, he discovers that Kathie has returned to
Whit on her own volition. Jeff has, of course, violated his contract with Whit
and gone into hiding. And as Frank Krutnik has convincingly demonstrated in
a psychoanalytic reading of film noir, Jeff has violated the Law of the Father
by attempting to take "mother" (Kathie) away from "father" (Whit).[13]

By the time Jeff reencounters Kathie with Whit, the audience is made to
assume that he no longer loves her and that he has become attached to Ann,
a much less problematic object choice. When Kathie and Jeff have a brief
moment alone in Whit's house, she tries to convince him that she had no
choice but to go back to Whit. Jeff expels her from his room, saying, "I have
to sleep in this room. Let's just leave it where it all is. Get out." After Kathie
leaves the room, the audience hears a version of the song played, for the first
time, in a minor key. This version of "The First Time I Saw You" segues into
a brief cue for a theremin that sounds curiously reminiscent of music for the
horror cinema. In fact, Roy Webb did the music for all of Jacques Tourneur's
horror films, including *Cat People* (1942), *I Walked with a Zombie* (1943), and
The Leopard Man (1943). Like the vast majority of Hollywood composers,
Webb was not above recycling bits of melody and orchestration, and he surely
found the theremin cue to be as appropriate for Mitchum dealing with his

"Baby, I Don't Care"

Just as Jeff is deciding to turn on Whit and protect Kathie, she lies to him by saying that she did not take the forty thousand dollars from Whit. She then asks, "You believe me, don't you?" Rather than question her veracity, Jeff simply says, "Baby, I don't care." When Lee Server named his biography, *Robert Mitchum: "Baby, I Don't Care,"* the phrase was almost surely designed to exploit the star image of Mitchum as irreverent and rebellious, someone who didn't give a shit.[1] On one level, Jeff is in fact acting in a devil-may-care manner by choosing Kathie over Whit. He can be both transgressive and sexy as he shifts allegiance from his job to his desire. But on another level, he has given up masculine control by submitting to a woman he must at least suspect of being something other than a paragon. For Krutnik, Jeff's declaration that he does not care is part of a position that can be associated with clinical masochism.[2] In fact, Krutnik's reading of film noir acknowledges that in the years during and immediately after World War II, American men were in a crisis of masculinity, trying desperately to live up to impossible ideals first as fighting men and then as family men. The men who went to see *Out of the Past* in 1947 could certainly identify with a character who gives up the fight and submits to a beautiful, dangerous woman. At its conclusion, *Out of the Past* is a moral fable about the dangers of getting too close to a femme fatale. But for a few lovely moments in the middle, the film allows the male viewer to fantasize about the forbidden pleasures of complete submission to a woman: Baby, I don't care what a real man is supposed to do. The lyrical strains of "The First Time I Saw You" make the fantasy all the more available.

Notes

1. Lee Server, *Robert Mitchum: "Baby, I Don't Care"* (New York: St. Martin's, 2001).
2. Krutnik, *In a Lonely Street,* 103–12.

conflicted memories of Kathie as for scenes in which a character in a horror film encounters the uncanny.

After migrating to a minor key, "The First Time I Saw You" might seem to have served its purpose in *Out of the Past.* But the affair between Jeff and Kathie is not actually over, and the song is heard briefly on two final occasions. First, when Jeff sees Kathie at the party just after he has hidden the body of the attorney Eels in hopes of outsmarting Whit in his attempt to pin the murder on Jeff. Realizing that Jeff is aware of a scheme in which

Kathie Moffat (Jane Greer) thinks she is in control as she prepares to run off with Jeff (Robert Mitchum) in *Out of the Past* (1947).

she plays a significant role, Kathie desperately tries to convince him that she is innocent and that she has never stopped loving him. The music is heard on the sound track as they kiss. The music now stands for their contaminated romance but also for Jeff's masochistic infatuation with Kathie and even for her manipulative attempts to make him the fall guy.

Finally, audiences can hear a brief phrase from the song after Kathie has killed Whit and coolly told Jeff that she is now in charge. The listener has to pay close attention to hear a few faint phrases from the tune played slowly in a score that is designed to represent Jeff's predicament and the murderous behavior of Kathie rather than any revival of their love. This is the last time "The First Time I Saw You" can be heard, and it is barely recognizable.

Of course, Kathie and Jeff soon die together in a spectacularly unromantic fashion. As Luhr points out, Kathie actually shoots Jeff in his crotch.[14] In the film's final moments, the love song has vanished. Instead, Webb has recycled the pastoral music associated with the mountains and lakes around Bridgeport and with Jeff's romance with Ann. This is the music of the paradise we saw at the beginning, to which Jeff was hoping to return. The music takes on a note of pathos as the audience has one last look at "the Kid," the young deaf mute played by Dickie Moore, who has apparently lost the one person in Bridgeport who looked after him. As Miklitsch points out, the film ends with the Kid's silent salute to Jeff and with a great deal more silence about what the film cannot say in its last moments.[15] Roy Webb's lush score tells us as much as we are allowed to hear from the film as it winds down.

The Reporter and the Innocent Woman

The Blue Gardenia begins with its love song playing over the opening credits, and as in *Out of the Past,* the melody segues into a new set of motifs that will be heard throughout the film. But *The Blue Gardenia* has no pastoral settings. The film takes place entirely in Los Angeles. Appropriately, over the opening credits, "Blue Gardenia" gives way to the music of big-city hustle and bustle as the newspaperman Casey Mayo (Richard Conte) and his photographer sidekick Al (Richard Erdman) drive through the streets of Los Angeles. The audience will soon learn that Casey has an address book full of the names and phone numbers of the many women he has dated, while Al can only dream of sexual success. Appropriately, Casey is driving as Al sleeps in the passenger seat.

Just as "The First Time I Saw You" is not heard until fifteen minutes into *Out of the Past,* the audience does not hear "Blue Gardenia" until the film is twenty minutes old. During the first minutes of the film, Harry Prebble (Raymond Burr) gets close enough to the telephone operator Crystal Carpenter (Ann Sothern) to get her phone number, and Norah Larkin (Anne Baxter) receives a letter from her fiancé in Korea telling her that he has fallen in love with a nurse and that he is going to marry her. Norah is alone in the apartment she shares with Crystal and Sally (Jeff Donnell) when she sits down to an elaborate dinner with her absent boyfriend, having arranged it as the appropriate setting to read what she assumes is a heartfelt love letter. When Harry calls for Crystal, Norah has just read the letter with its unexpected message. She takes the call intended for Crystal, and in a moment of despair-driven devil-may-care, she accepts his invitation to dinner. They agree to meet at a Polynesian restaurant, also known as the Blue Gardenia.

The entertainer at the restaurant is Nat King Cole, who sings with a small group on camera as well as with an invisible orchestra playing an arrangement written especially for the film by Nelson Riddle. The scene designer has created an elaborately detailed set for the restaurant that suggests decadence and something less than good taste—or, as Tom Gunning has phrased it, "50s bad taste exoticism."[16] Even Cole and his sidemen are wearing tacky flowered leis. Cole sits beneath a large mirror that seems designed to show

In a pseudo-Polynesian club called the Blue Gardenia, Nat King Cole sings "Blue Gardenia" in a film called *The Blue Gardenia* (1953).

the audience his fingers on the keys but adds to the strained exoticism of the mise-en-scène. Before Cole sings "Blue Gardenia," Prebble is plying Norah with a drink called a Polynesian Pearl Diver. In the seconds just before Cole begins to sing, the audience hears a bit of the song nondiegetically as the blind woman who sells flowers in the restaurant approaches Norah and Prebble's table. Although Cole endows the song with his usual elegance, "Blue Gardenia" has already been associated with the inelegance of a restaurant with the same name as his song.

After Cole does a complete performance of "Blue Gardenia," Prebble takes Norah to his apartment for more drinks, but only after he has placed Cole's recording of "Blue Gardenia" on the turntable. At first, the music on the record player is standard seduction fare. But it soon provides what Gorbman has called an "anempathetic" background as Prebble becomes more aggressive.[17] Cole goes on singing, and the orchestra goes on making romantic music, as if they were oblivious to the imminent rape of Norah. But when a desperate and intoxicated Norah strikes at Prebble with a fireplace poker, the composer Raoul Kraushaar plays several expressionist variations on the song, taking it from diegetic to nondiegetic. The recording of "Blue Gardenia" abruptly ends, even though there is no indication that the turntable has been bumped or somehow turned off. Instead, the score provides a dissonant version of the song and then various iterations of the melody's first phrase played against a repeated motif from a harp. The music at this point complements images of swirling liquid and animated pinwheels that are superimposed over Norah as she tries to overcome the effects of too many Polynesian Pearl Divers. The expressionist camera work in this scene does not last long, however. Most of the film is dominated by the highly professional, naturalist cinematography of Nicholas Musuraca, who coincidentally also shot *Out of the Past*.

Kraushaar continues to inject the song into his score throughout most of the rest of the film. In fact, there are more cues with fragments of "Blue Gardenia" in *The Blue Gardenia* than there are cues from "The First Time I Saw You" in *Out of the Past*. After the scene in Prebble's apartment, the audience next hears "Blue Gardenia" while Casey interviews the blind woman who had sold the blue gardenia to Prebble at the restaurant. In this scene, much of the song is heard without the lyrics in a fairly straightforward arrangement, as the film reencounters the sweet old woman who was briefly associated with the song even before it was sung by Cole. The romance in the song is now shifted to pleasant feelings for the blind woman.

A few minutes later, motifs from the song are dropped into the score much more discordantly as Norah becomes increasingly paranoid about being discovered as the murderer of Prebble. Lang sets up the sequence by filming each of the three roommates in bed. Sally is shown first, sleeping peacefully with the latest slasher novel by "Mickey Mallet" resting on the covers of her bed. (Audiences in the 1950s would have had no trouble associating Mickey Mallet with the notorious but widely read Mike Hammer novels of Mickey Spillane.) Crystal appears to be dreaming, smiling and moving suggestively as she mutters the name of her ex-husband Homer, with whom she is presumably having a more active sex life than when they were married. But Norah is surreptitiously listening to the radio to hear the latest news about the murder she thinks she has committed. She then climbs out of bed to burn the dress she wore on the night she was in Prebble's apartment. As Janet Bergstrom has suggested, Norah does not live in a supportive, homosocial woman's world.[18] And Gunning writes, "The fantasy life of these frustrated and lonely young women consists of sex and violence and perhaps involves an equation between the two."[19] I would add that the roommates are only minimally attentive to Norah. Meanwhile, Norah sees police everywhere she turns. It is into this environment that Kraushaar inserts several fragments of the song.

"Blue Gardenia" is heard bombastically a few minutes later when Casey writes a newspaper story, "Open Letter to an Unknown Murderess," in hopes of locating the woman who has become known as "The Blue Gardenia" because of the flower from the restaurant that was left behind in Prebble's apartment. The music plays prominently over shots of a newspaper printing press. As variations on the song appear in the score, Lang creates a montage with people from various walks of life reading their copy of the *Los Angeles Chronicle* with Casey's headline taking up the entire front page. An oboe plays an eroticized version of a motif from the song as the camera briefly shows a louche, blonde woman smoking while she reads the paper in bed. When the montage ends, Norah is alone in her apartment reading Casey's story. As Bergstrom points out, Norah reads the "letter" written to her by Casey in a camera setup deliberately designed to recall her position at the table when she read the breakup letter from her fiancé. Bergstrom even produces a passage from *The Blue Gardenia*'s shooting script explicitly stating that the second scene should recall the earlier one.[20] Although Norah believes that Casey is writing to her with sincerity, the film clearly suggests that he is betraying her as surely as she was betrayed by her fiancé.

When Casey actually meets Norah in a diner, he plays the Nat Cole recording on the jukebox. Practically the entire song with Cole's vocal can be heard behind their conversation. For a moment it seems as if "Blue Gardenia" might become the love song that unites Norah and Casey, driving out the film's association of Norah with the oleaginous and murdered Prebble. But Casey is motivated almost entirely by his narcissistic need to file a hot story, and he is ultimately responsible for setting up Norah to be arrested. The second-to-last time the audience hears the "Blue Gardenia" theme is more than ten minutes before the end of the film. Just the first four notes of the melody are played as the sleazy counterman at the restaurant where Casey and Norah had met acknowledges that he is the one who overheard their conversation and phoned the police. The exact same version of the cue plays a few seconds later when Norah is being fingerprinted at the police station. Appropriately, it's just a smattering of the melody in this farewell to the tune.

As in *Out of the Past*, audiences do *not* hear "Blue Gardenia" in the final moments of *The Blue Gardenia*. Rather, they hear several cues in quick succession: the triumphant march that anchors the justice insignia on the floor of the courthouse; the fluid melody that connotes camaraderie among the three female roommates; the music of big-city bustle as the camera cuts back to Mayo; the chromatic descending tones that accompany Casey's address book full of women's names and phone numbers as it flies into the waiting hands of Al; the appropriate wolf-whistle effect as Al pages through the address book; and finally, a symphonic gesture of closure that recycles the big-city music that was played over the opening credits. This closing music suggests that Casey and Norah may have a new beginning without the baggage of a

A Wagnerian Dénouement

Before the final scene of *The Blue Gardenia,* there is some remarkable use of "Liebestod" from Richard Wagner's opera *Tristan und Isolde.* The familiar love/death motif is kicked back and forth between the diegetic and nondiegetic registers in a fascinating example of how flexible a film score can be in the hands of the right artists. As with the title song, the music is both inside and outside the world of the characters, but in much more complex patterns than is typical of Classical Hollywood. Just as "Blue Gardenia" is tied to Norah the supposed murderer, Wagner's music is tied to the actual murderer, Rose (Ruth Storey). The music twice begins diegetically, on a phonograph and as piped-in music at an airport restaurant, and is then shifted to the background score. In another case, it begins as background music and is subsequently assimilated as the diegetic sound of a phonograph record. At one point it seamlessly moves between two diegetic sources, from the airport speakers to the record player in Prebble's apartment. During a four-minute period, as the action switches between past and present, each moment of Wagner's music is cued to specific emotions, indicating Rose's dawning resignation as the police close in and then, in a flashback, the pain of her unrequited love for Prebble. Casey's feelings for Norah are tied to the same sounds a few moments later, just after the music has provided a melancholy tone to accompany Rose's confession after her suicide attempt. In a flashback, when the audience sees Rose attack Prebble with the fireplace poker, she strikes him just as the music climaxes, a moment that strongly recalls the scene in Luis Buñuel's *Un chien andalou* (1929), when a passage from *Tristan und Isolde* plays as "The Man" collapses after he is shot by his double. In both films Wagner's music "Mickey Mouses" a climactic act of violence.

murder and Norah's arrest. The certainty of reconciliation and a romance, however, is undermined by a camera setup in the final scene: "[T]he insignia of the Hall of Justice appears to descend over Norah's head like a noose."[21]

Knowing the Score

Except for the vanishing love songs, there is nothing unusual about the music in *Out of the Past* and *The Blue Gardenia.* Both films are suffused with music for approximately half of their running time, and the constant reappearance of bits of melody throughout the films is standard operating procedure for the Classical Hollywood score. Each time a familiar melody reappears, it seems to have been carefully orchestrated to fit the dramatic circumstances. The rest of the score includes several motifs that are not taken from the opening song but that are similarly designed to "anchor" the meaning of the action with music.[22] Again, none of this is unusual. Consider the case of Max Steiner, perhaps the most typical composer for Classical Hollywood. As Gorbman has shown in some detail, Steiner regularly recycled themes throughout one of the many films he scored at Warner Bros., Michael Curtiz's *Mildred Pierce* (1945).[23] After identifying five principal themes that dominate the score, Gorbman writes, "The melodies are treated in conventional ways to fit each narrative context in which they appear. Variations in tonality, register, harmonic accompaniment, time signature, rhythm, and instrumentation alter their sound and mood."[24] Much the same can be said of countless scores for films, both old and new. Think of the themes by John Williams that we know so well from *Star Wars* films and how they are so clearly designed for specific characters and places.

The music for *Out of the Past* and *The Blue Gardenia* functions according to these same rules, and as a result, both films seem to require that their love songs disappear. On the one hand, the songs have been contaminated by their connection to romances that turn murderous, and there is no place to put the music as the films conclude. On the other hand, one cannot ignore the fact that both songs are introduced diegetically by African American artists. In this sense, it can be argued that they were "contaminated" from the outset. By no means am I suggesting that the writers, directors, or producers of either film were racists who deliberately used black people to connote darkness and crime. Quite the contrary. As Thomas Cripps has exhaustively demonstrated, Hollywood made serious attempts to find work for African Americans and often to portray them in positive ways.[25] Hollywood liberals were especially determined that movies should strive to integrate blacks into the mainstreams of American life. The dignified behavior of the black characters at the nightclub in *Out of the Past* and the charm and romance projected by Nat King Cole in *The Blue Gardenia* surely testify to the filmmakers' good intentions.

Nevertheless, the filmmakers were creatures of their era, and even though neither Jacques Tourneur or Fritz Lang was raised in America, they were immersed in the deeply entrenched conventions of the Hollywood cinema. Whether they were fully conscious of it or not, they did not shake the boat as they navigated the ideological waters. As I mentioned earlier, William Luhr has argued that in *Out of the Past*, Jeff's journey through the underworld of African Americans and Mexicans to find Kathie suggests that she belongs to that world much more than to the normative world of white Americans. In this sense, it does not matter how dignified the blacks at the nightclub appear to be or how much respect Jeff grants them. Of course, Jose Rodriguez

(Tony Roux) is treated as a mostly comic character out for a quick buck. The important thing is that blacks and Mexicans were consistently othered in postwar American culture, and the codes of the cinema were working according to plan when the femme fatale Kathie is associated with them.

Nat Cole was among the few black entertainers to have real appeal for white Americans in the 1950s. He even had his own television program on NBC for an entire year in 1956 and 1957. It was the first time that a major network had starred a black performer in a regularly scheduled program, and there would not be another television program with an African American host until Sammy Davis Jr.'s brief tenure on NBC in 1966.[26] In spite of Cole's cross-racial appeal, in *The Blue Gardenia* he could easily be associated by whites with the tacky exoticism of the Polynesian restaurant and with the unscrupulous womanizing of Harry Prebble. In the popular imagination, black musicians, especially black jazz musicians, lived in a world of drugs, heavy drinking, and loose sexuality. Cole's voice is present, after all, at the opening of that extremely paranoid film noir, Robert Aldrich's *Kiss Me Deadly* (1955), which starred Ralph Meeker as Mike Hammer. Harry Belafonte has a prominent role in Robert Wise's late noir *Odds against Tomorrow* (1959), but Nat King Cole is surely the single most seen and heard black performer in all of film noir. In *The Blue Gardenia*, Cole is constantly beneath the bizarrely tilted mirror that foregrounds him—he was after all, an extremely popular entertainer with a long list of hit records. But the mirror also marginalizes him, turning him into a part of the commodified and suspect exoticism of the restaurant.[27]

No one associated with *Out of the Past* or *The Blue Gardenia* was objectively trying to slow the progress of African Americans toward full equality. They invited talented black musicians into their films and let them display their talents in full. They did not ask Gerald Wilson, Nat Cole, or any other black performer to act out minstrel stereotypes. But on a deeper level, the filmmakers were unable to free themselves from myths that were still present in postwar America. And they were certainly unwilling to assault the prejudices of the many whites in their audiences. Ultimately, the love songs in *Out of the Past* and *The Blue Gardenia* were contaminated at least in part by race, and therefore they had to vanish, even in an industry that was almost as interested in promoting popular songs as in promoting popular films.

Notes

1. For what it's worth, the novel on which *Laura* is based was written by Vera Caspary, who also wrote the short story that is the source for the plot of *The Blue Gardenia*.

2. Jeff Smith, *The Sounds of Commerce: Marketing Popular Film Music* (New York: Columbia University Press, 1988).

3. Ibid., 17.

4. Christopher Palmer, *The Composer in Hollywood* (London: Marion Boyars, 1990), 169.

5. Robert Miklitsch, *Siren City: Sound and Source Music in Classic American Noir* (New Brunswick, N.J.: Rutgers University Press, 2011), 20.

6. Mark Cantor, e-mail message to author, February 6, 2011.

7. Jans Wager, *Dames in the Driver's Seat: Rereading Film Noir* (Austin: University of Texas Press, 2005), 57.

8. Richard Dyer, "White," *Screen* 29.4 (1988): 44–65.

9. James Naremore, *More than Night: Film Noir in Its Contexts* (Berkeley: University of California Press, 1998), 240.

10. William Luhr, *Film Noir* (Malden, Mass.: Wiley-Blackwell, 2012), 114.

11. Ibid., 113.

12. Claudia Gorbman, *Unheard Melodies: Narrative Film Music* (Bloomington: Indiana University Press, 1987), 73.

13. Frank Krutnik, *In a Lonely Street: Film Noir, Genre, Masculinity* (New York: Routledge, 1991).

14. Luhr, *Film Noir*, 105.

15. Miklitsch, *Siren City*, 254.

16. Tom Gunning, *The Films of Fritz Lang: Allegories of Vision and Modernity* (London: British Film Institute, 2000), 400.

17. Gorbman, *Unheard Melodies*, 24.

18. Janet Bergstrom, "The Mystery of *The Blue Gardenia*," in *Shades of Noir*, ed. Joan Copjec (New York: Verso, 1993), 109.

19. Gunning, *Films of Fritz Lang*, 403.

20. Bergstrom, "Mystery of *The Blue Gardenia*," 108.

21. Ibid., 107.

22. Gorbman has taken the term "ancrage" from Roland Barthes's comments on how captions beneath photos in magazines *anchor* polysemous images to specific meanings. Similarly, movie music "enforces an interpretation" of a complicated set of images. See Gorbman, *Unheard Melodies*, 32.

23. Ibid., 91–98.

24. Ibid., 95.

25. Thomas Cripps, *Making Movies Black: The Hollywood Message Movie from World War II to the Civil Rights Era* (New York: Oxford University Press, 1993).

26. Krin Gabbard, *Jammin' at the Margins: Jazz and the American Cinema* (Chicago: University of Chicago Press, 1996), 245.

27. I thank Robert Miklitsch for suggesting this reading of the scene.

4

Radio, Film Noir, and the Aesthetics of Auditory Spectacle

NEIL VERMA

> What does it mean for a being to be immersed entirely in listening, formed by listening or in listening, listening with all his being?
>
> —Jean-Luc Nancy, *Listening*

This essay asks what to make of the fact that the classic era of film noir and the golden age of American radio drama overlap so closely. Many think of radio as a novel technology of the 1920s, but radio culture on a national scale actually arose in the Depression, achieving mass saturation around 1940, when the U.S. Census Bureau found that 82.8 percent of families had sets at home. By 1944, according to the Nielsen service, more than twenty-five million families listened each weeknight.[1] So while classic noirs began to flourish at the cinema, most Americans listened to radio for about four hours a day (more in the evening, and in rural areas) over some nine hundred stations, most of which were affiliated with one of four large commercial networks that centralized content. During these years, drama formats were second only to music as the most common network offering in the evening. Crime and mystery shows prospered especially well. Although constituting only 13 percent of evening drama in the mid-1930s, the category rose to 33 percent during the war, and by the 1950s crime stories could be up to half of all plays

Clifton Webb as radio commentator Waldo Lydecker in Preminger's *Laura* (1944), pictured with a Zenith radio set by the bathtub, where we can readily imagine him immersed in the sound of his own voice.

on air on a given evening.[2] Many shows used scripts, themes, characters, music, and voices linked with film noirs, often to promote movie releases, especially after 1938, when the networks opened new centers in Hollywood, including Columbia Square, the CBS hub on the old lot of Nestor Studios at 6121 Sunset. Seen in aggregate, noir on the radio adds up to tens of thousands of hours of material heard by tens of millions of listeners from 1937 to 1955, the most active years for auditory drama on American airwaves ever.

Tempting as it is, it would be overenthusiastic to chalk a cinema of shadows up to *The Shadow*, proposing that radio culture was the "true" source of what Frank Krutnik calls the "noir phenomenon," particularly after so many candidates for that role have emerged over the decades that the candidacy itself has become a cliché.[3] Still, a better handle on radio culture might aid our historical grasp of these films at least as well as does a firm understanding of *Black Mask* magazine, the Production Code, psychoanalysis, or German expressionism. Unfortunately, the multifaceted connection between film and radio has been rarely pursued by noir critics, who often narrow their comments on the matter to an offhand note that Litvak's *Sorry, Wrong Number* (1948) started out as a radio play. One reason for this short shrift is the way that discourse on noir emerged through historical decontextualization. The films we call "noir" were named thus in the immediate postwar by French critics who, as James Naremore has shown, saw much of their own sensibilities reflected in the wartime American crime melodramas that reached their cinemas late and all at once.[4] These writers had a far narrower sense of quotidian American life during the 1940s, and particularly of commercial radio culture, and thus understandably made little note of it in their writings. When "noir" was imported as a term and became a subject of debate in the United States in the 1960s and 1970s, the golden age of radio was over, and critics were more invested in assessing the merits of thematic analysis versus those of visual stylistics, and the question of whether noir ought to be understood as a "genre" or "cycle." Only after subsequent studies synthesized and surpassed the terms of those debates was room prepared for a recent wave of historically oriented books—such as those of Edward Dimendberg, Sheri Chinen Biesen, and Robert Miklitsch—that broadened the question of noir's context.[5] At the same time, radio history came of age, as researchers began to use digital formats to obtain programs in the quantities needed to produce robust accounts of radiophonic experience.[6] Ironically, we had to wait until the digital era to begin to unpack an expressive form emblematic of the predigital era. So just as "noir" as a discourse once emerged in a backward glance, radio plays have become "thinkable" in a historical echo; as critical subjects, both come "out of the past." These developments have also made it possible to view film noir "from the perspective of radio." That's what I propose to do below.

A Radiophonic Cinema

No single prominent noir thematizes radio culture directly, yet many clearly address a society immersed in (even formed through) mass radio listening. One way of doing so was to feature radio listeners, broadcasters, and sets, which often stand as ciphers for social regulation and subversions thereof. In noir, a radio technician might be a killer, like Richard Basehart as Roy Morgan in Alfred L. Werker's *He Walked by Night* (1948); a radio actor might be a setup man, like Lloyd Corrigan as McKinley in John Farrow's *The Big Clock* (1948); a false broadcast report might manipulate a fugitive from afar, as in Ida Lupino's *The Hitch-Hiker* (1953); or a radio bulletin might also signal a crisis resolved, as in Elia Kazan's *Panic in the Streets* (1950). Derisive references to radio personalities pepper passages of banter. In William Wyler's *Detective Story* (1951), Lieutenant Monaghan (Horace McMahon) quips that he threw his radio out the window because he "hates mysteries," contrasting his humdrum labors with swashbuckling radio serials like *I Love a Mystery*.[7] When the detective Bradford Galt (Mark Stevens) runs out of leads in Henry Hathaway's *The Dark Corner* (1946), he cracks that it's time to call the "Quiz Kids," referencing NBC's showcase of child prodigies. By calling policemen "Happiness Boys," the diner owner Gus (James Whitmore) in John Huston's *The Asphalt Jungle* (1950) sneeringly likens them to singing radio candy salesmen of the 1920s, also linking radio with reform-era policing in a film that begins with the sound of a radio car on a manhunt and ends with a reformer's exhibit of radio-based surveillance as a force of modern civilization.

Some Film Noirs Heard on Radio

"The Big Clock" (*Screen Director's Playhouse,* July 8, 1949); "Call Northside 777" (*Hollywood Sound Stage,* January 24, 1952); "Criss Cross" (*Screen Director's Playhouse,* October 10, 1949); "The Dark Corner" (*Lux Radio Theater,* November 10, 1947); "Deadline at Dawn" (*Suspense,* May 15, 1948); "Double Indemnity" (*Screen Guild Theater,* March 5, 1945; *The Ford Theater,* October 15, 1948; *Lux Radio Theater,* October 30, 1950); "The House on 92nd Street" (*Screen Guild Theater,* June 10, 1946); "Key Largo" (*Lux Radio Theater,* November 28, 1949); "Laura" (*Lux Radio Theater,* February 5, 1945; *The Ford Theater,* May 30, 1945); "The Maltese Falcon" (*Academy Award Theater,* July 3, 1946; *Screen Guild Theater,* September 20, 1943); "Mildred Pierce" (*Lux Radio Theater,* June 6, 1949); "The Ministry of Fear" (*NBC University Theater,* January 23, 1949); "Murder, My Sweet" (*Lux Radio Theater,* June 11, 1945); "The Night Has a Thousand Eyes" (*Screen Director's Playhouse,* February 27, 1948); "The Phantom Lady" (*Lux Radio Theater,* March 27, 1944; *The Globe Theater,* ca. 1945); "The Postman Always Rings Twice" (*Screen Guild Theater,* June 16, 1947); "Shadow of a Doubt" (*Academy Award Theater,* September 11, 1946; *Screen Director's Playhouse,* November 9, 1950); "Spellbound" (*Lux Radio Theater,* March 8, 1948); "The Spiral Staircase" (*Screen Director's Playhouse,* November 25, 1949); "The Strange Love of Martha Ivers" (*Screen Director's Playhouse,* June 23, 1950); "Strangers on a Train" (*Lux Radio Theater,* December 3, 1951); "Street of Chance" (as "The Black Curtain," *Suspense,* December 2, 1943); "The Third Man" (*Lux Radio Theater,* April 9, 1951); "This Gun for Hire" (*Lux Radio Theater,* January 25, 1943).

Other Related Programs

The Adventures of Philip Marlowe (1947–51); *The Adventures of Sam Spade* (1946–51); *Big Town* (1937–52); *Boston Blackie* (1944–50); *Bold Venture* (1951–52); *Broadway Is My Beat* (1949–54); *Casey, Crime Photographer* (1943–55); *Dragnet* (1949–57); *Escape* (1947–54); *Gangbusters* (1934–57); *Michael Shayne, Private Eye* (1944–53); *Molle Mystery Theater* (1943–54); *Richard Diamond, Private Detective* (1949–53); *Suspense* (1940–62); *That Hammer Guy* (1953–54); *Yours Truly, Johnny Dollar* (1943–62).

Some Film Noir Stars Often Heard on Air

Dana Andrews, Lucille Ball, William Bendix, Joan Bennett, Ingrid Bergman, Humphrey Bogart, William Conrad, Joseph Cotton, Brian Donlevy, Jose Ferrer, Cary Grant, Sydney Greenstreet, Susan Hayward, Rita Hayworth, Alan Ladd, Burt Lancaster, Charles Laughton, Peter Lorre, Frank Lovejoy, Ida Lupino, Fred MacMurray, Victor Mature, Mercedes McCambridge, Ray Milland, Lloyd Nolan, Dick Powell, Vincent Price, Robert Ryan, Claude Rains, Edward G. Robinson, Everett Sloane, Barbara Stanwyck, James Stewart, Clifton Webb, Jack Webb, Orson Welles, Richard Widmark.

Diegetic broadcasts and radio sets could alternately offer filmmakers auditory stylizations and visual gimmicks. In Orson Welles's *The Lady from Shanghai* (1947), for example, a radio ad for "Glosso Lusto" hair tonic ("Pleases your hair . . . Pleases the man you love") airs as a sonic shock between Rita Hayworth's haunting siren song and her recitation of a love proverb.[8] In Michael Curtiz's *The Unsuspected* (1947), the sound of a radio show starring the crime raconteur Victor Grandison (Claude Rains) dramatically sets up a system of correspondences between inner and outer states, while fusing realism with formal expressionism, as Robert Porfirio has argued.[9] In Otto Preminger's *Laura* (1944), when the radio commentator Waldo Lydecker (Clifton Webb) first appears on screen—a scene of what Michel Chion terms "de-acousmatization," in which we seem to visually acquire the source of a disembodied voice—he sits in a coffinlike bathtub in front of a Zenith radio wall-unit.[10] The shot foreshadows his downfall in a concluding sequence that "re-acousmetizes" a dead Lydecker, whose prerecorded broadcast emanates from a radio set, persisting on the airwaves as he expires on screen.

Film noirs often feature sonorous and structural details whose effectiveness rests on their resemblance to tropes and techniques that many viewers likely knew from radio. In an oft-cited remark in Billy Wilder's *Double Indemnity* (1944), for instance, Walter Neff (Fred MacMurray) swears that while walking at night he can't hear his own footsteps on the asphalt. The absence is eerie in part because footsteps were then by far the most frequently used sound effect in radio, part of a registry of sonic figures (gunshots, screams, sirens, storms, animal sounds, cars) used across mass media, a subject to which Miklitsch has given new critical attention.[11] On the airwaves, as a rule, footsteps gave beings corporeality; a character that can be heard to walk is "really there," whereas one who does not may be a voice from beyond. Neff's retrospective narration fascinates us precisely because it's neither one nor the other, which is why he calls his steps "the walk of a dead man." And what about that retrospective voiceover narration? For decades, writers have argued that this curious convention represents a deviation from established Hollywood norms in that it tends to be used by unsympathetic and powerless narrators.[12] But perhaps that contrast is the wrong approach. As Fredric Jameson has noted, a "radio aesthetic" is at the heart of this feature of hard-boiled writing.[13] From the Depression to the cold war, thousands of radio plays used this narrative device to catch listeners liable to tune elsewhere, an approach favored by Orson Welles on *The Mercury Theater on the Air.* The convention dominates radio detective serials. *The Adventures of Sam Spade* uses first-person retrospective narration despite the fact that neither Dashiell Hammett's *The Maltese Falcon* (1930) nor the 1941 John Huston film does.

Like *The Adventures of Philip Marlowe, Sam Spade* extends the mythology of the detective primarily by trivializing it. But radio's trivializations aren't entirely trivial; they often yield great insight on the genre, illuminating its comic dimensions especially well. In "To Be Edward G. Robinson" on *Suspense,* for instance, Edward G. Robinson plays several characters: (a) himself; (b) Homer J. Hubbard, a weakling who wants to become like Robinson and murder his wife; and (c) gangster characters from the Robinson oeuvre over which Hubbard fawns. It's as if the play reimagined the existential crises of Robinson's many noir characters as a farce. Another insight on noir emerges through the introduction of unique radio conventions. When *The Screen Guild Theater* presented a version of *Laura* on air in 1945, the studio audience tittered audibly at Clifton Webb's lines and the excessive splashing sounds in the bathtub scene. The bawdy subtext of the cinematic version is exposed, so to speak, the moment Lydecker asks Dana Andrews for a towel.

Elsewhere I've considered a few dimensions of how radio shows like *Suspense, Marlowe,* and *Broadway Is My Beat* appropriated and rearranged noir tropes and motifs.[14] Here I'd like to press deeper into a few canonical films with a new idea in mind. If film noirs were phenomena "of the radio age," and if the experience of broadcasting played a role in conditioning a taste for noir, then we can look to these films not only for radios onscreen but for clues about how listening *itself* was understood in the period. After all, radio is an idea as well as a gadget, just as the radio play is a dramaturgical principle as well as a dramatic form, and only by considering these complexities in the context of films can their full implications emerge.[15] For radio-age Americans, mass-mediated listening was a pastime, a vice, a form of power, and a social condition, but the vigorous economy of affects surrounding all that is hard to grasp because we can neither watch people listen nor access how they inwardly pictured what they heard. We can do precisely that with classic film noirs, where characters often spend a great deal of time listening in, putting on "sound-plays" for one another, discovering themselves to be suddenly audible, or producing audibility where it did not previously exist—all features seen less often in revivals of the noir style. Understood this way, the genre is a miracle for radio history, turning the inaccessible phantom public of the period from a hypothesis into a projection, making ordinary auricular habits into choreographed performances, and rendering perceptible the invisible openness of space to audition. If that is right, then classic noir can be understood as the showcase of a world-listened-to, a way of beholding beings "in" listening, and ultimately as the privileged bearer of a radiophonic unconscious hidden within classical American cinema.

The Listener as Exhibit

In *Voices in the Dark*, J. P. Telotte points out that a common "human force" in noir is the effort to speak, however failed that effort may be.[16] This force has a logical corollary in a drive to listen, whose regulation is contemplated in many noir films. After all, one of the things we watch most routinely in noir is a being "doing" listening, the visual rhetoric of which can be amazingly dressy. Think of the Great Stanton (Tyrone Power) in his mentalist routine in Edmund Goulding's *Nightmare Alley* (1947), standing tuxedoed and masked at the center of the dance floor in a posh supper club, listening for coded intonations in his assistant's voice, sartorially elevated from the work clothes with which he began the film and the rags in which he will end it. His listening is "active," belying the distinction between active looking and passive listening, but it is also "all an act," a performance-within-a-performance intended to attract the gaze of others. "The Great Stanton" is a man blindfolded yet spotlighted, a spectacle of listening-made-visible that exhibits how noir made auditory capabilities into supple emblems.

Edward Dmytryk's *Murder, My Sweet* (1944) starts out with another blind-folded man in a spotlight, this time Philip Marlowe (Dick Powell), his eyes scorched by a gunshot flash, who tells the tale of the film to Police Lieutenant Randall in a flashback that begins and ends at the moment of his own statement. The film "is" the temporal span of the act of narrating, but it is also the duration of an act of listening on the part of the love interest, Ann Grayle (Anne Shirley), hidden in the room until the finale, when she is exposed to us in a visual burst, a pan so swift that it oversteps the mood of the setting. It is the same pan that Preminger uses when Lydecker appears in *Laura*, although here the reveal doesn't disclose an "acousmêtre" but his addressee. That kind

Russ Tamblyn as Bart Tare in the opening of Lewis's *Gun Crazy* (1950), the first of two shots in the film in which the ear of the marksman becomes a target for the voices of others, and for the camera.

of latent actuation—a narration whose true narratee becomes "real" at the last moment—was a common device on suspense radio, where it was not unusual to suddenly learn that the implied listener was the next victim of a killer. Had we always been aware of *someone else* in that over-small room of gruff men in *Murder, My Sweet*, of a sympathetic listening presence that is a corollary to Marlowe's speaking presence? In retrospect, the narration hints all along at what Chion calls an "ear supposed by the voice," a private ear for a private eye.[17]

Listening, be it active or passive, is always inaudible and invisible. On air, radio dramatists typically convey it using narration, filters, and other sonic exaggerations. In film, actors use gestures, affects, and habits. A vivid example is Walter Neff as he prowls the Pacific All Risk offices in the second half of *Double Indemnity* during the film's investigation phase, listening as if from afar, leaning on walls, folding his arms, gnawing a matchstick, resting his hands uneasily on his thin belt. Alfred Hitchcock's *Shadow of a Doubt* (1943) has another character often shown externalizing troubled listening, Charlie Newton (Teresa Wright), who spends long periods of the film lingering in the upstairs hall and kitchen of her home, frowning, with downcast eyes, hearing her suspicious uncle (Joseph Cotten) speaking elsewhere in the house. Other characters find themselves compelled to listen while performing gestures of emasculation. In Preminger's *Fallen Angel* (1945), the sadistic ex-cop Mark Judd (Charles Bickford) beats a suspect, aware that his actions are audible just past the curtain in the next room where a powerless Eric Stanton (Dana Andrews) manhandles a stuffed toy in disgust. The infantilizing quality of listening also resonates in a powerful scene in Hathaway's *Kiss of Death* (1947), when Nick Bianco (Victor Mature) awakens to a banging screen in the night, as he lay unsleeping, afraid that the maniac gangster Tommy Udo (Richard Widmark) is coming for his family. In the next shot, light from an opening door, a shadowed figure in its center, crosses the bed of the sleeping Bianco children, and we wonder if Udo has come for revenge, proving ourselves as susceptible to ambiguous shadows as Nick is to ambiguous sounds, turning his paranoid hearing into our paranoid vision. Then a reverse shot proves that our fears are unfounded. It is the shadow of Nick, after all. Back in bed, Nick's wife Nettie (Coleen Gray) asks why he is so jumpy. "You've been listening for something," she pleads. "All night you've been lying there listening for something."

As the nursery shot suggests, wherever actors could not use gestures to render the energy of active listening visually available, the camera could. In the opening of Joseph H. Lewis's *Gun Crazy* (1950), for instance, we see Bart Tare (Russ Tamblyn) sitting before a judge, after having stolen a handgun from a shop, his sister pleading for leniency. A flashback brings us to an episode in Bart's childhood in which he killed a chirping chick with his air rifle and wept remorsefully. Later, two of Bart's friends testify that, despite his marksman-ship, he has an aversion to killing. The next flashback depicts Tare a little older on a camping trip with the boys. The trio is presented with a line of sight on a mountain lion. Pressured by his cronies to shoot, Tare lines up the rifle, but as we cut to close-up, we hear an extradiegetic bird chirp, seemingly from the boy's memory, now a signal of childhood remorse. Tare lowers the gun. The acute marksman is overwhelmed by sound, a sensitivity underscored in the next moment, when one of the other boys lets off three shots, and we see Bart's hand spasm in a flinch at each report. Tare reestablishes visual prowess immediately. "Think I can't shoot when I want to?" he cries, tossing a canteen in the air and hitting it three times before it lands, then stalking up the hill, his friends following in awe, an ascent emphasized by a low-angle shot appropriate to this adolescent male ritual of eye and trigger. Back in the courtroom, the judge explains to Tare that he must be sent to a reformatory for his theft. The verdict fades into reverb, as if moving down a hallway, the judge's voice "entering" Bart's mind like the cry of the chick. As the words resound, the camera closes in on his head from behind, his ear snapping into focus at the center of the frame. That vulnerable ear appears once again later in the film, when Bart's bride Annie Starr (Peggy Cummins) convinces him to turn to crime. In the scene, Tare covers his eyes as Annie berates him from behind, doubly invisible. The ear again takes up the frame, like a target struck dead center.

Sleepwalkers

Many acts of listening transform readily into pictorial form, but sound ex-perience also always contains an energy that can't be fully reprocessed into an image without blockage or remainder. Indeed, some of the most indelible pictures of listeners in noir are of audile beings transfixed by a mysterious auditory surplus that the camera cannot quite give us. Perhaps that is why listening is often linked to autoeroticism in the genre. Think of Mike Ham-mer (Ralph Meeker) enjoying "honey-talk" in taped seductions in Robert Aldrich's *Kiss Me Deadly* (1955), of Waldo Lydecker in *Laura* listening to his broadcast of poetry as if wooing himself, or the similar autophonia scene in the conclusion of Preminger's *Whirlpool* (1949), when the lurking hypnotist David Korvo (Jose Ferrer) luxuriates in the sound of his own recorded voice, bleeding. These characters are what Elisabeth Weis calls "otakoustophiles," beings excessively enamored with listening in, marked by an unwillingness to participate in other kinds of exchange.[18] I would argue that otakoustophilia is an extremely common affect in noir, one that helps explain, for example, the kind of noir acting that Robert Pippin has recently highlighted, in which dazed characters act in environments where agency seems unable to bring

Barbara Stanwyck as Phyllis Dietrichson in *Double Indemnity* (1944), listening to her husband dying. We have a distressing closeness with Phyllis's hypnosis in this moment. Where does her "mental picture" of the murder end and ours begin?

about outcomes, yet outcomes happen anyway.[19] And although we see them listen—sometimes only to themselves—something about each listening act remains decidedly unobservable. The Great Stanton, Walter Neff, and Eric Stanton perform visual acts that capture the content of their listening, while *Murder, My Sweet, Kiss of Death,* and *Gun Crazy* use camera work to link the act of listening to a visual token. But the sum of the exhibit of listeners like Korvo and Lydecker lies in the elsewhereness in their eyes, a picture of the invisible process of picturing inwardly.

Double Indemnity employs such exhibits at key moments, including the murder sequence. Events begin when Walter Neff sneaks into the Dietrichson garage and climbs into the back of the couple's car. Phyllis Dietrichson (Barbara Stanwyck) enters with her husband (Tom Powers) and mouths a silent greeting to Neff while stuffing bags in the rear. As they drive we see Neff, his hand poised clawlike on the rear of the front seat, listening silently. The car turns down a dark street and Phyllis scans the road from left to right, then honks the horn in a prearranged signal. Neff reaches over the seat and kills Dietrichson. The murder is offscreen, just the span of a frame away. Phyllis bobs slightly as her seat jerks with the scuffle. The script reads: "There are struggling noises and a dull sound of something breaking. Phyllis drives on and never turns her head. She stares straight in front of her. Her teeth are clenched."[20] Staring forward, yet not really looking, she is in a state of . . . what? Trance? Titillation? The shot of Phyllis recalls Foster Hirsch's description of her as a "reptilian" figure, a kind of somnambulist.[21] Elisabeth Bronfen sees more complexity in the close-up, identifying three distinct phases to it: "Determination initially turns to sad acceptance of the death she has provoked, then becomes a quiet joy that indicates her own satisfaction and the completion of her plan."[22]

However we read her complicated expression, the more perplexing issue is why Phyllis elects to listen to something that she may easily observe.[23] She wants to see her husband dead, yet it's more chilling that, when given the chance to do so, she'd rather hear it instead. And in spite of the fact that we do not face the same choice as Phyllis, her desires are not easily extricated from ours. For the viewer, the events in the next seat are a sound-play whose parameters are spelled out, with specifics left to our imagination. We visualize within semantic bounds shaped by acoustic information—a swell of music, the sound of struggle, a faint choke—picturing an event in a place we cannot see. But our "viewing" is complicated by the fact that we do it as we watch her face and imagine what she imagines, hypnotized. The picture in our mind at once includes and meshes with the picture in her mind as we suppose it to be. In this way, the shot lures us through Phyllis's otakoustophilia back to our own overactive audile imagination, which is echoed back at us as a perversion. There is something about this moment that indicts the gratuitousness of radiophonic experience, with its fascination with making pictures in the mind, turning them around in our heads, dwelling on them to excess. In radio versions of *Double Indemnity,* the scene is sped over, as if dangerous. In a 1945 version on *Screen Guild Theater,* the scene is merely described by Walter Neff in his narrated memorandum, here typed (and thus sonified) rather than recorded. In the 1948 radio version on *The Ford Theater,* the scene is reduced to an auditory haiku—three honks of the horn, a muffled cry, and a vocalization: "Oh, Walter."

In his monograph on *Double Indemnity,* Richard Schickel justly points out that the murder is a weak point in the film, straining credulity.[24] But viewed as an expression of a radiophonic unconscious, it's richer than expected. Not only is this parable of audile surplus commenting directly on the ethical treachery of picturing, of living too much inside one's imagination, but beneath that allegory there is also an insight into noir epistemology. Jean-Luc Nancy has argued that listening is different from looking or merely hearing in that it represents a state of not-knowing-yet, a straining toward meaning that is withheld or not available for some other reason. "To be listening," he writes, "is always to be on the edge of meaning, or in an edgy meaning of extremity, and as if the sound were precisely nothing else than this edge, this fringe, this margin."[25] To have an "edgy" relationship to meaning, Nancy reasons, is to be on the lookout for a resonance of return, or "relation to self." That idea captures the noir predicament exactly, particularly in moments like this one in *Double Indemnity,* where characters choose of their own feeble volition to listen without hearing, and thus to remain always at the edge of meaning, to forestall a relation to self, to abjure *knowing,* even when—especially when—they have the chance.

Phantom Audiences

One thing that makes radio drama different from other programming is that unlike speakers in a newscast or a speech, those in a drama seem to ignore us.

That's a ruse, of course. The actors know that we are out here, and we know that their words, oriented toward one another, are really for us, resulting in a subtle but persistent aesthetic of coyness, a background pretense of diverted speech. We do not eavesdrop at all, but it's crucial that we listen *as if* eavesdropping. It is no surprise that dramas thematize that situation frequently. Indeed, tall tales of enemy eavesdropping were particularly important in wartime, as a device to underscore government-sponsored stories associated with the "Don't Talk" poster campaign. At the same time, whatever their overt social purposes, depictions of eavesdropping necessarily worked out a deep fantasy about the listener at home, the unwelcome presence that is (not-so-secretly) the guest of honor.

Many film noirs also experimented with the larger social meaning of pervasive eavesdropping. In film noir, eavesdroppers are often tyrants, both real, like Earl Janoth (Charles Laughton) in *The Big Clock* or Victor Grandison in *The Unsuspected,* and perceived, like Adele Cross (Rosalind Ivan) in Fritz Lang's *Scarlet Street* (1945). But "listening in" is also often shown to be inherent to the texture of modern life. That sense is conveyed well by the opening montage of Jules Dassin's *The Naked City* (1948), in which we hear humdrum inner monologues of the denizens of the city, until the prerogative to do so is turned over to authority figures as the sequence concludes at the Bureau of Telegraph, where sonorous reports are received in a city not so much watched as listened in on. Eavesdropping is also used for exposition in noir. In the opening of Jacques Tourneur's *Out of the Past* (1947), Joe Stefanos (Paul Valentine) overhears gossip in Marny's diner about Jeff Bailey, learning precisely what he needs to know about the former private eye, until he begins to chat with Marny (Mary Field) himself, telling the audience what we need to know about him. No sooner have we watched an astoundingly obvious eavesdropper at work than we begin to behave just like him.

In noir, eavesdropping is often that which links characters in the main struggle of the film to secondary or tertiary characters at an observational remove in an ever-shifting social geography. We can think of many film noirs as dramas that include "phantom auditors"—beings who listen at an elastic proximity to central plot events, as the camera witnesses them being overlooked. There is a good example in Lang's *The Big Heat* (1953). Halfway through the film, the rogue cop Dave Bannion (Glenn Ford) visits the Victory Auto Wrecking yard in search of Slim Farrow, a mechanic who helped murder Bannion's wife. The yard boss Mr. Atkins (Dan Seymour) claims that Farrow is dead and refuses to provide information, fidgeting with a soda straw, shifting on his stool, a "scared rabbit who doesn't see anything," as Bannion puts it. Their colloquy has an eavesdropper who hears it all, the secretary Selma Parker (Edith Evanson), who sits unnoticed by Bannion and Atkins but not by the camera. When Bannion mentions his dead wife, we cut to Parker, who

Colleen Alpaugh as the Little Girl with the Slide
Whistle, one of a dozen eavesdroppers in the dark
corners of Hathaway's *The Dark Corner* (1946).

looks up, awareness crossing her features. When Atkins crosses the room
to get another soda, Parker is framed between the stony Bannion and the
doughy Atkins as she pretends to work on her books. When Atkins claims,
"All I know about Slim is that he's dead," Parker seems to be on the cusp of
interjecting, then sinks back, unnoticed. Moments later, however, as Bannion
walks along the fence beyond the yard, Parker hobbles out from the detritus
of old machinery (looking over her shoulder to be sure *she* is not overheard),
truncating their social distance and giving him a clue to bring down the gangsters responsible for his wife's death. As Tom Gunning has pointed out, the
scene demonstrates how Bannion "uses" others (in a nonpejorative sense) to
move toward objectives.[26] But Bannion also humanizes Parker by asking her
name, as the score offers a few sentimental notes. Like many eavesdroppers
in noir, Parker is essential because she receives and redistributes information
in directions that its speaker did not intend, helping these tales bring about
resolutions in spite of their manifest epistemological pessimism. Because
knowledge is often impossible to obtain when it is actively sought in noirs,
these films require the accidents of reveal that eavesdropping readily provides.

The larger a "phantom audience" is in noir, the more the story reads like
a radio play remediated into the cinema. Consider *The Dark Corner*, a film
in which each major character eavesdrops on at least one other. The wildly
complicated plot begins just after a thug, Stauffer (William Bendix), is hired
by an art dealer, Hardy Cathcart (Clifton Webb), to spy on detective Brad
Galt (Mark Stevens) and his secretary Kathleen (Lucille Ball). The move is

a ploy to lure Galt into a fight with his erstwhile partner Tony Jardine (Kurt Krueger), who is having an affair with Cathcart's wife Mari (Cathy Downs). Galt takes the bait and attacks Jardine, while we see Mari in the next room, listening through the door. Later, in the basement of his museum, where he keeps a treasured portrait of Mari, Cathcart listens in on the two lovers plotting to run away together. Soon Jardine is dead, and Galt is framed and on the run, searching for leads in darkened apartments as Kathleen waits in the hallway, listening. In the conclusion, Galt is cornered in the basement of Cathcart's museum, where Galt and Cathcart are overheard by Mari (unnoticed upstairs with a gun), who shoots Cathcart, miraculously saving the detective.

Dark Corner is about putting people in frames, literally and figuratively, but on many occasions it's also about how eavesdroppers on the outside of those frames—often women—rupture them. That is true for the film as a whole, too. All of the characters mentioned above form a picture surrounded by a perimeter of seemingly unimportant secondary characters also involved in the unregulated circuit of misdirected speech: a mouthy cabbie speaks just loud enough for Galt to overhear, a newsboy emerges from a listening throng to provide a partial license-plate number, a box-office saleswoman overhears Kathleen's titillating banter and leans in to hear more, a girl in the hallway at Stauffer's apartment plays a pennywhistle and eavesdrops on his dealings on the phone with Cathcart. Everywhere in *The Dark Corner*, working-class ears listen as if to a radio play, an inbuilt audience reaching for hints. Indeed, it is only when Galt steps out of the inner circle of characters to speak to the girl with the whistle, thereby shrinking the social separation in the film between participant and eavesdropper (just as Bannion does with Parker), that he is directed to Cathcart's museum and the narrative resolves. Siegfried Kracauer once described that girl in the hall as an apparition.[27] She is doubly so, a mimic of the circle of eavesdroppers, an echo of the audience in the theater, and a metaphor for the abbreviation of distance that the radio age seemed to promise. It is an abbreviation that the cinema could evoke best. When *The Lux Radio Theater* presented an adaptation of *Dark Corner* in 1947, virtually all of the scenes of eavesdropping were eliminated and filled in by new dialogue alluding to them, smoothing down the rich texture of the drama, and even denying the little girl her whistle.[28]

Odd Abilities

In noir, eavesdropping is often misrecognized as voyeurism because it has a way of securing impressions of the latter, and it does so in a genre long mined for ideas on the psychopolitics of the gaze. An interesting example occurs in

Robert Mitchum as Jeff Bailey, spying on Kathie Moffat in Tourneur's *Out of the Past* (1947). In this first of three shots, do we see what Bailey sees, or see what he hears?

the San Francisco sequence in *Out of the Past*. Jeff Bailey, aware that he is in the midst of being framed for the murder of the lawyer Ernie Eels (Ken Niles), sneaks into the back of the flat of Meta Carson (Rhonda Fleming), where the femme fatale Kathie Moffat (Jane Greer) is at a party in the next room. Bailey is searching a desk when the phone rings. He hears a key unlocking the door and retreats into an adjacent darkened bedroom, his arm just leaving the light as Kathie enters. Having recognized the call as her cue, Kathie takes the phone, dialing Eels's apartment and asking the doorman to check on him so as to prompt the recording of a time of death that would implicate Bailey. It is one of the rare moments in the film when we see Kathie alone, or believing herself to be.

Whether or not Bailey sees her during this sequence is not clear. In the scene, the camera focuses on Kathie but cuts back to Bailey in the bedroom three times. In the first cut, he is seen from a point just a few feet inside the lighted room. There are two conspicuous sources of light: one from a bedroom window, giving definition to Bailey's neck, nose, and chest, and another from the bright room bisecting his face, suggesting that his left eye is able to see in. But Bailey's left shoulder rests flush against the edge of the doorway, suggesting that at no point can he or Kathie see one another. In the second shot, the camera has moved to the inside of the dark room, just a few feet to the right of where Bailey stands. The screen is now showing both rooms, with Bailey part of a dark frame and Kathie dazzling before a mirror as she lights a cigarette and crosses the room, her fur coat swinging. The shot quotes Kathie's first appearance in the film, framed in a doorway and coming out of the sun before Jeff's gaze in the La Mar Azul café in Mexico. Unlike the café scene, however, here Jeff has no obvious angle of sight leading to Kathie—unless he catches her when she crosses to a refrigerator on the far wall toward the end of the shot, a possibility implied by the next shot, which could be his point of view. Kathie begins fixing a drink, as the camera shifts to a high angle in a far corner in the room. Then comes the third, and shortest, cut to Bailey. This one is like the first, but much closer, providing a look at his face from the lighted room at an acute angle relative to the wall, suggesting that he can see Kathie, as the new intentness in his eyes indicates. But the line of light across his face, which represented its trespass into the doorway in the first shot, has disappeared. At this angle, if he could see her, then she would likely see him, which would render hiding useless. Soon, the camera returns to the high angle in the far corner, a signature noir rat-in-a-maze shot, and pans following Kathie back toward the phone, sweeping across the doorway. Just when we had been most persuaded to suppose that we would see Jeff looking in, there is no sign of him. In fact, the bedroom is more brightly lit than in our previous cutaways, suggesting that the angle was filmed separately from the others. Robert Mitchum may not even have been on set. At any rate, the camera then cuts to a closer shot of Kathie at the telephone learning that Eels's body is not in his apartment. She calls Stefanos to see what has gone wrong but is unable to reach him. Just as she turns to resume making her drink, Bailey steps out of the shadows. In a magnificent shot, Kathie's eyes widen, her eyebrows rise, and her lips and teeth part. It's a face that says *I've been overheard.*

The ambiguity of Bailey's eyeline is interesting because our alignment with his audition is so clear. The "ear" of the film rests just where Bailey would be projecting his hearing—to a point near Kathie—in the kind of auditory interpellation of the viewer that, as Rick Altman has explained, at once limits the possible hearings of the space and also gives a sense of control.[29] But it simply isn't clear if the "eye" of the camera and Bailey's eyes coincide. So how should we arbitrate our troubled sense that Bailey's visual observation of Kathie is there and yet not there? The question recalls a colloquy in the opening of the film, when the diner owner Marny gossips about Jeff with a local state official: "I just see what I see," she says. "Are you sure you don't see what you hear?" he replies. Of course, as Chion has often pointed out, in filmgoing we "see what we hear" and "hear what we see" all the time. Because we are looking at a listener and at the object of his listening at once, we superimpose our look on Bailey's listening and fuse them. Understanding it that way wouldn't be an "error" but a normal reading of how a classical Hollywood film smoothes together heterogeneous elements at the service of narrative. After all, isn't it precisely by overhearing Kathie that Jeff "sees through" her? The ambiguity of visual perspective, however, leaves a residual charge in the scene that it would not otherwise possess, hiding an oneiric reading behind the normative realist one. If Bailey cannot see Kathie, then we have two mutually isolated stories before us at once, one of an audile Jeff in the midst of imagining, and another of Kathie, alone. In that case, perhaps the images we see of her beyond the doorway stand in for a sound-play, a fantasy projected in (and mediated through) Bailey's mind.

However we read this moment of *Out of the Past*, it is clear that Kathie's surprise at the end of the scene arises from a sudden (and ironic) realization of her own audibility. The vulnerable ears of the passive men on the other end of the phone line are hers to activate and manipulate, but the ear of the man in the dark (like those of an audience) are not. She is unwittingly in a state of acoustic exposure, the auditory equivalent of nakedness, a situation whose precariousness is accentuated when she "clothes herself" in a new persona to curry sympathy when Jeff emerges. The scene reminds us that all audition requires a preexisting state of audibility (one may only hear things that can be heard in the first place), but that audibility can be imposed on us too, invisibly and without consent. The capacity to show the "making" of audibility, to provide images that examine the ineffable awareness of acoustic exposure—the uncanny sense that "someone is listening"—is perhaps the oddest power of film noir in the radio age.

To explore the point a little, think of the scenes at the house on Laverne Terrace, a key setting in Howard Hawks's *The Big Sleep* (1946). We arrive at the house early in the film, when Philip Marlowe (Humphrey Bogart) follows the phony book dealer Arthur Geiger (Theodore von Eltz) to the unremarkable home. The image fades to mark elapsed time, and cricket sound fills the air. Marlowe reclines, smoking and watching. There is a flash in the window and a scream so loud that it disturbs the artifice of the scene. The house is a kind of amplifier and will retain a certain to-be-listened-to-ness throughout the film. Marlowe rushes to the door and hears gunshots, not yet understanding what they mean. He enters to find the body of Geiger on the floor and Carmen Sternwood (Martha Vickers) seated giggling in an otherwise quiet room. Although the room's drapes and hidden camera indicate a crude set for shooting pornography, it's not hard to think of the space as a studio for a radio drama, particularly in the original 1945 version of the film, in which Marlowe spends the remainder of the long scene sonifying inert objects—opening doors, clinking glasses, upsetting beads, fingering splintered wood, flicking switches, handling keys, opening drawers and a squeaking lockbox, and paging through a notebook. In this version and the theatrical release, the house on Laverne Terrace is a hyperaudible place around which auditors accumulate and where sounds tell stories, two properties confirmed the next day when Marlowe returns to the house, and Eddie Mars (John Ridgely) whistles for his thugs waiting outside, who come running. That's the third of five visits to Laverne Terrace, the broadcasting studio from which the drama constantly radiates and to which it inevitably retreats.

By the conclusion of the film, a hastily structured contest between Marlowe and Mars hinges on the dynamics of that studio's audibility. Marlowe wins the contest in three ways. By proposing a meeting on Laverne Terrace and arriving first, Marlowe controls who is inside and who is outside, orchestrating the asymmetry of audibility to his liking. Second, Marlowe elects what sounds will issue toward the attentive outsiders, asking Carmen Sternwood to stop the sound of a rustling bead curtain to hide their presence, then letting out three gunshots intended for the ears of the thugs outside, thus doing with sound just what David Bordwell has argued Hawks does with the camera: restricting knowledge.[30] Third, and most curiously, Marlowe the "sound-effects man" controls the *interpretation* of those gunshots, which is identical with controlling life or death. "What do you think's gonna happen now, now what are your boys gonna think?" Marlowe sneeringly remarks to Mars after firing, a phrase echoing back on itself. Having drawn an audience for a sound show, Marlowe prompts a gross misinterpretation of its narrative elements, completing his transformation from an auditor stymied by ambiguous sounds to a broadcaster shaping them. In the moment Eddie rushes to his death-by-audience (a compelling fantasy on its own), Marlowe's "radio play" induces the same kind of panic in Mars's men as Orson Welles once inspired with a play about monsters from Mars. Like the famous "War of the Worlds" episode—or our public memory of it—*The Big Sleep* exaggerates the world-making power of auditory information by way of a show of catastrophic mishearing, thereby evincing a profound ambivalence about any society "in" listening. The power to listen to stories on the air—the core of radiophonic experience, if there is one—produces a double vulnerability, rendering the unsuspecting world acoustically exposed and, at the same time, exposing the critical defenselessness of any ear before which that mediated world is audible.

Notes

1. See William C. Ackerman, "The Dimensions of American Broadcasting," *Public Opinion Quarterly* 9 (Spring 1945): 1–18.

2. See Neil Verma, *Theater of the Mind: Imagination, Aesthetics, and American Radio Drama* (Chicago: University of Chicago Press, 2012), 170–71.

3. Frank Krutnik, *In a Lonely Street: Film Noir, Genre and Masculinity* (New York: Routledge, 1991), ix–xiv.

4. See James Naremore, *More than Night: Film Noir in Its Contexts* (Berkeley: University of California Press, 1998), 9–39.

5. Edward Dimendberg, *Film Noir and the Spaces of Modernity* (Cambridge, Mass.: Harvard University Press, 2004); Sheri Chinen Biesen, *Blackout: World War II and the Origins of Film Noir* (Baltimore: Johns Hopkins University Press, 2005); Robert Miklitsch, *Siren City: Sound and Source Music in Classic American Noir* (New Brunswick, N.J.: Rutgers University Press, 2011).

6. See Verma, *Theater of the Mind*, 7–9.

7. I thank Tom Gunning for pointing out this allusion to me.

8. See Miklitsch, *Siren City*, 246–47.

9. Robert Porfirio "*The Unsuspected* and the Noir Sequence: Realism, Expressionism, Style," in *Film Noir Reader 4*, ed. Alain Silver and James Ursini (Pompton Plains, N.J.: Limelight, 2004), 66–77.

10. Michel Chion, *The Voice in Cinema*, trans. Claudia Gorbman (New York: Columbia University Press, 1999), 27–29.

11. Miklitsch, *Siren City*, 53–83.

12. See, for example, Karen Hollinger, "Film Noir, Voice-over and the Femme Fatale," in *Film Noir Reader*, ed. Alain Silver and James Ursini (New York: Limelight, 1996), 246–60.

13. Fredric Jameson, "The Synoptic Chandler" in *Shades of Noir*, ed. Joan Copjec (London: Verso, 1993), 36.

14. Verma, *Theater of the Mind*, 91–114, 181–202.

15. See Kate Lacey, "Ten Years of Radio Studies: The Very Idea," *Radio Journal* 6.1 (February 2009): 21–32.

16. J. P. Telotte, *Voices in the Dark: The Narrative Patterns in Film Noir* (Urbana: University of Illinois Press, 1989), 218.

17. Michel Chion, *Film, a Sound Art*, trans. Claudia Gorbman (New York: Columbia, 2009), 302.

18. Elisabeth Weis, "Eavesdropping: An Aural Analogue of Voyeurism?" in *Cinesonic: The World of Sound in Film*, ed. Philip Brophy (Sydney: Southwood Press, 1999), 80.

19. Robert Pippin, *Fatalism in American Noir: Some Cinematic Philosophy* (Charlottesville: University of Virginia Press, 2012), 12–21.

20. Billy Wilder and Raymond Chandler, *Double Indemnity: The Complete Screenplay* (Berkeley: University of California Press, 2000), 63.

21. Foster Hirsch, *The Dark Side of the Screen: Film Noir* (New York: Da Capo Press, 1983), 1–8.

22. Elisabeth Bronfen, "Femme Fatale—Negotiations of Tragic Desire," *New Literary History* 35.1 (Winter 2004): 110.

23. The problem does not arise in Cain's novel, which gives no details about the gaze of Phyllis. See James M. Cain, *Double Indemnity* (New York: Vintage Crime, 1992), 44.

24. Richard Schickel, *Double Indemnity* (London: British Film Institute, 1992), 45.

25. Jean-Luc Nancy, *Listening*, trans. Charlotte Mandell (New York: Fordham University Press, 2007), 6.

26. Tom Gunning, *The Films of Fritz Lang: Allegories of Vision and Modernity* (London: British Film Institute, 2000), 426.

27. Siegfried Kracauer, "Hollywood's Terror Films," *New German Critique* 89 (Spring–Summer 2003): 109.

28. In the film, a key piece of dialogue involves the girl mistaking the name "Cathcart" for cascara, a laxative. No doubt aware that "bodily function" advertising was touchy on network, writers shrewdly changed Cathcart's name to Wickett, and the mixup became Wickett/ticket.

29. Rick Altman, *Sound Theory/Sound Practice* (New York: Routledge, 1992), 60–61.

30. David Bordwell, *Narration in the Fiction Film* (Madison: University of Wisconsin Press, 1985), 65–66.

5

Disney Noir

"Just Drawn That Way"

J. P. TELOTTE

Attempting to excuse her vampish looks and reputation, the "toon" Jessica Rabbit of the Disney production *Who Framed Roger Rabbit* (1988) explains to the detective Eddie Valiant that "I'm not bad; I'm just drawn that way." It is a memorable and evocative line, particularly given how excessively "bad" she indeed looks and the jaw-dropping effect that this "drawn" character clearly has on the various males in this neo-noir hybrid of live action and animation. That self-description recalls the almost equally—and literally—stunning impact of a range of femme fatales from the film-noir canon: Phyllis Dietrichson (Barbara Stanwyck), as she first appears wrapped in a towel in *Double Indemnity* (1944); Gilda (Rita Hayworth) doing her striptease in *Gilda* (1946); Kathie Moffat (Jane Greer) dressed all in white and walking out of the sun in *Out of the Past* (1947). At the same time it might remind us of what Janey Place describes as the "highly stylised and conventionalised" way in which so much of film noir operates,[1] the form's exaggerated construction not only of its women but of the world and even the narrative itself that, as *Who Framed Roger Rabbit* illustrates, easily "draws" a kind of kinship between the noir form and the equally stylized realm of animation. Yet even in its heyday, and thus long before the retro efforts of a work like *Who Framed Roger Rabbit*, the film noir was already inflecting American animation, lending its character types, atmosphere, and narrative strategies to the cartoon in ways that reveal much about its contemporaneous impact.

Pursuing that relationship between the film noir and animation, we might add that Jessica's complaint about being "drawn that way" also suggests a level on which she has been framed, not quite in the manner that, as the title offers, her husband Roger has (i.e., for murder), but simply by being presented as something she is not. In her wildly drawn curves, abundant cleavage, and other attractions—all stylizations of those already rather stylized noir femme fatales noted above—she has been effectively framed by *style,* by the nature of the film type that she inhabits. But as she tries to explain, she is—very much in the tradition of figures like Phyllis Dietrichson, Gilda, and Kathie Moffat—rather more, or at least different, than she initially appears; or, as Alan Cholodenko simply puts it, "[S]he is bad as well as not bad at the same time."[2] It is a difference or doubleness that also marks the film noir's intersection with and impact on classical animation, as the American cartoon industry in various ways sought to draw in the characters, visual stylings, and narrative techniques that noir was popularizing in the late World War II and immediate postwar era, to draw on the energies that noir had brought to the cinema, even as it also tried to maintain its own difference from that often troubling form.

For much of the World War II era, at a time when the major studios were already producing some of the classic noir films with their insistently dark view of the American cultural landscape, most of the animation industry had rather different concerns. The cartoon industry, largely controlled by the major studios, "enthusiastically embraced and promoted the war effort,"[3] providing audiences not only with overt propaganda—as we can see demonstrated in a host of titles, including *The Ducktators* (Warner Bros., 1942), *Japoteurs* (Fleischer, 1942), *Der Fuehrer's Face* (Disney, 1943), and *Bugs Bunny Nips the Nips* (Warner Bros., 1944)—but also with a comforting humor in the face of shared homefront concerns like shortages, rationing, censorship, and bond drives. Thus Michael Shull and David Wilt note that "rarely" in American film history do we find cartoons "made with the singlemindedness of purpose that was prevalent in Hollywood between 7 December 1941, and 2 September 1945."[4] And while the film noir was hardly immune from propaganda elements during the war years—and here we might quickly note some of Fritz Lang's efforts, such as *Manhunt* (1942) and *Ministry of Fear* (1944)—its hard edge, its fundamental concern with problems within our culture, its persistent *self-critique* of American life, together with the Office of War Information's general prescriptions against overstated criticisms of the homefront,[5] would seem to have made noir an unlikely inspiration for the period's animators.

And yet, as the war drew to a close, and certainly in the period immediately following, that distinction began to wane, not because noir was losing its popularity—that was far from the case—but precisely because the form had become such a key part of our cultural imaginary and had also entered into what we might term "high fashion." In fact, Hollywood itself would eventually transpose the noir look, atmosphere, and characters into a variety of other film genres, including the western (*Rancho Notorious* [1952]), the science-fiction film (*Invasion of the Body Snatchers* [1956]), the musical (*Lady in the Dark* [1944]), and especially the comedy, as the studios discovered various—although especially comic—potentials in the very extremes of noir, such as those that *Who Framed Roger Rabbit* plays up. It thus began to parody the form in such live-action efforts as Danny Kaye's *Wonder Man* (1945); Bob Hope films like *They've Got Me Covered* (1944) and *My Favorite Brunette* (1947); several Bowery Boys films, including the tellingly titled *Hard Boiled Mahoney* (1947); and especially the "Girl Hunt Ballet" sequence of Vincente Minnelli's *The Band Wagon* (1953). As James Naremore observes, such parodistic practice was fairly common to Hollywood and to American popular culture, and it generally had "less to do with the ridicule of a dead style than with an attempt to capitalize on a wildly popular trend."[6] For one example of animation's effort at capitalizing on the form, we need only recall the title of a UPA Mister Magoo cartoon, *Trouble Indemnity* (1950), which evoked one of the most famous, darkest, and seemingly least open to comic treatment of all film noirs, Billy Wilder's *Double Indemnity.*

But through the late war years and into the postwar era, we also begin to see a number of elements of classical noir narrative gradually filtering into the animation that emerged from several of the major studios. Obviously, the violence of film noir, with characters being shot, stabbed, or "sapped," relatively easily transferred to the comic world of animation, wherein over-the-top violence—with no lasting damage to the cartoon characters—had traditionally been part of the appeal. But sex, especially as connected to the threatening figure of the femme fatale that we have described above, increasingly surfaced in late war-era and postwar cartoons, and it would find especially iconic embodiment in Tex Avery's "Red" character of *Red Hot Riding Hood* (1943), *Swing Shift Cinderella* (1945), *The Shooting of Dan McGoo* (1945), *Wild and Woolfy* (1945), and *Little Rural Riding Hood* (1949), among others. Other key figures like the detective—particularly as embodied in the classical noir narratives centered on Sam Spade and Philip Marlowe—would also relatively easily translate into cartoons, as evidence Avery's *Who Killed Who?* (1943), as would the iconic gangster, a recurring character type in postwar Bugs Bunny cartoons like *Racketeer Rabbit* (1946), *Bugs and Thugs* (1953), and *Bugsy and Mugsy* (1957). And while the noir preference for darkly lit and deeply composed images would seem a more challenging translation into the Technicolor and inherently flat world of the cartoons, it too would find some place, as we see in the Fleischer Bros./Paramount Studio's short-lived Superman cartoons (1941–43), which combined a Technicolor palette with an almost expressionist design, in part because of a desire to capture something of the comic-book styling of the original, but also in a determined effort to make that fantasy figure fit into the darker context that the World War had thrust upon audiences and that had naturally become central to the plots of many of these films.[7]

Yet perhaps the most unlikely evidence of that influence—if also perhaps the most telling—can be found in the work of the Walt Disney Studio, which produced some of the most pointedly noir-styled cartoons of the period, most notably a series of Donald Duck films, *Donald's Crime* (1945), *Duck Pimples* (1945), and *The Trial of Donald Duck* (1948). In these cartoons we gain a sense of just how deeply a noir aesthetic had penetrated American culture, for they repeatedly plunge Disney's top "star" of the period not into the world of oversaturated colors that Disney had pioneered in American animation, or musical-style narratives in which the studio had lately starred him—such as the features *Saludos Amigos* (1943) and *The Three Caballeros* (1945)—but into a consistently dark, strangely composed, and highly subjective realm, one that consistently recalls Naremore's description of noir as a "liminal" territory, a "borderland" that, in our normal lives, we usually try to avoid.[8]

I suggest that the Disney Studio is a rather surprising place to find that influence in such force because of the company's reputation in this period— a reputation grounded in the studio's success with fairy-tale narratives, its established family audience, and even its reputation for a realistically styled rather than overtly exaggerated approach to animation. Underscoring that unlikely convergence, Robin Allan suggests that, with the appearance in close proximity of such feature films as *Fantasia* (1940), *Dumbo* (1941), and *Bambi* (1942), the studio had early in the World War II period come to develop an "accent on sentimentality and baby appeal," with its primary audience seen as composed of women and young children.[9] However, its films were, at the time, being released by RKO, a company especially noted for producing some of the key noir films of the mid to late 1940s, including works like *Murder, My Sweet* (1944), *Cornered* (1945), and *Out of the Past* (1947). And since it was common practice to match cartoons with features in terms of subject or theme—in some cases, even to design cartoons to fit with a planned feature release—the appearance of works such as *Donald's Crime, Duck Pimples,* and *The Trial of Donald Duck* becomes somewhat less surprising. In fact, Disney's featuring of the studio's top star of the period, Donald Duck, in all of these works, as well as the Academy Award nomination that the first of these films earned, should suggest the attention that the studio gave to these cartoons.

We might also note a few other impulses that may have influenced this noir inflection at Disney, since they speak to influences that were being felt in the other animation studios in this period as well. In 1945 Disney released the hybrid (live-action and animation) feature film *The Three Caballeros*, a work in which the reviewer John Mason Brown saw signs that Walt Disney seemed to be having "audience trouble," that "he could not make up his mind whether he was appealing to the young or the old" anymore.[10] And certainly the overt sexualizing of Donald Duck in that film, as we find him chasing after—but never catching—a succession of beautiful live-action women, including a beach full of bathing beauties, well illustrates his point. Barbara Deming, whose book *Running away from Myself* offered one of the first assessments of the noirish turn in 1940s American cinema, would describe that film in terms that she usually reserved for a more serious, live-action cinema. Clearly evoking the world of noir, she describes *The Three Caballeros'* "nightmare realm . . . where visions tantalize but deceive, what seems substantial may prove insubstantial."[11] Neal Gabler adds a further rationale for this development, as he notes that, given the changing atmosphere—one colored by the wartime violence, a rise in cultural emphasis on sexuality, and a pervasive sense of insecurity—the Disney Studio, like other cartoon producers in this shifting climate, was suddenly finding that *all* of its cartoon stars "needed to be revitalized"[12] to fit in and retain their appeal with a postwar audience.

Certainly there is some sense that a revisioning is at work in a film like *Donald's Crime*. The cartoon largely discards what had become the typical—and highly predictable—Donald Duck narrative formula, wherein the serious and always quite enterprising Duck undergoes a series of trying encounters, which inevitably result in frustrations, and which prompt him to explode in a sputtering, incoherent temper tantrum—all of it belying the theme song that had been adopted for the Duck series that ironically asks the question, "Who's got the sweetest disposition?" But in this case the narrative trajectory seems modeled on that of a typical film noir, as Donald prepares for a date with his girlfriend Daisy, realizes that he does not have the money to impress her, and so proceeds to rob a bank—appropriately for a comedy, the piggy bank belonging to his nephews Huey, Dewey, and Louie—to finance an evening of nightclubbing that culminates in Daisy kissing him and dubbing him her "Big Shot." The second half of the film comments on this first, exploiting the nighttime setting to take Donald through a dark and menacing cityscape, as if he were being pursued for his "crime." He is, in fact, being driven by an accusing conscience, as he imagines himself a true criminal and slinks through the shadows, while looking out for the police and envisioning "Wanted" posters calling for his capture "Dead or Alive." It is a situation that culminates with him in despair over his seemingly doomed plight, and one that clearly evokes a number of other noir "trapped" and "doomed" scenarios with which audiences of the period would have been familiar, such as *Double Indemnity, Scarlet Street* (1945), and *Detour* (1945). The fact that Donald partially redeems himself—by stumbling on a help-wanted ad for a dishwasher and then working all night to replace the stolen money—is itself ironically undercut when the next morning his nephews discover him putting coins back *into* their bank and assume he is in the process of stealing from them. The closing reminder from Donald's conscience in voiceover, that "crime doesn't pay," only renders obvious what was already one of the most common motifs running through this cartoon's live-action counterparts.

While this narrative trajectory obviously suggests a comic trivializing of a familiar noir plot, wherein the weak male succumbs to robbery or even murder in order to obtain wealth or impress his girl, that was hardly the common stuff of cartoons in this period, especially those emanating from Disney. Moreover, the way that this narrative unfolds, its complex styling, is equally noteworthy. *Donald's Crime* is indeed "drawn that way"—it incorporates, and stresses, all of the common noir visual markers: a pervasive darkness, constant shadows and facial modeling, an urban landscape with buildings rising at impossible angles, high- and low-angle shots to frame the Duck in unusual or unstable compositions, street lamps producing a chiaroscuro effect, and slotted blinds casting bar shadows on the Duck, as if he were already wearing a convict's uniform. Done in a quick-cut fashion with repeated movements on a diagonal or into the frame—rather than in the horizontal plan of more conventional period animation—the cartoon reminds us how quickly the noir style had become a common part of our film parlance and an effective way of evoking that "nightmare realm" that Deming describes.

As I have argued elsewhere, more than a distinctive visual style marks the noir universe,[13] and that point is underlined in this film through the use of another frequent signature of the form, a voiceover narration—here the voice of Donald's conscience—and the larger sense of subjectivity that dominates much of the film and that would prove one of noir's key contributions to postwar American cinema. From the point at which Donald first recognizes that he lacks the funds to play a "big shot," the voice of his conscience drives the narrative, prompting him to take his nephews' money, reassuring

Donald's Crime (1945) shows the Duck trapped in an expressionist-inspired underworld. Copyright Walt Disney Pictures.

him that "nobody's going to know," and telling him that Daisy expects and deserves a "good time." After he breaks the boys' piggy bank—for a bounty of $1.25—that voiceover gains a parodic edge by *inflating* the attendant noirish atmosphere: accusing the Duck and calling him a "gangster," "bank robber," and "public enemy." This element of hyperbole builds with the dark look and the expressionistic treatment of the cityscape to effectively transport the narrative into a subjective realm, a world where, as Donald sees it, he now has no place. Seeing another kind of "wanted" sign, this one for a dishwasher, he tries quite literally to *earn* his way back into the world of light and right behavior by laboring through the rest of this dark night. However, his comically speeded-up washing of a seeming mountain of dishes—another subjective flourish—only adds to the larger effect of exaggeration, for we also gather that this is how Donald interprets his efforts at making things right. And that lingering subjective element at the conclusion, as he puts the money back into a now-repaired piggy bank and the voiceover intones that "crime doesn't pay," leaves us with a sense of Donald as a figure not only of unstable *temper* but of unstable *character*, unable to control either the world around him or the world within. He thus becomes a new kind of comic character, one whose instability forecasts a Jessica Rabbit, a figure who is, after all, "bad as well as not bad."

Appearing later in the same year, Disney's second effort in this vein, *Duck Pimples*, builds on the same subjective foundation, although in this instance the film points less directly to the cinema than to other media strands—the radio, the novel, the pulp magazine—all of which also made significant contributions to the key texts of film noir. It begins on a dark and stormy night with Donald listening to a series of crime shows on the radio—shows in the tradition of *Lights Out* (1934–47), *Inner Sanctum* (1941–52), and especially *Suspense* (1942–62), a program that would launch a number of scripts in this period that would later become noir films, most notably *Sorry, Wrong Number* (1948). A narrator for one of the shows invites the listeners to "let your imagination go," and Donald readily accepts that invitation, only to become nervous and unsettled by what he hears, as he begins to imagine that characters from the mysteries are reaching out from the radio or already in the room with him, and so he turns the radio off. A sudden knock on the door amplifies that sense of foreboding, as it introduces a large and menacing man selling books and magazines with titles like *Murder, Thriller,* and *Crime*. The open door also lets the storm—like the strange man—into Donald's now very insecure home; and he is left with a variety of titles, in one of which he begins to immerse himself. But as he reads, the figures in the story—like those on the radio—literally pop out of the book, involving him in its plot of murder, a theft of pearls, a missing seductress (who looks and acts remarkably like

A femme fatale, recalling Tex Avery's "Red," literally pops out of a noir novel in *Duck Pimples* (1945). Copyright Walt Disney Pictures.

Avery's popular "Red" character, as well as Jessica Rabbit), and a cop named Hennessy. As Donald becomes engulfed in this narrative, his house is gradually "drawn this way," metamorphosing into a dark cityscape, much like that depicted in *Donald's Crime,* and the Duck himself takes on a similar coloring, as he becomes the subject of investigation and accusations until finally the author of the story pops out of the book, correcting any misperceptions and revealing that Hennessy, a crooked cop, is the real criminal. When the cop fires several shots at Donald and makes his escape, all of the other characters follow, jumping back into the book and leaving the Duck quaking while another voiceover, recalling the initial radio narrator as well as the voice-of-conscience in *Donald's Crime,* not very reassuringly offers, "Well, *possibly* it was only your imagination."

As with *Donald's Crime, Duck Pimples'* mise-en-scène readily establishes the familiar noir world, providing a look and an atmosphere that prompts us to expect to encounter sudden crimes, a femme fatale, a crooked cop, and a wrongly accused man—or duck. In this instance, the film traces that world back to its earlier roots in pulp fiction and radio mystery, while also drawing out some of the techniques that these sources had helped bring into cinematic practice, including the first-person narrator/voiceover, the introduction of numerous minor characters to add atmosphere and move the narrative along, and the convoluted, puzzle-like shape of the narrative, most famously demonstrated in a noir like *The Big Sleep* (1946).[14] But even more than in the previous cartoon, *Duck Pimples* emphasizes the narrative's subjective dimension, from its initial injunction that Donald let his "imagination go" to the far-from-restorative conclusion that these dark events were "possibly" only the product of his imagination. This imaginative framing of the story reminds us of how Disney often tried out new narrative patterns, even to the point of drawing audiences into the subjective world created for the cartoon—much as he had done in a more famous, Academy Award–winning nightmare film only two years prior, *Der Fuehrer's Face,* wherein Donald dreams that he is a citizen of Nazi Germany. Criticized a few years earlier for producing animation that too slavishly followed realistic film conventions—in fact, commenting on Disney's *Dumbo,* Siegfried Kracauer had attacked the film because he felt that animation should emphasize "the dissolution rather than the reinforcement of conventional reality"[15]—the studio here, as in *Donald's Crime,* demonstrated that it could construct a narrative precisely around the sudden "dissolution . . . of conventional reality" into the fantastic realm of the imagination, leaving the Duck clearly, and disturbingly, within the "liminal" territory that Naremore describes, a realm wherein only the author's sudden appearance can sort out whether the duck is, in fact, "bad" or "not bad."

However, a third film in this mode, *The Trial of Donald Duck,* suggests that only a few years later Disney was beginning to pull back from this sort of noir-inflected experimentation. Still drawing the Duck into the realm of urban crime, still relying on a distinctly noir visual scheme for a large part of the narrative, and still employing a voiceover flashback mechanism, this cartoon offers a far less complex narrative, albeit one that recalls *Donald's Crime* in the way that it tries to exaggerate a commonplace noir situation for—limited—comic effect. In this instance the film focuses on Donald's arrest and trial, resulting, we eventually learn, from the seemingly inconsequential act of not paying the bill at a fancy French restaurant. That rather slight "criminal" material gains in impact from being framed in what was by 1948 a familiar noir situation, the ponderously presented trial of a seemingly innocent figure, and from the circumstances being recounted in flashback—both elements central to a key noir film of the same year, Orson Welles's *Lady from Shanghai* (1948). Here that difficult determination between "bad" and "not bad" seems, from the start, to be the central issue.

But instead of employing the common noir conventions to build an atmosphere of foreboding and to open onto Donald's subjective responses, *The Trial of Donald Duck* from the start problematizes that atmosphere, milking it for comic effect by emphasizing its very construction, underscoring how carefully things are "drawn." Recalling a film often cited as the "first" film noir, *Stranger on the Third Floor* (1940), *The Trial of Donald Duck* begins with a highly stylized courtroom scene. In fact, we never see the dark courtroom in its entirety; rather, it is fashioned through a series of quick cuts from extreme high and low angles that disorient and fragment the scene. The judge remains invisible behind the height of his bench, represented only by the gavel that we see pounded on his desk. And the defense lawyer similarly remains offscreen while describing his client, the Duck, as "a mere victim of circumstances." Yet when Donald mounts the witness stand that seems to loom high above him like a gallows, he strikes an angelic pose, his hands poised as if in prayer; when he is sworn to "tell the truth," we see in close-up his fingers crossed;

and as his lawyer announces that he will shed the "light of truth" on events, Donald slyly pulls open a Venetian blind to shift its bar-like shadows into a shaft of bright light cast on his figure. Even the introduction of his accuser, the restaurateur Pierre, follows this pattern, as the calmly seated Pierre turns into a raging figure when Donald covertly hits him with a peashooter, and when the defense attorney describes him as coldhearted, a cutaway to Pierre depicts him as blue and frozen in attitude, like a block of ice. Once the flash-back account of the events leading up to the trial concludes, we hear the attorney proclaim "the injustice of it all," while we see Donald crying behind bars—actually slumped behind the railing surrounding the witness stand, an effect that the judge then reverses as he pronounces a sentence of "ten dollars or ten days washing dishes," while his own hand is seen drawing the blinds to again impose bar-like shadows on the Duck.

As a result of this repeated emphasis on the construction—or "drawing"—of effects, especially the play with the signature bar shadows of noir narra-tive, it actually becomes more difficult to read the center of this narrative, the flashback scenes in Pierre's Café. For those scenes lose much of what Paul Schrader famously described as the defining characteristics of noir, its emphasis on "subtle qualities of tone and mood."[16] Unlike the narrative's framing portions, here we find no play with shadows, no facial modeling, no outsized settings or unusual angles. Rather, the scenes take on the bright coloring and suggest the sort of casual action of practically any Donald Duck cartoon of the late 1940s, with Donald "ducking" into Pierre's Cafe to avoid a sudden shower and then comically confronting the pretensions and prices of a high-class restaurant when he has only a nickel in his pocket. This extended flashback and the at-torney's voiceover, detailing the events of the supposed crime, certainly give no hint of noir's "love of romantic narration"[17] but rather emphasize Donald's embarrassment, while also priming us for something more familiar, the eventual comic explosion on which the film ends: Donald is found guilty, sentenced to wash dishes for ten days, and then he unleashes his well-known duck temper, breaking most of those dishes that he washes. It is, in sum, a return to type for Donald, a return to a version of the character with which the Disney animators were certainly familiar but in whom they had also begun to recognize limita-tions. As the key Disney animators Ollie Johnston and Frank Thomas note, most at the studio had come to feel that the character was too "broad" for the period: "We had grown up" as artists.[18] But the noirish framing of this film, as the narrative's emphasis on the construction of visual and narrative effects suggest, was itself just another effect, a calculated effort at injecting narrative interest into a character with whom the animators were becoming bored, at inflecting—for one last time—what was, as the postwar mood lifted, coming to seem a rather conventional cartoon series.

At least for a time, though, these Disney cartoons, as well as some from other studios noted above, would take an important lead from the popular film noir. They would obviously find new possibilities for parody—a strategy given special effort at Warner Bros., where the animation unit was encouraged to reference the studio's live-action films as a kind of synergistic promotion,[19] resulting in works like the Bugs Bunny cartoon *The Big Snooze* (1946), appearing shortly after the studio's feature *The Big Sleep* (1946). But they would also gain new directions for narrative development, especially by incorporating reflexive and subjective components into their stories. Of course, there was already a kind of reflexive tradition in American animation. As Donald Crafton notes, many early cartoons incorporated what he terms "self-figuration," that is, the "tendency of the filmmaker to interject himself into his film"[20]—a practice that was consistent with the form's links to avant-garde cinema and easily exploited for comic effect. But by the late 1930s, that dimension had lost its fashion, especially in light of the Disney Studio's industry-leading "illusion of life" aesthetic, with which it would have clashed. And the subjective element had never quite taken hold in the nation's cartoons, despite nightmarish scenarios found in some of the Fleischer Studio's work and even in some early Disney. Rather, the common tendency was to evoke the world of conventional experience with its impressions of stability and solidity, for caricaturing and lampooning that world was enough; its overturning had proved a most satisfactory strategy—especially satisfying for Depression-era audiences who had lived through an era of cultural instability and unpredictability.

The Disney cartoons discussed here managed to link both impulses, to work in a self-conscious way, focusing on how characters and situations were "drawn"—even giving audiences a rather un-Disney-like seductress in the "missing" girl of *Duck Pimples*—while also foregrounding an unreliable subjectivity. That linkage allowed the studio to stretch the boundaries of its "illusion of life" approach, as it would also try to do with another experimental and highly subjective narrative, the short *Destino* that the studio began as a collaboration with Salvador Dali in 1945.[21] That connection also let Disney recast Donald Duck, at least for a time, as something other than a fowl with a foul attitude. Not really bad or merely bad-tempered, he was, rather like Jessica Rabbit years later, only—but repeatedly—framed, "just drawn that way," and these films let audiences see him as something more: a figure of some internal complexity who inhabited just the sort of unstable and at times frightening world as did his audience. If that characterization did not last—if Disney, as well as the other cartoon studios, did not make more of that noir influence—it is probably because American animation of the 1950s, at least that produced by the major studios, would become less and less open to experimentation, certainly less likely to follow the patterns of live-action cinema, especially as it began to look toward a future as a quickly and cheaply produced product for the new medium of television.

And yet that noir influence did not disappear from American animation—or from Disney. During the rise of neo-noir in the 1980s and 1990s, when films like *Body Heat* (1981), *Blood Simple* (1985), *The Grifters* (1990), and *L.A. Confidential* (1997) remixed the visual style and sense of pervasive corruption found in classical noir with a highly self-conscious attitude, animation would again draw with some success on that narrative and stylistic richness. Disney would release Robert Zemeckis's *Who Framed Roger Rabbit,* and its combination of live-action and animation would in turn inspire Ralph Bakshi's similarly styled *Cool World* (1992). In these films, but especially the former, we see Hollywood resurrecting the noir settings, atmosphere, and iconic character types—particularly the detective and the femme fatale—not only to evoke a noirish aspect of the contemporary cultural landscape, much as the live-action neo-noirs were already powerfully doing, but also to develop the sort of reflexive dimension that we have noted in both *Duck Pimples* and *The Trial of Donald Duck,* employing it in large part to talk about the very nature of animation.

Seen at a temporal distance, as well as through the lens of animation, the very exaggerations that had so marked film noir of the 1940s and 1950s—of lighting, atmosphere, dialogue, and broadly drawn character types—would stand out and even seem appropriate to the stylized world of animation. In *Who Framed Roger Rabbit,* for example, the private detective Eddie Valiant's interactions with a—literal—"big gorilla" at the Ink and Paint Club clearly echo Philip Marlowe's confrontations with Moose Malloy (played by one of Hollywood's consummate "big gorillas," Mike Mazurki) in *Murder, My Sweet,* as well as numerous other instances in which the rational detective or investigator suddenly confronts a stark physicality; and the world of Toontown, with its streets and buildings that come alive, that twist and turn, enfolding characters like the stuff of nightmares, seems almost a literal interpretation of

Cool World's live noir detective is tested by a seductive animated world. Copyright Paramount Pictures.

Raymond Chandler's oft-cited—and oft-cinematized—vision of the American cityscape as a world of "mean streets."[22] But these hybrid films evoke that earlier cinematic vision, frame it by matching up live and animated action and characters, in part because noir's cultural darkness so tellingly parallels the darkness that settled on animation itself in that late 1940s era in which *Who Framed Roger Rabbit* is set—a period when various studios began to shut down their animation units or started to shift into the production of low-quality work for the new television market. *Roger Rabbit,* and to some extent *Cool World,* looks nostalgically back at and laments the lost world of "toons"—and perhaps too the lost possibilities of the noir-like cartoons discussed here. For they offered audiences a world and characters that were indeed "drawn" in ways that, for a time, allowed for more complexity and experimentation than was typical of period animation and in fact complemented the film noir and its own distinctive form of cinematic speech.

Notes

1. Janey Place, "Women in Film Noir," in *Women in Film Noir,* ed. E. Ann Kaplan (London: British Film Institute, 1980), 36.

2. Alan Cholodenko, *"Who Framed Roger Rabbit,* or the Framing of Animation," in *The Illusion of Life: Essays on Animation,* ed. Alan Cholodenko (Sydney: Power Publications, 1991), 230.

3. Michael S. Shull and David E. Wilt, *Doing Their Bit: Wartime American Animated Short Films, 1939–1945,* 2nd ed. (Jefferson, N.C.: McFarland, 2004), 14.

4. Ibid., 79.

5. For a brief discussion of the Office of War Information's impact on cartoon narrative during the war years, see Stefan Kanfer, *Serious Business: The Art and Commerce of Animation in America from Betty Boop to* Toy Story (New York: Da Capo, 1997), 144–45.

6. James Naremore, *More than Night: Film Noir in Its Contexts* (Berkeley: University of California Press, 1998), 200.

7. Background on the history of the Fleischer/Paramount Superman cartoons of 1941–43 can be found in J. P. Telotte, *Animating Space* (Lexington: University Press of Kentucky, 2010), 100–12.

8. Naremore, *More than Night,* 139.

9. See Robin Allen, *Walt Disney and Europe* (London: John Libbey, 1999), 44.

10. John Mason Brown, "Mr. Disney's Caballeros," *Saturday Review,* February 24, 1945, 23.

11. Barbara Deming, *Running away from Myself: A Dream Portrait of America Drawn from the Films of the Forties* (New York: Grossman, 1969), 121.

12. Neal Gabler, *Walt Disney: The Triumph of the American Imagination* (New York: Knopf, 2006), 422.

13. J. P. Telotte, *Voices in the Dark: The Narrative Patterns of Film Noir* (Urbana: University of Illinois Press, 1989), 10.

14. The director Howard Hawks's discussion of *The Big Sleep*'s convoluted and confusing narrative and of his effort to have Raymond Chandler explain it has often been recounted. In an interview with Joseph McBride, Hawks says, "I just decided I wasn't

going to explain things. I was just going to try and make good scenes"—a tactic that would seem to describe the approach of many cartoon narratives of the period. Joseph McBride, *Hawks on Hawks* (Berkeley: University of California Press, 1982), 104.

15. Siegfried Kracauer, *"Dumbo," The Nation,* November 8, 1941, 463.

16. Paul Schrader, "Notes on Film Noir," in *Awake in the Dark: An Anthology of American Film Criticism, 1915 to the Present,* ed. David Denby (New York: Random House, 1977), 279.

17. Ibid., 284.

18. Frank Thomas and Ollie Johnston, *Disney Animation: The Illusion of Life,* rev. ed. (New York: Disney Editions, 1995), 80.

19. See Leonard Maltin, *Of Mice and Magic* (New York: New American Library, 1980), for commentary on how "references to Warner Brothers . . . became commonplace" in the studio's cartoons (230).

20. See Donald Crafton, *Before Mickey: The Animated Film, 1898–1928* (Cambridge: Massachusetts Institute of Technology Press, 1982), 11.

21. Neal Gabler makes a similar assertion about the *Destino* project, identifying it as one of several efforts by Walt Disney at "trying to stretch the bounds of animation by bringing a new, more subjective sensibility to the medium" (415). For additional commentary on this project, abandoned in 1946 but eventually completed by Walt's nephew Roy Disney in 2003, see Gabler, *Walt Disney,* 414–16.

22. See Raymond Chandler, *The Simple Art of Murder* (New York: Ballantine, 1972), 15.

6

Detour

Driving in a Back Projection, or Forestalled by Film Noir

VIVIAN SOBCHACK

I borrow my subtitle from the great critic David Thomson, who uses it to introduce a short meditation not directly about film noir but about the experience of driving in Los Angeles.[1] For Thomson, driving in Los Angeles means always imagining oneself in a movie, even in bright sunlight, and his thoughts seem noirish as he evokes Walter Neff's confessional Dictaphone recording in *Double Indemnity* (1944) when he writes: "I would like to say that this piece was composed—written or dropped into the spirals of a recorder on the front seat—when driving in Los Angeles." However, Thomson makes a slight but significant detour as he continues: "Of course, I might have managed it, if the car were still, the dangers abstract, and the roaming, unstable city just imagery behind me in a back projection, . . . the square of receding street seen through the back of a car [that] never moves, no matter how persistently the background assures . . . escape."[2]

Indeed, the very first image of Edgar G. Ulmer's 1945 minimalist film noir, *Detour,* is such a back projection: a deserted desert highway receding into the distance as seen by someone looking out the back of a car rather than forward at the stretch of road ahead. From the beginning and throughout the film's sixty-seven-minute running time,[3] as its questionable protagonist Al Roberts (Tom Neal) attempts to travel west toward an idealized California future, that receding road assuring escape reveals itself to be a fabulation, a lie, a metaphoric stand-in for—and forestallment of—the "real thing": real and present forward movement in space and time. It is no wonder that, insofar as cinematic point of view is concerned, this back-projected opening shot, seen under the credits, is detached from any of the film's characters yet nonetheless, in a retrospective foreshadowing, comments on them all—letting us know from the beginning that escape is impossible and that apparent movement forward will lead only to reversal, repetition, and eternal return. However far Al travels in *Detour*, he goes nowhere. His "automobility" (whether as hitchhiker or driver) is immobility, returning him always as the same person to the same place.

In a series of flashbacks that begin and end in a greasy-spoon diner, the film is narrated by Al, its self-serving and unreliable protagonist, who tells the story of how, in an attempt to hitchhike from New York to a sunny reunion in California with his songstress fiancée Sue (Claudia Drake), his future was—and is—forever forestalled. Picked up by a man named Haskell (Edmund MacDonald), a blowhard with a convertible and money, Al takes his nighttime turn at the wheel while Haskell sleeps, but then, when Al stops to trade turns driving and opens the passenger side door, the man falls out of the car and fatally hits his head on a rock. Initially afraid of being accused of murder, Al "solves" the problem by assuming Haskell's identity and car. The next morning, however, in one of those noir coincidences marked as "fate," he picks up a female hitchhiker, who, hostile, fierce, and tough as nails, reluctantly gives up her name as Vera (Ann Savage). Having had an earlier (and nasty) encounter with Haskell, she quickly realizes that Al is an imposter and just as quickly blackmails him into using his new identity for further profit. Eventually they reach Los Angeles and hole up in a stuffy apartment, where the two bicker and impatiently wait to "score" on an inheritance due to Haskell. Here, Al is virtually Vera's prisoner—until she ends up drunk one night and, in a highly surreal scene, accidentally tangles herself in a telephone cord and is strangled to death in a mishap that involves a clueless and innocent Al. Now afraid of being accused of Vera's death, Al escapes into the night. He has nowhere to go; his identity as either Al Roberts or as Haskell is linked to a possible murder. Sitting in the greasy spoon once more, Al bitterly speculates that, one way or another, the police will find him—and, as he speaks in voiceover, the film ends with images that literally, if ambiguously, realize his "future past tense" scenario. However, whether we are looking at an illustration of his imagined prediction or at his actual arrest is of little consequence, since he has been forestalled—arrested—from the beginning. There is no escape for Al.

Low-budget, and with a good portion of its "action" spent in a car that, as Thomson writes, "never moves," *Detour* not only begins with back projection but also relies on it throughout. A stock Hollywood practice during the studio years, it enabled in-camera and on-set compositing, then called a "process shot." Pro-filmic performers were photographed against a pre-filmed background (a "transparency" if static and a "plate" if moving), using either stock footage or specific material shot by a second-unit crew. Back—or rear-screen—projection was so-called because of the projector's position behind the projection screen, where it cast reverse images that were seen properly by the camera filming the combined action in front of the screen.[4] Although in use much earlier, the practice became prominent in the 1930s after several significant technological developments emerged in the late 1920s in relation to sound film. These included motors able to synchronize the shutters of camera and projector, more powerful projection lamps that made the projection screen more reflective and thus brighter, and panchromatic film stock that produced a brighter image of the projected footage on the negative.[5] Nonetheless, given the distance of the projected material from the foreground live action, as well as the fact that its imagery would register on film as second-generation in relation to that first-generation action, back projection often appeared washed out and blurred in comparison to whatever was going on in front of it.[6] Moreover, when vehicles were involved, the lack of synchrony between movement in the projected images and the mock-up vehicles (as well as the actors in them) was also often quite noticeable.

Despite these flaws, back projection became "the primary special effects composite technology in the Hollywood studio system from about 1935 to about 1970," valued most for its efficiency, its low cost in comparison to that of either location shooting or postproduction optical effects, and the level of control it afforded cinematographers and directors.[7] However, during and shortly after World War II, the period that also marks the emergence of classic Hollywood noir, the use of back projection greatly increased—a consequence of, as Thomas Schatz writes, "wartime shortages and restrictions [affecting] the availability of raw film stock," which was needed for military training films.[8] These shortages resulted not only in "more careful preproduction planning" and "fewer takes of individual scenes being shot" but also in the more frequent use of stock footage.[9] Moreover, in late 1942, new travel restrictions curtailed location shooting and "made it almost impossible to leave the back lot."[10] Thus, as Schatz puts it, "[T]he war-induced confinement to the studio, owing to the myriad restrictions and the demand for production economy and efficiency, led . . . to something of a break with the classical film style."[11] Marc Vernet also points to the influence of the period's economic restrictions on the different "look" of Hollywood cinema, noting, among other stylistic changes, the period's "tight framing," which, during the first half of the 1940s, shrinks the frame "to a sort of claustrophobic space."[12] Indeed, given these external constraints, film-noir "style," including its extensive use of back projection, would seem to emerge less from aesthetic vision or existential angst than from the contingent necessities dictated by the war's impact on film production. Nonetheless, as Vincent Brook argues, the "rationing of lights, electricity, and film stock, and the need to recycle sets and props encouraged *noir*'s emblematic low-key lighting and sparse décor."[13] The rationing of film stock and restrictions on location shooting also encouraged noir's emblematic use of back projection.

For various reasons, including the greater control of sound recording it afforded, back projection was most commonly used for driving scenes—hence, its particular importance to noir, in which cars figure prominently, and as Mark Osteen notes, often, as in *Detour,* "serve as the engine of narrative itself."[14] It is thus apposite that Thomson, driving in Los Angeles, a prime location for noir, imagines himself in a back projection. Musing on the edge of a major insight, he tells us: "Movies full of entertaining lies stiff with intent and controlled telling are also spilling over with helpless, neglected phenomena, and the least doctored . . ., the most available, are visible background."[15] Certainly, among these neglected phenomena is back projection. Critics and scholars, if they mention it at all, have tended to do so in only in passing—and, except in rare instances, pejoratively.[16] Only recently, with the advent of digital filmmaking and seamless green- and blue-screen postproduction compositing, has back projection enjoyed some small attention as having positive aesthetic effects rather than as a distracting, tacky, low-budget device. Laura Mulvey writes in 2007, "As so often happens with passing time, rear projection's disappearance has given this once-despised technology new interest and poignancy." Meditating on its spatial effects, she eloquently concludes: "This paradoxical, impossible space, detached from either an approximation to reality or the verisimilitude of fiction, allows the audience to see the dream space of the cinema. But rear projection renders the dream uncertain: the image of a cinematic sublime depends on a mechanism that is fascinating because of, not in spite of, its clumsy visibility."[17]

Critical attention to the frequent use of back projection in film noir is scarce despite its clumsy, if cinematically "sublime," visibility and the thematic relevance of its rendering "the dream space" of noir cinema "uncertain." Like Thomson's reference to many other things visible in the background of the image, it suffers neglect, but it is hardly as "helpless" as he suggests. Even used as a contingent necessity and thus not "stiff with intent," like noir's more prominent stylistic devices, it exerts a good deal of "control" over noir's "telling." As Hugh Manon notes, the use of back projection need not be "intentional artifice" for its "formal flaws (occurring for whatever reason) [to] directly complement [a] film's scripted plot." Although his point is well taken, his inherent assumption that the use of back projection is a "formal flaw" leads to his description of those moments in which it serves a narrative or thematic function as "successful failures."

But why assume back projection's use a formal flaw or failure at all? Particularly in film noir, its attempts at deception function to significantly complement narrative, characters, and theme. As a spatial "lie," back projection hides the "dream space of the cinema" in plain sight. And, in doing so, it makes the metaphoric terms so often used in critical readings of noir (particularly of a psychoanalytic kind) *literal* and, as Thomson suggests, materially available *in* the film rather than somehow *behind* it. Back projection externalizes and makes visible not only an interior but also an anterior "projection." Washed out and dreamlike, it functions as a phantasmatic "screen" image. Moreover, installed as a deceptive "cover-up" for the lack of a real or "primal scene," it constitutes a visible "blind spot"—not only for characters but also for viewers. In sum, back projection, like noir's other noted stylistic and narrative elements, works to temporally forestall and spatially foreclose any sense of the characters' existential "freedom" and to make this constriction sensually, as well as cognitively, intelligible to viewers. Back projection makes noir's abstract themes of claustrophobia and entrapment, of "claustration" (a word to which I will return), spatially concrete.

With particular emphasis on *Detour,* I want to argue that back projection is to film-noir space what flashbacks are to film-noir time. Not merely a tacky effect of low-budget production, back projection is an aesthetic element that well serves noir's philosophical worldview, transforming it not only into something literal and materially realized but also producing a subtle, yet significant, effect on the viewer's sensual comprehension of cinematic meaning. Conjoining sensation and sense, *Detour* is an exemplary work through which to explore what is regularly evoked in film criticism by commonly used and spatially hermetic words and phrases to describe noir's narratives and style. These include "pinched," "confined," "murky and close," "oppressive," "cramped," and "claustrophobic." Marc Vernet emphasizes 1940s "tight" framing, and George Lipsitz refers to noir's "cramped quarters," "rooms without windows," and "closed automobiles" in which "the inner world of psychological torment finds external expression."[18] Writing specifically of *Detour,* James Naremore notes that the film's low budget "produces an atmosphere of pinched difficulty and claustrophobia."[19] And Dana Polan tells us that the film's "pared down narrative and visual 'style' . . . echoes the constricted field of options in which its characters move about. Immersing itself in a minimalism that is intense and claustrophobic, [the film is] not that removed from the despairing existential effort of a Jean-Paul Sartre in . . . 'No Exit.'"[20]

In noir more generally and *Detour* in particular, characters express their sense of constriction. They are in "tight spots," see "no way out," or feel they are "going nowhere." In *Detour,* Al is trapped in the Los Angeles apartment Vera has rented. At the beginning of their perverse domesticity (initially so as to sell Haskell's car, but then to wait further for his ill father to die so they can claim the inheritance), Vera won't even let Al open the window when he says it's "stuffy." She keeps the key not only to the apartment but also to the bedroom door. Al talks about being "cooped up," bitterly says that his "favorite sport is being kept prisoner," and, in one of his frequent voiceovers, says that he knows he's "in a spot." But we really don't need such dialogue to see and sense Al's confinement, his "claustration"—a word I prefer to "claustrophobia" or "claustrophilia," as I think we experience repulsion and attraction as major perverse pleasures of noir. Defined by the *Oxford English Dictionary* as "the action of confining in a cloistered or enclosed space,"[21] "claustration" also seems a more accurate description of the various technical and aesthetic choices made in the films, many of these *not* experienced by characters but solely by viewers. Characters may experience the low lighting of "stuffy" hotel rooms or purposefully hide in the shadows, for instance, but they do not experience their tight framing in close-ups or "driving in a back projection," even as these devices visibly enclose them in film-noir space for us. However, I also prefer the word "claustration" because it evokes and challenges "castration," that metaphorical charge directed by noir's psycho-analytic critics toward gender relationships such as Al and Vera's—he, her weak male victim, and she, arguably the most aggressive and dominating femme fatale in all of noir. Given all the psychoanalytic readings of noir, "claustration" makes me laugh not only because of its oblique rhyme with "castration" but also because it refuses the metaphoric sense of being "cut off" for a much more literal description of what we actually see on screen as noir's forestallment and foreclosure of its characters' desires, ambitions, and plans.

This claustration and cutting off of spatial escape and existential options is a pervasive element of noir, seen in such narrative scenarios as characters having to "hole up" somewhere, waiting in motel or hotel rooms to be killed like the Swede in *The Killers* (1946), or to "score" like Al and Vera in their grim parody of a domestic apartment. Noir characters are often forestalled from automotively escaping their narrative fate by roadblocks and detours, or by picking up a hitchhiker like Al Roberts, or by ending up where they began like Bart and Laurie in *Gun Crazy* (1950), their apparent mobility, as Mark Osteen suggests, "merely geographic, never social, and even that movement . . . circular."[22] Furthermore, noir's claustration and forestallment are not only narrative difficulties; just as significantly, they are what Dana Polan calls "a difficulty at the level of the image itself"—that is, "not only what [happens] in a space but what that space itself is."[23]

In *Power and Paranoia*, Polan suggests that, "to a large degree, forties narrative is nothing so much as a vast meditation on place and space, on the field in which action and meaning are constituted."²⁴ The "new space of modernity," with its interstate highways, motels and diners, and "the new alienations of endless roads all looking the same," becomes a central site for "the staging of space as [an] ambivalent force."²⁵ The putative protagonists in many 1940s film narratives (including, and perhaps especially, Al Roberts) find themselves separated "from a grounding in a space that could give individual actions a sense."²⁶ Although he focuses on another 1940s protagonist, Polan might well be describing Al when he writes: "Space is a space of others, a force that turns on him, that betrays his projects and transforms them into nothingness."²⁷ And Polan might also be describing *Detour* and the spatial confusions it generates at the level of the image through its pervasive use of back projection, rearview mirroring, and other dreamlike reversals and repetitions when he tells us: "At the very center . . ., there's a certain decenteredness, an inability to make geography anything more than a fleeting, unsure, insubstantial site."²⁸ Nonetheless, in his discussion of this decenteredness, Polan never mentions back projection, despite its hiding in plain sight. Yet back projection is "a difficulty at the level of the image"—a decentering device that, in film noir, not only makes geography "a fleeting, unsure, insubstantial site" but also betrays and belies the characters' forward momentum and future projects, foreclosing and forestalling both as phantasmatic. As Julie Turnock notes, although back projection was "perfectly consistent with the Hollywood studio production system" because of its efficiency and low cost, its degraded second-generation imagery was not at all consistent with that system's "ideal seamless aesthetic" of transparent realism.²⁹

In *Detour*, phantasmatic automobility is the film's narrative engine, and back projection necessarily goes along for the phantasmatic ride. As mentioned earlier, a goodly portion of the film's running time was shot in a mockup convertible (rumored to be Ulmer's own car³⁰) shot against back-projected footage of Arizona and California desert highways at day and night, a vague nightscape identified in a small sign as Reno, Nevada, and an abrasively sunny Los Angeles. We see this prefilmed and ambiguously unmarked geography not only, as in the very first image, in the doubled-back projection of an empty receding road shot from the back of a moving vehicle, but also as a reversed back projection of the road stretching forward as seen through a car's front windshield. Adding to our sense of claustration and the spatial foreclosure of Al's movement, such projections are also seen obliquely from out of the car's side windows, blurring, and also significantly flattening, the landscape. Indeed, if one includes the "fourth wall" of the screen that opens only to absorb the viewer, any "real" mobility is forestalled on all sides. Just as Al's flashbacks and voiceover narration produce visible and audible temporal events that take place in the *interior* space of his self-serving and possibly unreliable consciousness, *Detour*'s back projections constrain Al and us in an *exterior* space that is similarly confining, oneiric, and unreliable—or, as Mulvey puts it, "uncertain."

Several of the film's devices are particularly dreamlike, unstable, and literally disproportionate to Al's present and supposedly "real" circumstances, perhaps the most dramatic (other than Vera's surreal strangulation) occurring in the greasy-spoon diner that plays a significant and recurrent spatial role in the narrative. Early on in the diner, Al's white coffee cup suddenly looms large in the image (this not a mere close-up but a purposeful effect, as Ulmer switched an oversize model for the ordinary cup) and, as we look down from above at its circular form and the black coffee, it takes us through rhyming close-ups of two other dark circular objects into Al's first flashback. Many scholars who write about *Detour* describe this sequence as "eerie," "vaguely surreal," and "dreamlike," thus preparing us for the nightmarish narrative to follow, but only Naremore has suggested, however briefly, something similar, as well as hyperbolic, about the film's use of back projection. Writing that Ulmer "may be the only Hollywood director of the period—aside from Orson Welles—to deliberately exploit the artificiality of back projection," he goes on to tell us to "notice the scene when Haskell falls asleep while Al is driving his car [and] the white rails or fence posts on the side of the road become hugely magnified, flashing past in a hypnotic blur."[31] There are other similar moments of such disproportion that transform quotidian geography into something suddenly oneiric: "fleeting, unsure, insubstantial." When Haskell and Al drive in front of the back projection of the Reno gas station and diner (where Al's first flashback occurs, in which Haskell buys Al dinner, and where, in another at the end, Al contemplates his fate), the buildings' dimensions are asynchronous with the size of the men and their car. However subtly, the angle at which we see the buildings' exterior is at odds with the orientation of the car. The same is true of the suburban houses Al and Vera pass as they first drive into the Los Angeles area, before reaching the city.[32]

The only scholar to even suggest that back projection functions aesthetically and sensually in the film, Naremore describes *Detour* as "radically stylized" and "so far down on the economic and cultural scale of things that it . . . can be viewed as a kind of subversive or vanguard art."[33] Pointing to Ulmer's "severe budget limitations," he praises the director for overcoming them "by means of process screens, sparsely decorated sets," and "old-fashioned but highly effective use of optical devices such as wipes and irises."[34] For Naremore, Ulmer's "cost-cutting," "studio-based expressionism, . . . careful attention to camera movement and off-screen space, and [the film's] intensely subjective narration" result not only in a "breathtaking minimalism" but also in a sense of constraint and "claustrophobia" that "reinforces the theme of social and cultural impoverishment" and the knowledge that none of the characters, all "pretenders" or "imposters," "has a chance of success."[35]

However, the characters are not the only pretenders and imposters in the film. There are other, more formal ones that create "difficulties at the level of the image" and that, like back projection, are generally regarded as technical flaws and indices of Ulmer's low budget. These too construct *Detour*'s themes of cultural and psychological entrapment as well as its viewers' (albeit not its characters') embodied sense of claustration—our feeling that, while we are watching, there is no way out of this noirscape, which, at every deceptive turn, transforms the merely contingent into what seems a predetermined and *prefilmed* fate and spatiotemporal experience. It is through these other "difficulties at the level of the image" that we, if not the characters, see and sense, however latently, the reversals of time and space and negative circularity that forestall the characters as they foreclose the film's form.

Along with the back projections that are deceptively anterior to Al's present existential project, Ulmer uses several rearview-mirror shots that reverse Al's look forward into a projection that turns his gaze backward not only toward us but also toward himself. Rather ironically in a film in which any real movement is phantasmatic, these mirror shots are composited into the surrounding image through the use of what are called "traveling mattes." Different from but often coupled with back projection, because both were frequently used in driving scenes, this process shot allowed a doubled in-camera exposure of the negative. A selected area of the negative is masked or matted (here, the rearview mirror) for the first exposure in Haskell's car, and then the masked areas are reversed for the second exposure, allowing only Al's eyes to register in the now unmasked mirror. As with the back projections, temporality and spatiality are often in uncertain synchrony in the composited image, and the superficial homogeneity of the narrative's "real" world is destabilized—the deceptive "opening" reflecting only itself in a solipsistic moment and movement that goes nowhere.

Thus, there is formal irony in the scene in which Al drives while Haskell sleeps, and we see Al's eyes reflected backward at us and himself in the rearview mirror as he says in voiceover, "I began to think of the future." Not only is the mirror image's visible orientation at odds with Al's words, but it also functions solipsistically so that, via his gaze, we enter his consciousness and yet another phantasmatic projection—an imagined flash-forward. Bookended by a return to the rearview-mirror shot of Al's eyes looking back at him, the flash-forward is an idealized vision of his fiancée Sue, who appears sequined and singing the couples' aptly titled love song, "I Can't Believe You're in Love with Me." Although Sue's dreams of Hollywood stardom have come to naught, and Al knows that she is actually "slinging hash" in the Los Angeles toward which he travels, his phantasmatic vision of the future denies reality through what amounts to a rejection of any trace of the exterior world. Caught between the reversals of the bookended rearview mirror shots, there is no place in this narrative for Al's vision of the future to go. In sum, Al claustrates Sue in an image isolated from *any* world, and, canted at an unstable angle that signals the phantasy's fragile grounding, sequined Sue obliquely stands alone in front of an empty backdrop with only the looming but insubstantial shadows of musicians as her company.

The phantasmatic spatial disorientations of back projection and mirror-shot reversals destabilize the image and decenter our vision (albeit not that of its characters), hiding in plain sight and supporting *Detour*'s theme of forestalled social and geographic mobility in an uncertain and hostile world. This theme is introduced most obviously as Al begins his journey, hitchhiking from New York toward California and Sue in a travel montage that denies not only geographical specificity but also existential direction. As Polan writes, "The camera pans westward over a succession of maps superimposed with shots of Roberts' feet walking: there are no arrows or lines to indicate where [he is]. Somewhere past Chicago, the maps cease to appear, eliminating even this abstract index of . . . spatial progression. The journey has taken Roberts to an uncharted no-man's land."[36] But this is not all. There is yet another, and even more disorienting, vagary of Al's westward journey—one certainly not noticed by Al. Most likely accidental but serving *Detour*'s mise-en-scène of entrapment and mise-en-abyme of forestallment, this is *a total reversal of the film's negative.* As Polan describes, "[Robert's] journey continues with a shot of [him] hitch-hiking from the wrong side of the road." As a consequence, although "the direction of Roberts' movement remains consistent, the logic of his actions, and that of the traffic around him, do not."[37]

Roger Ebert also notices this eerie negative reversal. Pointing out that "the first vehicles to give lifts to the hitchhiking Al seem to have right-hand drives . . . and the cars drive off on the 'wrong' side of the road," Ebert guesses that "with re-shoots being out of the question for such a low budget movie," the negative was, as he puts it, "flipped."[38] In all likelihood, the cars were shot "going from left to right, [but] then [Ulmer] reflected that a journey from the east to the west coasts, right to left, would be more conventional film grammar." And, Ebert adds, "Placing style above common sense is completely consistent with Ulmer's approach throughout the film." This is not a criticism, for Ebert calls *Detour* "haunting and creepy, an embodiment of the guilty soul of *noir*"; "no one who has seen it has easily forgotten it." Although he begins his review by saying that *Detour*'s "ham-handed narrative" is so full of "technical errors," including "shabby rear-projection," that "it would not earn the director a passing grade in film school," he ends by asking and answering the rhetorical question: "Do these limitations and stylistic transgressions hurt the film? No. They are the film. *Detour* is an example of material finding the appropriate form."

Indeed, Ulmer transformed financial necessity and extracinematic contingency into perverse aesthetic and sensual effect. However latent in our vision, the film's reversals spatially and sensuously play out the complex temporal turnings of the narrative that inevitably return Al to himself. Back projection, mirror shots, and reversals of the negative all spatially echo and reinforce the film's flashbacks and its imagined flash-forwards; Al's guilty dream sequence that repeats the events of Haskell's ambiguous death; and hitchhiker Vera's uncanny replacement of Haskell asleep in the convertible's front seat, and her abrupt awakening to gleefully recognize Al as an imposter—as if, Al says in voiceover, Haskell were "sitting right there in the car laughing like mad while he haunted me." These moments further confuse *Detour*'s tense and temporality, past and future becoming one in the same recurrent present—exemplified in a convoluted line of Al's dialogue articulated in future past tense. In a flashback, after hiding Haskell's body and convincing himself to take the man's money, clothes, and car, Al bitterly says in voiceover, "By that time, I'd done just what the police said I did, even if I didn't."

Polan writes, "*Detour* builds its whole structure around the deferment of actions," creating "an endless cyclicity of defeat" played out "against the trajectory of the already read future."[39] Thus Al's purported existential project of reaching an idealized Sue is forever deferred, the future forever forestalled. As he tells us back in the diner, toward the film's end, "I had to stay away from New York for all time because Al Roberts was listed as dead and he had to stay there. And I could never go back to Hollywood. Someone might recognize me as Haskell. Then, too, there was Sue. I could never go to her with a thing like this hanging over my head." As we see him leave the diner for the last time in an ambiguously imaginary projection that ends the film even as it hasn't clearly happened yet, the prophecy of his voiceover is fulfilled by a police car that pulls into the frame as he tells us—using both present and future tense—"But one thing I know. One day a car will stop to pick me up that I never thumbed. Yes, fate or some mysterious force can put the finger on you, or me, for no good reason at all."

In regard to this ending that has not yet happened but is, like a back projection, prefilmed and projected for us to see, it is worth quoting Joan Copjec, a very fine psychoanalytic critic, who writes: "What *film noir* presents to us are spaces that have been emptied of desire."[40] Just like the back projection of an empty and receding road that begins *Detour,* this final image of Al projecting his own detainment in an imaginary flash-forward is emptied of all desire. As Copjec suggests, noir's spatial images, emptied of desire, indicate "less that there is nothing in them than that nothing more can be got out of them. . . . They will never yield anything new and cannot, therefore, hide anything. Primarily it is the hero himself who suffers the loss of a hiding place."[41] And, I would add, the loss of a future—stripped of desire, *pace* Al Roberts.

Unlike many other psychoanalytic critics, Copjec does not interpret noir's characters in terms of Oedipal or object relations, the search for origins, or the fear of castration. Her interest is in noir as a paradoxical psychic space that is both visually foreclosed and yet open for all to see. As she puts it, for both characters and viewers, noir "continually exposes the landscapes of privacy."[42] Once these interior landscapes are visibly emptied of desire, reality is "depleted," losing not only "the sense of solidity that ordinarily attaches to the social field" but also "the illusion of depth that underwrites this solidity" and assures us that reality "has no bottom."[43] Linking desire and depth, Copjec then tells us: "One must distinguish between the genuine illusion of depth—which is a matter of desire, of not knowing something and wanting, therefore, to know more—and the *ersatz* representation of depth—which is simply a matter of technical skill in rendering, of verisimilitude—if one wants to avoid being misled by the shadows and depth of field that so famously characterize . . . *noir* images."[44] It is possible that a major element of *Detour*'s power emerges from the fact that it never secures or sustains a credible illusion of depth. From the film's beginning, with that flat and barren back projection of a receding road, emptied of desire, we really know the end and are hardly misled. That image signals not illusion but disillusion. Indeed, all of the back projections that follow, as well as the traveling matte shots and reversed negative images, continually destabilize the film's spatial solidity, verisimilitude, and depth of field. What haunts us in *Detour* is its pinched emptiness and assertive flatness, which finally (although also from the beginning) seem beyond desire and depth, exposing not only Al's false consciousness but also the very philosophical essence of noir itself.

Although Copjec does discuss noir's visual techniques, she never mentions its frequent use of back projection and other devices that literally—rather than metaphorically—flatten noir space and rob the image of depth. Nor does she make any reference to noir's frequent driving sequences—even as she focuses on noir's attempts to detour and forestall its characters' psychic drives. Rather, she discovers noir's lack of depth "behind" images that would presumably deceive us through their apparent verisimilitude. She uncovers noir's "drive" not in literal automobility and its forestallment but rather in a psychic enervation in the narrative that cinematic verisimilitude and the illusion of depth cover up. The irony here is that we, in something like *Detour*'s own reversals, can read Copjec's psychoanalysis of film-noir space literally and against the grain of metaphorical terminology and psychoanalytic interpretation.

When Copjec writes that "the drive is not indifferent to symbolic intervention," we can point to the back projection, rearview-mirror shots, traveling mattes, and reversals of the negative that intervene and forestall Al's journey west as he hitchhikes and, yes, "drives." Unaware of these symbolic interventions that take place at the level of the image, Al nonetheless senses their effects on his own narrative journey. Thus, shortly after Haskell's death, he tells us in voiceover: "Something else stepped in and shunted me off to a different destination than I'd picked for myself." Moreover, Copjec writes that "the visual techniques of *film noir* are placed in the service of creating an artificial replication of depth in the *image* in order to . . . compensate [for] the absence of depth in the *narrative* spaces" and function as "a defense against the drive" and a substitute for and protection against the "dangerous, and potentially lethal, lack in the *noir* universe itself."[45] Again, I fully agree with her—pointing not metaphorically but literally to noir's narrative circularity rather than spatial depth, and to the spiraling convolutions that substitute for the characters' forestallment and lack of movement.

In this regard, it is worth noting the *Oxford English Dictionary*'s various definitions of "forestall."[46] As a past participle, it means "bespoken" or "taken beforehand," which is a literal description of the anterior nature of back projection and stock footage. Paradoxically, however, it can also mean "anticipated"—like AI and noir, mixing up its past and future tenses. Used as a verb, "forestall" can mean "the action of appropriating beforehand, obstructing," and "waylaying"—the literal effect of the back projections that, at every turn, thwart Al's journey west toward Sue. And used as a noun, "forestall" means "an ambush, plot," or (most aptly, and a form of cutting off) "intercepting in the highway"—giving weight to Al's lament, "That's life. Whichever way you turn, fate sticks out a foot to trip you."

Back projection not only waylays Al Roberts, flattening both his desire and the film's depth; it also constitutes an obstruction for the viewer. As Copjec suggests (albeit not of back projection or rearview-mirror shots or the negative reversals), it constitutes a phantasy substitute—not for "the drive" but for the real historical and social conditions it occludes in the process of turning its own metaphoricity into something literally visible. As such, back projection produces a "blind spot," not only for noir protagonists who think their desire is driving them somewhere but who ultimately travel nowhere but also for most viewers and scholars who think back projection as a means of noir travel is merely a low-budget cinematic device. This is how it is able to hide in plain sight—not *underneath* the film's other cinematic effects (for, to counter Copjec, when do we ever see noir as an example of verisimilitude?) and not *behind* the film as its psychic engine but right there before us *in* the film. What Naremore calls *Detour*'s "breathtaking minimalism" brings back projection into the foreground of our vision. We don't have to read the film to understand it; we just have to *see* it to make sense of it.

Detour was entered in the National Film Registry by the U.S. National Film Preservation Board in 1992, one of a select number of American films considered culturally, historically, and/or aesthetically significant. It was made at the Producers Releasing Corporation (PRC), a mini-studio on Hollywood's Poverty Row, where Ulmer worked from 1942 to 1946. PRC's average budget was twenty to thirty thousand dollars, and its average shooting ratio two—or, in *Detour*'s case, only one and a half—to one. Nonetheless, Ulmer preferred to work at such small studios "despite the lower budgets, tighter shooting schedules, and lesser talent" because they allowed him "greater autonomy."[47] Budgeted at eighty-nine thousand dollars, a sum "lavish by PRC standards," *Detour* was shot in a mere six days for the final "grand sum of $117,000."[48]

Just what is it about the film that justifies its canonical status? After all, as one Internet Movie Database (IMDB) viewer notes, "*Detour* is . . . bottom of the barrel, a cheap, sleazy movie about cheap, sleazy people. I respect the talent that went into it, but this is not a likeable film."[49] And yet it fascinates and haunts those who have seen it. Polan writes that the film, "a tawdry, even aesthetically and morally ugly work," rises to the occasion of "a philosophical lament admired for its obstinate avoidance of complacency, affirmation, and seductive visual and narrative pleasure."[50] For other critics and viewers *Detour* is seductive and does provide visual and narrative pleasure. One critic writes of the trancelike and sensuous effects of Ulmer's "whirlpool in a shoebox" and "aesthetics of hunger."[51] And an IMDB viewer posts that *Detour*'s "flaws only add to the dreamlike atmosphere" of a "film that will haunt you for the rest of your life."[52] Above all, however, it is the film's "minimalism" that seems the major source of its power. That is, for a large number of viewers, *Detour* is intensely pleasurable in its extreme *parsimony*. As a range of IMDB posters put it, the film "does what most films can't . . . it cuts to the chase";[53] it's "tightly and claustrophobically shot, in a world drained of all color or digression or respite, [and] fascinating . . . at every step";[54] it's " a great, terse, dark, little film! . . . it's simple and cuts to the bone";[55] it "manages to encapsulate, in 67 minutes, all the inchoate angst that informs the [noir] cycle, and [while] it may have been an accident, . . . it's the kind of accident you can't peel your eyes [from]";[56] and, it's "fascinating . . . like a work of art that has been abstracted down to the essence to produce a single effect, this film is the absolute essence of film noir."[57]

Amid the sleaze and tawdriness of its narrative and characters and because of the deceptions and impostures at the level of its images produced by economic necessity and Ulmer's inventiveness, *Detour* adheres to what has been called the "principle of parsimony" (sometimes referred to as "Ockham's Razor"). This principle is based on the presumption that "entities must not be multiplied beyond necessity," or, to put it more simply, "It is futile to do with more things that which can be done with fewer."[58] In *Detour*, more was done with less. Cutting the film to the bone, Ulmer restricted not only the action to four characters and few settings but also his means to a few "cheap" devices: an oversize coffee cup and his own car, back projections, rearview-mirror shots, and even a mistaken negative. The consequential result of such "parsimony" is a narrative and spatial condensation that constructs a noir of driving minimalism and aesthetic complexity. Thus, however cheap *Detour*'s budget and however "tawdry" and "sleazy" its narrative and characters, driving in a back projection, they and this sixty-seven-minute film attain a counterintuitive force and exhilarating elegance.

Notes

1. David Thomson, *Beneath Mulholland: Thoughts on Hollywood and Its Ghosts* (New York: Vintage Books, 1997), 76–82.

2. Ibid., 76.

3. There is some question about the running time at release. The American Film Institute online catalog lists it as sixty-seven to sixty-nine minutes (accessed November 10, 2013, http://afi.com/members/catalog/AbbrView.aspx?s=&Movie=24756), whereas the Internet Movie Database and a number of other sources list it at sixty-seven minutes only, including the Alpha Video DVD used as reference for this essay. I have used that latter duration here.

4. See Raymond Fielding, *The Technique of Special Effects Cinematography* (New York: Hastings House, 1968), 259–304; and Raymond Fielding, *A Technological History of Motion Pictures and Television* (Berkeley: University of California Press, 1983), 141–49. Although mentioned throughout trade journals, all technical information in the notes below comes from these volumes.

5. Back projection was used sporadically in the 1910s and 1920s, but it became standard practice in the 1930s after the advent of sound.

6. The distance at which the projector was set behind the screen so it could throw a sufficiently large image upon it also increased the visibility of the film image's "grain," another factor in the sense of its "irresoluteness."

7. Julie Turnock, "The Screen on the Set: The Problem of Classical-Studio Rear Projection," *Cinema Journal* 51.2 (Winter 2012): 157.

8. Thomas Schatz, *Boom or Bust: American Cinema in the 1940s*, vol. 6 of *History of the American Cinema* (Berkeley: University of California Press, 1997), 143.

9. Ibid.

10. Ibid., 144.

11. Ibid., 233.

12. Marc Vernet, "Film Noir on the Edge of Doom," trans. J. Swenson, in *Shades of Noir*, ed. Joan Copjec (London: Verso, 1993), 22.

13. Vincent Brook, *Driven to Darkness: Jewish Émigré Directors and the Rise of Film Noir* (New Brunswick, N.J.: Rutgers University Press, 2009), 14.

14. Mark Osteen, "Noir's Cars: Automobility and Amoral Space in American Film Noir," *Journal of Popular Film and Television* 35.4 (Winter 2008): 186.

15. Thomson, *Beneath Mulholland*, 77–78.

16. See, for these rare instances, Robin Wood, *Hitchcock's Films*, 2nd enlarged and rev. ed. (New York: Castle Books, 1969); Robin Wood, *Hitchcock's Films Revisited* (New York: Columbia University Press, 2002); Laura Mulvey, "Close Up: A Clumsy Sublime," *Film Quarterly* 60.3 (Spring 2007): 3; Hugh S. Manon, "Fantasy and Failure in

Strange Illusion," in *The Films of Edgar G. Ulmer*, ed. Bernd Herzogenrath (Lanham, Md.: Scarecrow Press, 2009), 165–66; Hugh S. Manon, "See Spot: The Parametric Film Noirs of Edgar G. Ulmer," in *Edgar G. Ulmer: Detour on Poverty Row*, ed. Gary Rhodes (Plymouth, U.K.: Lexingon Books, 2010), 111–12; and Turnock, "Screen on the Set." Wood summarizes—but also rejects—what he considers the ill-conceived critique of the director's frequent use of back projection as "absurdly clumsy, lazy, crude" and "used with a blatant disregard for realism" (*Hitchcock's Films Revisited* 173). It is worth noting that in her one-page homage to back projection, Mulvey too refers specifically to Hitchcock. Manon focuses on an Ulmer film that is not considered a noir and spends a page discussing the aesthetic effects of back projection (while the essay by David Kalat, "*Detour*'s Detour" in *The Films of Edgar G. Ulmer*, mentions it only once or twice with no elaboration whatsoever); and Turnock approaches back projection historically and suggests that audiences in the 1940s and 1950s had no objections to its use. The neglect of serious attention to back projection is best exemplified by an otherwise fine monograph in the British Film Institute's Film Classics series: Noah Isenberg's *Detour* (London: British Film Institute, 2008), where back projection is only referred to five times and always in passing.

17. Mulvey, "Close Up," 3.

18. George Lipsitz, *Time Passages: Collective Memory and American Popular Culture* (Minneapolis: University of Minnesota Press, 1990), 206.

19. James Naremore, *More than Night: Film Noir and its Contexts* (Berkeley: University of California Press, 1998), 149.

20. Dana Polan, "*Detour*," *Senses of Cinema*, Cinémathèque Annotations on Film 21 (July 2002), accessed November 10, 2013, http://sensesofcinema.com/2002/cteq/detour/.

21. "Claustration," *Oxford English Dictionary*, accessed November 10, 2013, http://www.oed.com.

22. Osteen, "Noir's Cars," 186.

23. Dana Polan, *Power and Paranoia: History, Narrative, and the American Cinema, 1940–1950* (New York: Columbia University Press, 1986), 228.

24. Ibid., 252.

25. Ibid., 232.

26. Ibid., 208.

27. Ibid., 252.

28. Ibid., 251.

29. Turnock, "Screen on the Set," 162.

30. Anthony Lane, "Critic's Notebook: The Road to Ruin," *New Yorker*, November 16, 2009, 10.

31. Naremore, *More than Night*, 148. *Citizen Kane* (1941) used a good bit of back projection; hence Naremore's reference to Welles.

32. This disorienting, if subtle, disproportion of size and angle is the result (accidental or intentional) of the fact that back-projection production in the studio used the projector and the filming camera positioned 90 degrees in relation to the screen; any inaccuracy would distort the image in relation to the live foreground action. Moreover, all the second-unit filming attempted to take this into account when shooting the plate material, but that too was not always accurate.

33. Naremore, *More than Night*, 148.

34. Ibid., 148.

35. Ibid., 148–49.

36. Polan, *Power and Paranoia*, 271 (emphasis added).

37. Ibid.

38. Roger Ebert, rev. of *Detour, Chicago Sun Times*, June 7, 1998, accessed November 12, 2013, http://www.rogerebert.com/reviews/great-movie-detour-1945. All subsequent quotations are from this source.

39. Polan, *Power and Paranoia*, 215, 219.

40. Joan Copjec, "The Phenomenal Nonphenomenal: Private Space in Film Noir," in *Shades of Noir*, ed. Joan Copjec (London: Verso, 1993), 189.

41. Ibid.

42. Ibid., 191.

43. Ibid.

44. Ibid., 192.

45. Ibid.

46. "Forestall," accessed November 10, 2013, Oxford English Dictionary, http://www.oed.com.

47. Brook, *Driven to Darkness*, 16.

48. Ibid., 156.

49. Telegonus (Brighton, Mass.), Internet Movie Database, user review of *Detour*, December 9, 2002, accessed December 17, 2013, http://www.imdb.com/title/tt0037638/reviews?start=21.

50. Polan, *"Detour."*

51. Fernando F. Croce, rev. of *Detour*, Cinepassion, accessed August 25, 2010, http://www.cinepassion.org/Reviews/d/Detour.html.

52. Timothy Farrell (Worcester, Mass.), Internet Movie Database, user review of *Detour*, December 31, 2006, accessed December 17, 2013, http://www.imdb.com/title/tt0037638/reviews?start=45.

53. Lydgate (Cambridge, U.K.), Internet Movie Database, user review of *Detour*, June 13, 2003, accessed December 17, 2013, http://www.imdb.com/title/tt0037638/reviews?start=12.

54. Allyjack (Toronto), Internet Movie Database, user review of *Detour*, August 23, 1999, accessed December 17, 2013, http://www.imdb.com/title/tt0037638/reviews?start=39.

55. Bucs1960 (West Virginia), Internet Movie Database, user review of *Detour*, July 26, 2002, accessed December 17, 2013, http://www.imdb.com/title/tt0037638/reviews?start=46.

56. Bmacv (western New York), Internet Movie Database, user review of *Detour*, July 14, 2004, accessed December 17, 2013, http://www.imdb.com/title/tt0037638/reviews?start=0.

57. Davidp41 (Temple, Tex.) Internet Movie Database, user review of *Detour*, October 22, 2000, accessed December 17, 2013, http://www.imdb.com/title/tt0037638/reviews?start=49.

58. William Kneale and Martha Kneale, *The Development of Logic* (London: Oxford University Press, 1962), 243.

7

Producing Noir

Wald, Scott, Hellinger

ANDREW SPICER

Introduction: Film Noir as Production Category

Scholars have tended to fasten on aesthetic features—chiaroscuro lighting, unbalanced compositions, oddly angled cinematography, complex patterns of narration and shifting, unstable time frames—as a way of characterizing film noir, whether it be to define it as a genre, a movement, a visual style, a prevailing mood or tone, or a transgeneric phenomenon. In part this reflects the characteristic tendency of film studies to privilege texts (and textual interpretation) over contexts where films are located as part of wider processes of production and reception. This general tendency is accentuated in the case of film noir because it is, notoriously, a retrospective category, one "invented" by French critics and not used by American studios or filmmakers themselves when the movies were actually made. In Steve Neale's view, this invalidates understanding film noir as a production category because its presence "cannot be verified by reference to contemporary studio documents, discussions or reviews, or to any other contemporary intertextual source."[1]

Neale's skepticism, while valuable in its requirement to adduce empirical data for the existence of film noir rather than work with loose invocations of a hypothetical category, misperceives the ways in which film noir operated as a production category, albeit one that went under other labels. As Sheri Chinen Biesen has demonstrated in her important study *Blackout: World War II and the Origins of Film Noir* (2005) through extensive contemporaneous documentation, "[T]he American film industry and domestic press recognized these *noir* pictures as a growing movement before they were formally acclaimed in France in 1946. By 1944 Hollywood studio publicity and critics in the United States had already identified these innovative films as a bold new trend called the 'red meat crime cycle.'"[2] As Biesen argues, the huge box-office revenue for Paramount's *Double Indemnity* (September 1944)—$2,500,000 in North American rentals alone—"offered studios tangible incentives for jumping on the *noir* band-wagon."[3] "Red meat" crime films could exploit a less-restrictive censorship regime that allowed greater latitude in the depiction of sex and violence, were able to disguise wartime constraints that reduced the sum that could be spent on sets and décor, and could also engage with contemporary anxieties generated by the war through their focus on social dislocation and psychological disturbance.[4]

This "red meat" trend—now known by its French label, film noir—exemplified what Richard Maltby argues is the characteristic tendency of Hollywood feature-film production: volatile cycles of films initiated by the success of an originating film or films (in this instance *Double Indemnity*) rather than the evolution of stable genres.[5] Such cycles radiate outward from a narrow base to incorporate the whole industry.[6] At its zenith, circa 1950, film noir represented—depending on the strictness of definition—between 8 and 15 percent of feature-film production, encompassing all the majors and also the smaller B-feature producers.[7] James Naremore has commented that most film noirs were "programmers," intermediate productions that fell somewhere between first and second features, commanding reasonable budgets but with far less market "hype" on their launch than a full A production.[8] As he argues, to understand film noir as a production cycle is not to deny its later construction as a discursive category but to recognize noir as both a body of films from a specific period and "an idea we have projected onto the past."[9]

This essay aims to augment the disturbingly slender body of literature on film noir as a production category.[10] Its distinctive focus is on the role played by three key producers—Jerry Wald, Adrian Scott, and Mark Hellinger—who helped initiate or transform the noir cycle. Since the rise of the auteur theory and its veneration of the director's creative role, producers have been given short shrift in film studies—frequently caricatured as philistine and venal, concerned only with the bottom line, a situation replicated by their absence from studies of film noir. However, their importance to the Hollywood film industry during this period is incontestable, as shown in Thomas Schatz's classic study, *The Genius of the System* (1989). Producers were the initiators and drivers of the production process, usually taking the key creative decisions. They were not, of course, autonomous agents but formed part of the "corporate art" of the studio that employed them.[11] However, there were pronounced variations within the structures of the majors—and the strength of their corporate "brand"—that affected the independence of individual producers and the extent of their creative control.[12] The studio system itself, as several commentators have argued, underwent a gradual but profound transformation during the "classic" noir period (ca. 1940–59) as the power of the majors waned and independent production increased significantly.[13] My three examples reflect these variations. Jerry Wald worked for a highly centralized studio, Warner Bros., in contrast to Adrian Scott at RKO, a company that was notoriously unstable and diffuse. Mark Hellinger was one of the pioneers of independent production. For reasons of space, rather than attempting a comprehensive assessment, this essay concentrates on the one or two key examples that defined each producer's particular take on film noir and their importance to the development of the cycle.[14]

Jerry Wald

Jerry Wald (1911–62), the son of a dry-goods salesman, was an energetic opportunist, widely thought to be the model for Sammy Glick, the ruthlessly ambitious hustler in Budd Schulberg's Hollywood exposé *What Makes Sammy Run?* (1941). Following an early career as a journalist, Wald worked for Warners as a staff writer from 1934 onwards. He cowrote the screenplays for three Mark Hellinger films, *The Roaring Twenties* (1939), *They Drive by Night* (1940), and *Manpower* (1941), the last from his original story, all of which typified Warners' hard-edged, socially oriented black-and-white urban crime melodramas (its "corporate art") that prepared the ground for the studio's shift into film noir. Hellinger recommended Wald for promotion to producer, judging that his indefatigable energy and restless mind, crammed full of possible scenarios gleaned from his omnivorous reading, would always be capable of generating interesting ideas.[15] It is this probing intelligence that makes Schatz's characterization of Wald as simply the company man, "expert at stroking Jack Warner's delicate ego," too narrow.[16] Although careful to keep right side of Hal Wallis, the authoritarian head of production whom he eventually replaced, Wald had an intuitive feeling for the new direction Warners films should take, already evident in his screenplay (with Robert Rossen) for *Out of the Fog* (1941)—in which John Garfield plays a small-time New York hoodlum who terrorizes a Brooklyn waterfront community—that starts to blend Warners' gangster formula with noir elements such as the pervasive sea mists that shroud the morally ambivalent action. Wald's sense of the possibilities offered by noir, always tempered by shrewd commercial considerations, is best shown in his production of one of the most influential early noirs, *Mildred Pierce* (September 1945).

Although Wald's screenplays indicated a noir sensibility—as did his production of *Background to Danger* (1943), adapted by W. R. Burnett from Eric

Ambler's 1937 dark spy thriller—Wald's reputation as a producer in 1944 was based on a series of action-orientated war films such as *Across the Pacific* (1942) and *Destination Tokyo* (1943). Shrewd enough to recognize that the tide was turning away from combat films, Wald judged that he needed a "woman's film" to demonstrate his ability to handle different subject matter, an opportunity that seemed to present itself when he was asked to assess the cinematic possibilities of James M. Cain's 1941 novel *Mildred Pierce* by Jack Warner, who was anxious to capitalize on Cain's reputation as a "sensational" writer.[17] In his detailed analysis of the film's production, Albert J. LaValley states unequivocally that Wald was "its most important shaping force. . . . *Mildred Pierce* bears many hallmarks of a strong and intransigent Wald, one who determined the basic direction and tone of the film . . . [and resolved] to shape it his way, to go beyond domestic drama and the women's movie and to move to a more lurid melodrama of murder and infidelity."[18]

From the outset, Wald wanted *Mildred Pierce,* set during the Depression and depicting the struggle of an ordinary working-class woman trying to make her way in a hostile world and raise a family without the support of a husband, recast as a murder mystery that would exploit the sex and violence that was the basis of Cain's reputation. He was also convinced that Cain's novel should be updated, thus providing audiences with a contemporary story that mirrored their own dilemmas. Wald hired Thomas Williamson to update the story, and his twenty-eight-page treatment (January 1944) uses a flashback technique to convey Mildred's narrative, a device LaValley attributes to Wald's influence.[19] However, Wald and Warner judged Williamson's adaptation too tame—lacking "red meat"—and Wald approached Cain himself as the best person to bring out the "adult themes" of his own novel. Cain was uncomfortable with Wald's approach, which he felt undermined and cheapened his serious study of the damage caused by the Depression. Cain kept in touch with the progress of the adaptation, writing to Wald on several occasions and objecting to his attempts to transform *Mildred Pierce* into another lurid and sexy "Cain thriller." Cain especially disliked the coarsening of Mildred's daughter Veda from an outstanding coloratura soprano to a "cheap little tart."[20]

Wald brought in Catherine Turney, a specialist "woman's writer," to complete a full adaptation, but she also objected to Wald's attempt to turn Cain's novel into a crime thriller. In particular, she chafed at his insistence on flashbacks, which she considered a gimmick. But Wald, having seen *Double Indemnity,* was more convinced than ever about their effectiveness, telling Turney, "From now on, every picture I make will be done in flashback."[21] By December 1944, he was confident enough to specify how particular scenes should be shot and the aesthetic possibilities of "low-key lighting."[22] Wald determined that *Mildred Pierce* should begin dramatically with the shooting of Monte Beragon, the shallow playboy Mildred has ill-advisedly married, a murder invented for the film. A flashback structure also made the story about moral retribution, which would help Wald in his negotiations with the censors who, although more receptive to "adult issues" following the decision to certificate *Double Indemnity,* still needed careful handling. Flashback narration also tightened the novel's loose, episodic structure, making for a much more dramatic film.

To further his conception, Wald brought in Albert Maltz, with whom he had collaborated on *Destination Tokyo,* to rework Turney's screenplay. However, Maltz, a socialist playwright who had joined the Communist party in 1935, was unhappy that the novel's social drama about the Depression had been lost and withdrew. After rejecting the work of three other writers—including William Faulkner—Wald eventually settled on Ranald MacDougall, who had written the screenplay for another Wald action film, *Objective Burma* (1945), as a safe pair of hands.[23] In the end, MacDougall, who worked on the script right up to the commencement of shooting in February 1945, was the only writer to receive a screen credit. Wald wanted to make the settings less tawdry and lower-class in order to transform Mildred into a more glamorous figure and persuaded Warner that *Mildred Pierce* should be a full A production, with a budget of $1,453,000. According to an article he wrote for *Photoplay,* "I Took One Look at Her," Wald saw Joan Crawford as Mildred, recognizing, from their first meeting, her potential to be "great dramatic actress."[24] There was a strong element of post hoc rationalization about this claim—Wald had approached *Double Indemnity*'s star Barbara Stanwyck and also Bette Davis, who had both declined the role—but having succeeded in persuading Crawford that the role would be her route back to stardom after a two-year hiatus, Wald overrode the objections of his director, Michael Curtiz, who considered Crawford to be a "temperamental bitch" with "high-hat airs," as well as those of his cinematographer Ernest Haller that he couldn't light her.[25] Wald insisted that the lighting and direction accent Crawford's allure, making Mildred a more stylish figure than in the novel, more sexually attractive and manipulative, aligning her with the femme fatale archetype and thereby allowing an audience to believe that she is indeed guilty of Monte's murder.

Lizzie Francke sees Wald's approach as frankly commercial: "Murder could make money, murder spiked with love and lust could make twice as much. With such ingredients added to *Mildred Pierce,* Wald deduced he would have a hot property on his hands since the film would appeal to more than just the women's audience."[26] Although the possibility of making a trenchant story about the Depression was indeed lost in the process, Wald's shrewd amalgamation of two previously separate genres—the murder mystery and the woman's picture—was highly successful. *Mildred Pierce* gained Academy

Award nominations for best script and picture; Crawford won for best actress. The film was a critical and commercial triumph, earning $3,470,000 domestically and another $2,141,000 worldwide.[27] Wald supervised its aggressive marketing as another of Cain's "sizzling bestsellers," presenting Crawford's Mildred as a glamorous femme fatale who shoulders the guilt and responsibility for what happens: "The kind of woman most men want—but shouldn't have!"[28]

Mildred Pierce was highly influential, opening up new possibilities for the woman's picture and the crime film that other filmmakers were quick to exploit, including Wald himself, who used his enhanced authority at Warners to make further film noirs starring Crawford—*Possessed* (1947), *Flamingo Road* (1949), and *The Damned Don't Cry* (1950)—developing Wald's particular slant on the noir woman's film. The most innovative was *Possessed*, which explores mental disturbance, a subject that had been, up to this point, a male preserve, most often associated with the maladjusted returning veteran.[29] Crawford received a second Academy Award for best actress. Wald was also instrumental in shifting Warners' crime films toward a postwar mood of disenchantment, as in *Key Largo* (1948) and *The Breaking Point* (1950). *Key Largo*, which Wald adapted with Richard Brooks, opposes Johnny Rocco, played by Edward G. Robinson as a reprise of his prewar gangster roles, against Humphrey Bogart's postwar veteran Frank McCloud. Although McCloud is initially world-weary and cynical, he eventually finds the moral courage to kill Rocco and start a relationship with Nora Temple (Lauren Bacall), the widow of one of his ex-soldiers. Speaking powerfully to contemporary audiences, *Key Largo* was another major hit; Wald received the Irving Thalberg award, presented periodically to "creative producers."

The seductive and sensual poster image for *Mildred Pierce* (1945), reflecting producer Jerry Wald's view of the film.

Wald's other Warners noirs—*Dark Passage* (1947), *The Unfaithful* (1947), *Caged* (1950), and *Storm Warning* (1951)—were powerful but less influential films. They continued to focus on women's predicaments: the social and sexual pressures on the "war widow" (Ann Sheridan) in *The Unfaithful*; the dilemma of Marsha (Ginger Rogers) in *Storm Warning* over whether she should tell her sister (Doris Day) that her husband is a member of the Ku Klux Klan; and the struggles of the inmates against a fascistic prison regime in *Caged*, an unusual prison-noir about women. Wald left Warners in 1950 to become an independent producer in partnership with the writer-director Norman Krasna. The company was relatively unsuccessful, but their one noir, *Clash by Night* (1952), was another Wald woman's noir, depicting the problems faced by a disillusioned city woman (Barbara Stanwyck) returning to her home town. Wald insisted that his director, Fritz Lang, concentrate on the emotional impact of the love triangle in the Odets play from which it was adapted rather than the social issues.[30] Wald continued to supervise noirs actively after his appointment as Columbia's vice president in charge of production in late October 1952. Most notable are two further films directed by Lang, *The Big Heat* (1953) and *Human Desire* (1954),[31] as well as a final film with Crawford, *Queen Bee* (1955), in which the actress enjoys caricaturing herself as the archetypal vamp.

Almost entirely absent from existing accounts of film noir, Wald needs to be recognized as an important influence on its development. Although his view of filmmaking was pragmatic rather than idealistic, he grasped, more clearly than most, the artistic as well as the commercial possibilities opened up by the emerging noir sensibility with its focus on disenchantment and ethical ambiguity.[32] Above all, he helped to reconfigure the woman's film away from the idealism and self-sacrifice that had characterized its prewar incarnations to encompass psychological problems, moral dilemmas, and the irrational power of sexual desire.

Adrian Scott

Adrian Scott (1912–73) was another writer-turned-producer, but his outlook differed radically from Wald's. In her informative analysis, Jennifer Langdon-Teclaw describes Scott as the "quintessential Popular Front Communist: committed to the tripartite agenda of anti-fascism, anti-racism, and progressive unionism, but inspired less by Marxism than by the American tradition of radical democracy."[33] From a middle-class Irish Catholic background, Scott spent his early career in New York writing for *Stage* magazine. When his ambitions to become a playwright were not realized, he moved to Los Angeles in 1938, joining the Motion Picture Guild, an independent group dedicated to making socially relevant documentaries and shorts.[34] Scott also became a member of the Screenwriters Guild, the Anti-Nazi League, and other progressive groups while working as a freelance screenwriter for MGM and Paramount before signing with RKO in 1942. The soft-spoken and charming Scott was hailed as a rising talent and quickly promoted to producer in 1943. In his own way as ambitious as Wald, Scott understood that this role offered greater control over the production process than he could ever have as a writer. For Scott, film was an art form and a powerful ideological tool capable of raising public consciousness and promoting a more tolerant and just society.[35] However, like any studio employee, Scott had to be mindful of the need to make films that would engage audiences.

In RKO's fluid system, with its hands-off head of production Charles Koerner, Scott was assigned his own small production unit and enjoyed considerable autonomy. RKO had purchased the rights to Raymond Chandler's *Farewell, My Lovely* in 1940, but its first adaptation, *The Falcon Takes Over* (1942), was a light comedy-thriller in which a suave George Sanders reconfigures Chandler's detective as a breezy socialite gliding through a well-lit, upper-crust world. Scott was convinced that the studio had missed an opportunity to capitalize on Chandler's novel, which, although hardly left-wing, is permeated by an acute sense of the iniquities of capitalism, exposing the deceit, greed, violence, and sexual corruption at work in the seedy underbelly of the City of Angels. Scott therefore decided on a radical reworking that, because Chandler's novel had been almost entirely jettisoned in the previous version, would never be spotted as such by Koerner or other RKO executives as a remake.[36] Scott worked closely with the writer John Paxton, a friend from the early days in New York, who recalled that the importance he was given in the production process by Scott was very unusual, exemplifying the producer's determination to work collaboratively rather than as taskmaster.[37] Encouraged by Scott, Paxton's adaptation was faithful to the novel's mood and retained much of its witty and acerbic dialogue. Paxton credits the innovative use of flashback sequences and voiceover narration to Scott's gift for "concepts and constructions," which, parallel with *Double Indemnity,* made *Farewell, My Lovely* a radical break with previous crime films.[38] Scott worked closely with his director, Edward Dmytryk—whom he had chosen for his first A feature on the basis of several tightly paced second features for RKO—and the cinematographer Harry J. Wild to develop Orson Welles's expressionist style in *Citizen Kane* (1941), using superimpositions, dream images, fogged or cobwebbed screens, odd angles, chiaroscuro lighting, and point-of-view shots to create a nightmarish atmosphere of paranoia and dislocation.

Scott did not, of course, enjoy complete autonomy. Koerner had responded to the RKO contract player Dick Powell's unhappiness at his typecasting as a song-and-dance performer by offering him the role of Chandler's world-weary detective Philip Marlowe.[39] Powell, in turn, gave a convincingly laconic, hard-bitten performance that nevertheless retained an engaging vulnerability during the course of a torrid investigation in which he is drugged, choked, knocked senseless, half-blinded, and shot. *Farewell, My Lovely* was judged to be something of a risk, deemed a programmer with a budget of under five hundred thousand dollars and a short shooting schedule, economies that are occasionally visible in the sets and peripheral scenes. Retitled *Murder, My Sweet* to avoid any possibility that audiences might expect a Dick Powell musical, studio publicity made much of the actor's new persona as well as emphasizing the seductiveness of Claire Trevor as the femme fatale Mrs. Grayle.[40] Scott had negotiated carefully with the censor Joseph Breen over her role, accommodating his insistence that she be punished for her crimes, in order to gain maximum latitude in the depiction of her predatory sexuality.[41]

Released in December 1944, only two months after *Double Indemnity*, *Murder, My Sweet* was a critical and commercial triumph, grossing $1,715,000 in domestic rentals.[42] Its success made Scott a hot property, the "new Thalberg."[43] Scott's increased stature gave him the confidence to make films that more directly reflected his left-wing politics. Scott had been assigned *Cornered* (December 1945) by William Dozier, the head of RKO's story department, a topical but conventional manhunt story by Ben Hecht and Herman Mankiewicz. It depicts the Canadian pilot Laurence Gerard, recently released from a POW camp, who sets out to avenge the death of his young war bride, a member of the Resistance, by tracking down the Vichy official who betrayed her. Scott hired John Wexley, a Communist and noted antifascist screenwriter, to rework the script. Wexley suggested shifting the action from the Caribbean to South America after reading about the Nazi sympathies of Juan Peron's oppressive regime in Argentina. However, as Langdon-Teclaw documents, RKO executives became alarmed at this development, which went against the United States' "good neighbor" ideology and could potentially jeopardize the distribution of RKO's films in Argentina by offending the Peron government.[44] Because Scott's director, Dmytryk, also had reservations, Scott reluctantly acceded to the studio's demand to remove Wexley from the production, engaging Paxton to rework the script. Although Paxton removed any suggestion that Argentina collaborated with the Axis powers or of the Peron regime's complicity in harboring ex-Nazis, Scott and Paxton fought hard to retain the film's location and a more general antifascist stance, trusting that audiences would pick up on what was being implied, especially by casting noted left-wing Group Theatre actors in minor roles as members of an underground network sworn to bring Nazis to justice. Powell gives his most accomplished noir performance as Gerard, a complex figure, brutalized, cynical, and manipulative but also vulnerable, crying at the memory of his dead wife and psychologically disturbed by his war service and incarceration. Although not quite the film Scott might ideally have intended, *Cornered* is an engaging and powerful film noir, more politically probing than Alfred Hitchcock's Nazi thriller *Notorious* (1946), set in Rio de Janeiro and released by RKO in August 1946.

Scott's defining film noir was *Crossfire* (July 1947), again directed by Dmytryk from a Paxton screenplay. Although the Richard Brooks novel on which it was based, *The Brick Foxhole,* centers on homophobia and had been comprehensively rejected by Breen, Scott always intended *Crossfire* to be a film about anti-Semitism. It was to be about personal as opposed to organized fascism, tackling a prejudice Scott felt was more widespread and also a subject he hoped to get past the censors. Scott had first proposed a film about anti-Semitism to Koerner and Dozier in 1945, arguing it could be made for only $250,000.[45] However, it was only when Dore Schary took over as RKO's head of production in January 1947 following Koerner's death that Scott received any encouragement; *Crossfire* was one of the first films Schary approved.[46] The son of Russian-Jewish immigrants and a New Deal democrat, Schary was involved in a number of progressive organizations espousing liberal and antifascist agendas and actively supported innovative and forward-thinking filmmakers. He was particularly keen to assist Scott's efforts, having lectured for the Army Special Services during the war about the dangers of anti-Semitism.[47] However, Schary was shrewd and experienced enough to recognize that *Crossfire* was something of a risk, decreeing that it should have a tight twenty-day shooting schedule and a budget of under five hundred thousand dollars.[48]

Despite these constraints, *Crossfire,* which depicts a group of GIs waiting in a Washington, D.C., hotel for their final release into civilian life, is the most comprehensive and ambitious of the numerous film noirs about the social and psychological problems of returning veterans.[49] The sensitive, confused, and vulnerable Mitchell (George Cooper) becomes wrongly suspected of murdering a Jew, Joseph Samuels, he met in a nightclub. His friend Sergeant Keeley (Robert Mitchum), cooperating with Detective Finlay (Robert Young), helps to prove that Samuels's actual killer is the bigoted and psychotic Montgomery (Robert Ryan). As in Scott's earlier *Deadline at Dawn* (1946)—adapted by Clifford Odets from a Cornell Woolrich novel about an amnesiac veteran accused of a crime he did not commit—the determination to ram home the social and political messages is at odds with the more diffuse and nebulous threats that permeate this noir world. *Crossfire*'s most memorable scene occurs when Mitchell encounters an unnamed man (Paul Kelly) who may be the husband of Ginny (Gloria Grahame), a dancer who

The publicity poster for *Crossfire* (1947) marketed the film as a sensational thriller. As RKO's head of production, Dore Schary's name is more prominent—above the title—than Adrian Scott's as producer.

has befriended Mitchell and lent him her apartment. "The Man" emerges out of the shadows, talks enigmatically about the meaningless posturings of his life, and later vanishes again from view. A spectral presence or "lost soul," Kelly's deracinated Everyman embodies the film's deeper sense of a restless, dislocated society that cannot be rectified by the humane and tolerant social justice embodied by Finlay. Scott's intention was to warn the American public that fascism "could happen here," and he described *Crossfire* as a "necessary and progressive picture."[50]

Crossfire was a critical and (modest) commercial success, nominated for five Academy Awards. Its reception confirmed Scott's faith that there was an audience for progressive films, not just entertainment: "The American people have always wanted and more than ever want pictures which touch their lives, illuminate them, bring understanding."[51] Scott compared his own film favorably with *Gentlemen's Agreement*, released in February 1948, which, he thought, emphasized the obvious lunatic fringe element of anti-Semitism as opposed to the pervasive presence *Crossfire* dramatized.[52] Its success also convinced Schary of the viability of an RKO "B" unit devoted to "experimental" films in which Scott would play a key role.[53] Before plans could come to fruition, Scott and Dmytryk were summoned to appear before the ultra-conservative and anti-Semitic House Un-American Activities Committee (HUAC) in 1947. Refusing to "name names," both were imprisoned as two of the "Hollywood Ten." Despite Schary's support, Scott was sacked by RKO. He sued for wrongful dismissal, but the case was dismissed in 1957. Although Scott survived by writing for film and television behind a front, he never produced another film, a dreadful waste of an exceptional talent.

Crossfire was Scott's monument and one of the best of the social-message film noirs that, as Brian Neve argues, were the outcome of the strong left-wing element in American filmmaking during this period—a development, as in Scott's case, that was ended by the predations of HUAC and Senator Joseph McCarthy's witch hunt.[54] Scott also needs to be remembered as the instigator of *Murder, My Sweet,* a highly influential early noir that helped pioneer the development of the dominant studio-based expressionist style of 1940s film noir. It opened up a subjective, existential dimension to the detective thriller with Marlowe musing on the baffling unreality of city life, the "dead silence of an office building at night—not quite real," before the hulking figure of Moose Malloy looms over him, reflected in the same pane of glass. This dual legacy makes Scott a highly significant figure in the history of film noir.

Mark Hellinger

When Mark Hellinger (1903–47) joined Warner Bros. in September 1937, his status as a celebrity New York columnist afforded him an open-ended contract stipulating duties of a "diverse nature, which will include writing, story consultant, possibly producing," on a salary of $1,100 per week plus ten thousand dollars for each original story he sold to the studio.[55] It was as a writer that Hellinger made his first contribution, providing an original story, "The World Moves On," for *The Roaring Twenties* (1939), which Jerry Wald cocrafted into a screenplay. Although this was judged too important a film for Hellinger to produce himself, its success persuaded Warners to make him the producer, working closely with the screenwriters Wald and Richard Macaulay, for two further crime films, *They Drive by Night* and *Manpower.* From the outset, Hellinger was a hands-on, go-getting producer whose restless temperament meant that he always pushed himself and others to work harder and faster—especially his writers, as he judged a good script to be the key to a successful film. Hellinger thought that Warners' output could be improved significantly through better writing and story construction.

The film that made Hellinger's reputation as a producer was *High Sierra* (1941), based on a novel by W. R. Burnett. The studio and the nominated star,

Paul Muni, both had doubts about the project, but Hellinger wrote to Wallis expressing his enthusiasm for this "superb romance" between an Indiana farmer who "wound up the last of the Dillinger mob" and the crippled girl "who is willing to die for the unattainable love of the strangest of men; a man who uses a gun even as he dreams of the stars."[56] Hellinger recognized that the pathos and psychological complexity of this tragic figure, compelled by forces beyond his control, shifted *High Sierra* from a typical Warners gangster picture into new terrain, expressive of the sensibility that was to develop into film noir. Accordingly, he asked Wallis to find him "someone who has just half of the enthusiasm I hold for this grand yarn."[57] That someone was John Huston, who, under pressure from a skeptical Jack Warner, Hellinger encouraged and cajoled to revise substantially Burnett's initial screenplay. Hellinger also insisted that director Raoul Walsh shoot as much of the film as possible on location even though this was more expensive, as Hellinger was convinced Warners' films needed to be less studio-bound.[58] After Muni declined the role and resigned from Warners, Humphrey Bogart was assigned the part of Roy "Mad Dog" Earle, a role that defined his subsequent career. Bogart conveys the hard-bitten pathos of a man who yearns for freedom yet is doomed to the inexorable fate that awaits the noir protagonist, and he is complemented by Ida Lupino's moving performance as the lonely misfit who falls in love with him.

High Sierra cost four hundred thousand dollars and grossed over four million dollars, making Hellinger a valued property at Warners.[59] However, he eventually became weary of the studio hierarchy and resigned, accusing Wallis of using his producers as "messenger boys and involuntary ass-kissers."[60] Hellinger went instead to Twentieth Century-Fox on an enhanced salary and guaranteed A-feature productions. He was assigned *Moontide* (1942) by the studio head Darryl F. Zanuck, an uneven early noir in which Lupino stars opposite Jean Gabin, who plays the prototypical working-class waterfront drifter that had been his hallmark in his French poetic-realist films. Hellinger felt uncomfortable overseeing a film that depended on mood and atmosphere rather than a strong story, complaining to Zanuck, "Every time I try for art . . . I fall on my prat."[61] Convinced that his strengths were not recognized or valued by the autocratic Zanuck, Hellinger resigned and returned to Warners. He made a number of other films with Bogart, with whom he had established a firm friendship on *High Sierra,* including the misfire *The Two Mrs. Carrolls,* a psychosexual domestic crime drama that was Wald's forté, not Hellinger's.

Although completed in 1945, *The Two Mrs. Carrolls* was not released until March 1947, by which point Hellinger had left Warners for a second time, setting up as an independent producer in August 1945 as Mark Hellinger Productions, which released through the recently merged Universal-International

(UI). Ambitious to achieve "big five" status, UI became a home for independent producers, including Diana Productions, the company formed by the producer Walter Wanger, the director Fritz Lang, and the star Joan Bennett.[62] UI talked up its association with the "celebrated" Mark Hellinger, giving him almost complete autonomy in choice of subject.[63] UI paid Hellinger twenty-five thousand dollars for script development and twenty-five thousand dollars to produce each picture, "loaning" Hellinger up to 50 percent of the production costs with a guarantee to find the remainder if necessary. The loan would be repaid to Universal once the film had been released, with Hellinger entitled to 25 percent of the profits.[64]

Declaring that writers were the most important part of his plans for independent production, Hellinger courted Ernest Hemingway, whom he had long admired for his spare style and realism. He purchased the rights to one of his lesser-known short stories, "The Killers," eleven pages long and consisting mostly of dialogue. Hellinger decided that Hemingway's narrative—in which Ole Andreson, a.k.a. "Swede," who, despite being warned, makes no attempt to run from the two hit men who have been sent to kill him—should only constitute the opening scene and hired Richard Brooks to provide the back story. Brooks was largely responsible for *The Killers'* complex structure of eleven separate but overlapping flashbacks that gradually reveal a portrait of the enigmatic central character who is never allowed his own voice as narrator.

Hellinger again used Huston to revise the screenplay, under the supervision of Anthony Veiller, who received the screen credit because Huston was under contract to Warners. Robert Siodmak, whose gothic noir *The Spiral Staircase* (1946) Hellinger admired, was hired to direct. Hellinger later admitted that he had been "lucky" in his choice, as Siodmak was responsible for many adroit transitions and subtle touches that weren't in the screenplay but which contributed significantly to the film's overall effect.[65] However, their creative collaboration went far deeper. Hellinger's desire that *The Killers* should have a "newsreel quality" was counterbalanced by the inescapable spiral of destruction that characterizes Siodmak's fatalistic romanticism.[66] Hellinger closely supervised the production, completed in June 1946 and fifty thousand dollars under budget, and oversaw the editing, having *The Killers* ready for release by August. This commendable efficiency was promoted by UI as exemplifying how the new company would work.[67] UI top-billed Hellinger in the film's publicity (as "Broadway's Master Storyteller"), followed by Hemingway, an unusual situation in which the producer was judged better copy than the film.[68] Although Hellinger was careful not to take credit for the screenplay, the film's critical and commercial success led commentators to debate the "Hellinger touch."[69]

Hellinger had been confident enough in his own judgments to cast the then-unknown Burt Lancaster as Swede, having been impressed by him during an interview.[70] He also cast another newcomer, Ava Gardner, as the voluptuous siren who lures Swede to his doom. Hellinger wanted a "brand new girl" with "the simplicity of Bergman, but in the end is a dirty looking slut."[71] Deeply impressed by Lancaster's performance, Hellinger used him again as the star in the harshly realistic and uncompromising noir *Brute Force* (June 1947). Hellinger insisted that Jules Dassin, directing from another Brooks screenplay, emphasize the brutality of prison life in a film that becomes a generalized allegory about authoritarian regimes with clear antifascist overtones, particularly through the venal Captain Munsey (Hume Cronyn), who presides over a sadistic regime in which humiliation and torture are commonplace. Despite its downbeat ending, in which the attempted escape ends in defeat and death, *Brute Force* was a major commercial hit, earning $2,200,000 in domestic rentals.[72]

Its success meant that Dassin was retained as the director of *The Naked City* (March 1948), the picture for which Hellinger is best remembered and the culmination of his drive for greater realism. It is the most ambitious of the "semi-documentary" noirs that blend noir themes with on-location realism, showing the profound influence of wartime documentaries—Hellinger had taken leave without pay from Warners to report on the war in the Pacific from 1943 to 1945—and Italian neorealism.[73] Hellinger was determined to make a film about his home town that would "reek of authenticity. It had to be so New Yorkerish that it would look like a documentary . . . my celluloid monument to New York."[74] He commissioned Jerry Wald's younger brother Malvin, who had just completed several years as a wartime documentarist, to spend a month with the New York Police Department to research a story, initially entitled "Homicide," drawn from actual police records. Aware of Hellinger's insistence on absolute accuracy, Wald ensured that his account of the painstaking nature of the police's investigation of the murder of a fashion model (an unsolved case and therefore capable of a fictional resolution) was meticulously correct.[75] His story was shaped into a screenplay by Albert Maltz, who shared Hellinger's belief in the persuasive power of realism, foregrounding "absolute authenticity" and the avoidance of any "forced melodramatics."[76]

Once UI had approved the project, the second unit was sent to New York in May 1947 for twenty-four days to film locations, after which Hellinger and Dassin spent a further eight weeks on the streets of New York, shooting "the buildings in their naked stone, the people without makeup," as Hellinger put it.[77] Dassin and his cinematographer William H. Daniels (who received an Oscar for his work on the film) used the new fast film stock and portable lighting units while filming in 107 different locations. Some scenes were photographed secretly through trucks panelled with two-way mirrors to avoid onlookers posing for the camera, thus capturing the "authentic" lives of ordinary New Yorkers sweltering during the hottest summer on record. Outside the four principal characters, including Lt. Dan Muldoon (Barry Fitzgerald) leading the investigation and the mendacious criminal Frank Niles (Howard Duff), the parts were filled either by New York radio or stage actors making their first film appearance or nonprofessionals.[78] It was a creatively shaped realism. Having bought the rights to *Naked City* (1945), the acclaimed collection by the freelance photographer Arthur H. Fellig ("Weegee"), whose stark, black-and-white news photographs of New York (often of violent happenings or of criminals) influenced the noir style, Hellinger instructed Dassin and Daniels to re-create Weegee's dramatic realism on celluloid. The editing—by Paul Weatherwax, who also received an Oscar—is dynamic, with constant changes of perspective, most expressively used in the nine-minute chase of the murderer Willie Garzah (Ted de Corsia) as he is hunted down on the Lower East Side.

   After suffering a mild heart attack in August, Hellinger had to monitor the remaining progress of the film from his hospital room. He was well enough to

Location filmmaking for *The Naked City* (1948), Mark Hellinger's "celluloid monument to New York."

supervise the editing in September and to record the voiceover narration.[79] This narration, scripted by Maltz but refined and enlarged by Hellinger, is highly distinctive, trading on his personal reputation: "Ladies and gentlemen, the motion picture you are about to see is called *The Naked City*. My name is Mark Hellinger. I was in charge of its production. And I may as well tell you frankly that it's a bit different from most films you have seen." Hellinger speaks as if confiding in the audience as a friend, making the narration radically different in tone and enunciation from the usual stentorian tone that characterised the semi-documentary cycle. As Sarah R. Kozloff argues, Hellinger's voiceover creates a complex persona: part lecturer, part tour guide, part barside raconteur, mingling the apparently objective with the highly personal, offering interpolated advice to characters, especially to Garzah during the dénouement, about their foibles and evasions.[80] Hellinger concludes the film by intoning: "There are eight million stories in the naked city—this has been one of them."

The Naked City was a highly successful film, perceived as the apotheosis of Hellinger's love affair with New York, but he did not live to enjoy its success, dying only three days after the film's Los Angeles preview on December 21, 1947.[81] As Carl Richardson notes, *The Naked City* was an ambitious and risky film. Semi-documentaries were still dubious box-office, and Hellinger had used

In DCA's re-release of *The Naked City* in 1956, Mark Hellinger's name is still the most important selling point.

his own private assets as collateral to secure a loan of $1.25 million from the Bank of America.[82] It was released despite the skepticism of Universal's executives who, according to Dassin, denuded the final version of much of the social commentary about inequality, impoverishment, and injustice that he and Maltz had carefully woven into its fabric.[83] Afterwards, Dassin was blacklisted, and Maltz, like Scott and Dmytryk, was imprisoned as one of the Hollywood Ten.

Hellinger had intended to film Don Tracy's 1936 pulp novel *Criss Cross,* a typically "strong story" involving gangsters, an elaborate robbery, and sexual

---

Mr. Broadway

Mark Hellinger was the son of a wealthy Park Avenue Jewish real-estate developer who wanted him to go into law. He rebelled, joining *Zit's Weekly,* a theatrical sheet, before moving to the *New York Daily News* in 1923, then the *New York Daily Mirror* in 1929. Like his close friend and fellow columnist Walter Winchell, Hellinger's great subject was the Broadway demimonde, the varied denizens of its theaters, nightclubs, restaurants, speakeasies, apartments, and offices. Hellinger was much more of a storyteller than Winchell, a prolific writer of plays, sketches, and above all short stories that were, like those of Broadway's other great chronicler, Damon Runyon, filled with streetwise argot but ending with an unexpected twist in the style of O. Henry. Hellinger was the archetypal fast-living, hard-drinking journalist, successful enough to become a minor celebrity in his own right but also avidly cultivating other celebrities, not only show-business people but gangsters. He dressed like a mobster in his trademark blue serge suit with deep blue shirt and white crepe tie. When he moved west in 1936 for a new career in Hollywood, he drove a bulletproof limousine that had belonged to Dutch Schultz. Attracted by beauty and glamour, Hellinger married a Ziegfeld showgirl, Gladys Glad, in 1929 and wrote sketches for *Ziegfeld Follies,* the lavish Broadway revues.

In his measured retrospective "Swell Guy" (the title of one of Hellinger's films), Richard Brooks portrays an ambivalent figure who loved and loathed the "entertainment jungle," at once open, generous, and supremely confident in his ability to succeed, settling contracts with a handshake, but also paranoid, secretive, continually apprehensive, never sure of his talents, longing always to be the great writer he knew he could never become. Ernest Hemingway, who became a close friend, once said that Hellinger "has death sitting on his shoulder": his heavy drinking and frenetic lifestyle compounded a congenital heart condition, and he died, aged only forty-four, from coronary thrombosis. Standing among the throngs of mourners at his funeral, Brooks said that it was "like being at the premiere of a movie."

betrayal, with Lancaster as the young man returning to his local neighborhood, Bunker Hill in Los Angeles. Hellinger's version would have featured
Los Angeles in a way that paralleled New York in *The Naked City*, but, during production, Siodmak became the driving force, shifting the focus from a
conspectus of Los Angeles life toward a more archetypal, if bitterly ironic,
romantic tragedy.[84] Released in January 1949, the film was sold to UI to settle
Hellinger's company debts; other noir projects were sold elsewhere: *Act of
Violence* to MGM, and *Knock on Any Door* to Bogart's company Santana
Productions. The intention to make a series of film noirs starring Bogart
adapted from Hemingway's stories was forestalled by Hellinger's demise.[85]

Conclusion: Documenting the Noir Producer

Hellinger's early death robbed film noir of one of its most active exponents,
but he left a powerful legacy. *The Killers* set new standards for flashback
narration, and *The Naked City* remained the epitome of the semi-documentary strand of film noir, spawning the popular television series *Naked City*
(1958–63). Hellinger also molded the careers of two noir icons, Bogart and
Lancaster, and gave opportunities to Dassin and Siodmak as directors. His
influence on the development of film noir as a production cycle was thus
far-reaching, as was that of Wald and Scott. What unites the work of these
very different men—the pragmatist, the ideologue, and the realist—was a
shared sense that film noir (a term, of course, they never encountered or used)
was a vehicle through which to realize their ambitions and a way to engage
contemporary audiences whose tastes were changing. Noir could explore,
with a frankness impossible for the previous generation of filmmakers, socio-
sexual problems and the seamier side of American life.

Each saw the producer's role as pivotal, straddling the worlds of commerce
and creativity, positioned to make the key decisions that shaped a film, choosing
source materials, collaborating closely with writers and directors, and overseeing casting and locations. Consequently they were able to retain the integrity
of their projects better than as writers. As I have emphasized, their work needs
to be understood within a volatile and changing Hollywood, one in which
opportunities arose for ambitious, talented, and creative men—occasionally
women—who could hope to influence studio policy and filmmaking practices.
However, a producer's significance remains invisible unless the focus becomes
the whole production process—from conception to exhibition—rather than the
interpretation of films as finished texts. I hope that what has been attempted
here will encourage others to take up and extend this approach, using archival
evidence to document the variegated range of other producers whose unseen
labors did so much to shape the course of film noir.

Notes

1. Steve Neale, *Genre and Hollywood* (London: Routledge, 2000), 153.

2. Sheri Chinen Biesen, *Blackout: World War II and the Origins of Film Noir* (Baltimore: Johns Hopkins University Press, 2005), 2, 189–219.

3. Ibid., 97.

4. Ibid., 12–13. See also Richard Sklar, *Movie-Made America: A Cultural History of American Movies* (London: Chappell), 252–53.

5. Richard Maltby, *Hollywood Cinema* (Oxford: Blackwell, 1995), 107.

6. Rick Altman, *Film/Genre* (London: British Film Institute, 1999), 59–62.

7. Andrew Spicer, *Film Noir* (Harlow: Longman/Pearson Education, 2002), 26–29.

8. James Naremore, *More than Night: Film Noir in Its Contexts* (Berkeley: University of California Press, 1998), 139.

9. Ibid., 39.

10. For an informative overview, see Geoff Mayer, "Film Noir and Studio Production Practices," in *A Companion to Film Noir*, ed. Andrew Spicer and Helen Hanson (Boston: Wiley/Blackwell, 2013), 211–28.

11. Jerome Christensen, *America's Corporate Art: The Studio Authorship of Hollywood Motion Pictures* (Stanford, Calif.: Stanford University Press, 2012).

12. See Ethan Mordden, *The Hollywood Studios: House Style in the Golden Age of Movies* (New York: Simon and Schuster, 1988).

13. For a recent account, see Denise Mann, *Hollywood Independents: The Postwar Talent Takeover* (Minneapolis: University of Minnesota Press, 2008), which notes that this shift was clearly discerned by commentators at the time.

14. I'm conscious that all three are men. This reflects the patriarchal assumptions underpinning the Hollywood industry at this time, but there were occasional opportunities for women to become producers. See Sheri Chinen Biesen, "Joan Harrison, Virginia Van Upp, and Women behind the Scenes in Wartime Film Noir," *Quarterly Review of Film and Video* 20 (2003): 125–44. In the 1950s, Ida Lupino became an important independent producer of film noirs.

15. Jim Bishop, *The Mark Hellinger Story: A Biography of Broadway and Hollywood* (New York: Appleton-Century-Crofts, 1952), 271. See also Richard Brooks, "Swell Guy," *The Screen Writer* 3.10 (March 1948): 15.

16. Thomas Schatz, *The Genius of the System: Hollywood Filmmaking in the Studio Era* (New York: Simon and Schuster, 1989), 321.

17. Roy Hoopes, *Cain: The Biography of James M. Cain* (Carbondale: Southern Illinois University Press, 1987), 350.

18. Albert J. LaValley, "*Mildred Pierce*: A Troublesome Property to Script," in *Authorship in Film Adaptation*, ed. Jack Boozer (Austin: University of Texas Press, 2008), 43.

19. Ibid., 47.

20. Hoopes, *Cain*, 348–49.

21. LaValley, "*Mildred Pierce*," 52.

22. Biesen, *Blackout*, 142.

23. Faulkner's screenplay was "outlandish and gothic," departing radically from the novel. LaValley, "*Mildred Pierce*," 55.

24. Qtd. in Hoopes, *Cain*, 351.

25. Ibid.

26. Lizzie Francke, *Script Girls: Women Screenwriters in Hollywood* (London: British Film Institute, 1994), 50.

27. Biesen, *Blackout*, 143.

28. See Mary Beth Haralovich, "Selling *Mildred Pierce*: A Case Study in Movie Promotion," in *Boom and Bust: American Cinema in the 1940s*, by Thomas Schatz (Los Angeles: University of California Press, 1997), 198–200.

29. See Spicer, *Film Noir*, 86–87; Robert Francis Saxe, *Settling Down: World War II Veterans' Challenge to the Postwar Consensus* (New York: Palgrave Macmillan, 2007).

30. Patrick McGilligan, *Fritz Lang: The Nature of the Beast* (London: Faber and Faber, 1998), 388–90.

31. For details of Wald's role in the Lang films see ibid., 405–9.

32. LaValley notes sympathetically that Wald was particularly attracted to works that combined artistry with a frank depiction of sexuality, including adapting Faulkner and D. H. Lawrence, and that he was working on a version of James Joyce's *Ulysses* when he died unexpectedly at the early age of fifty. LaValley, "*Mildred Pierce*," 44.

33. Jennifer Langdon-Teclaw, "The Progressive Producer in the Studio System: Adrian Scott at RKO," in "*Un-American" Hollywood*, ed. Frank Krutnik, Steve Neale, Brian Neve, and Peter Stanfield (New Brunswick, N.J.: Rutgers University Press, 2007), 152.

34. Bernard F. Dick, *Radical Innocence: A Critical Study of the Hollywood Ten* (Lexington: University Press of Kentucky, 1989), 122–23.

35. Langdon-Teclaw, "Progressive Producer," 153.

36. Edward Dmytryk, *It's a Hell of a Life but Not a Bad Living* (New York: Times Books, 1978), 58–62.

37. Langdon-Teclaw, "Progressive Producer," 155–56.

38. Ibid., 155.

39. Biesen, *Blackout*, 115.

40. Mary Beth Haralovich, "Selling Noir: Stars, Gender and Genre in Film Noir Posters and Publicity," in *A Companion to Film Noir*, ed. Spicer and Hanson, 246–64.

41. Biesen, *Blackout*, 113–14.

42. Ibid., 116.

43. Langdon-Teclaw, "Progressive Producer," 154.

44. Ibid., 157–59.

45. Brian Neve, *Film and Politics in America: A Social Tradition* (London: Routledge, 1992), 96.

46. Ibid., 98.

47. Dore Schary, *Heyday: An Autobiography* (New York: Berkley Books, 1981), 159.

48. Ibid.

49. See n. 28.

50. Langdon-Teclaw, "Progressive Producer," 165–66.

51. Ibid., 167.

52. Neve, *Film and Politics in America*, 99.

53. Ibid.

54. Ibid., esp. 198–202.

55. Bishop, *Mark Hellinger Story*, 304.

56. Qtd. in A. M. Sperber and Eric Lax, *Bogart* (London: Phoenix, 1998), 120.

57. Ibid.

58. Bishop, *Mark Hellinger Story*, 254.

59. Ibid., 261.

60. Ibid., 307.

61. Ibid., 281.

62. See Matthew Bernstein, *Walter Wanger: Hollywood Independent* (Minneapolis: University of Minnesota Press, 2000).

63. Ibid., 310.

64. Schatz, *Boom and Bust*, 387.

65. Deborah Alpi, *Robert Siodmak* (Jefferson, N.C.: McFarland and Co., 1998), 154.

66. Ibid., 159.

67. Schatz, *Boom and Bust*, 388.

68. Bishop, *Mark Hellinger Story*, 316.

69. Ibid., 318. *The Killers* earned $2,500,000 in the domestic market and three million dollars worldwide. Schatz, *Boom and Bust*, 388.

70. Alpi, *Robert Siodmak*, 156.

71. Qtd. in Joseph Greco, "The File on Robert Siodmak in Hollywood, 1941–1951" (Ph.D. dissertation, State University of New York at Stony Brook, 1995), 91.

72. Schatz, *Boom and Bust*, 388.

73. See Spicer, *Film Noir*, 56–59; Carl Richardson, *Autopsy: An Element of Realism in Film Noir* (Metuchen, N.J.: Scarecrow Press, 1992), 84–85, 187–90.

74. Qtd. in Bishop, *Mark Hellinger Story*, 328, 330.

75. Malvin Wald, "The Making of *The Naked City*," in *The Big Book of Noir*, ed. Ed Gorman, Lee Server, and Martin H. Greenberg (New York: Carroll and Graf, 1998), 55–64.

76. Schatz, *Boom and Bust*, 390.

77. Qtd. in Richardson, *Autopsy*, 88.

78. Ibid., 84.

79. Schatz, *Boom and Bust*, 390.

80. Sarah R. Kozloff, *Invisible Storytellers: Voice-Over Narration in the American Fiction Film* (Berkeley: University of California Press, 1988), 84.

81. Ibid.; Richardson, *Autopsy*, 87. It grossed $2,400,000 in domestic rentals and was among the top fifty films of its release year. Schatz, *Boom and Bust*, 390.

82. Richardson, *Autopsy*, 98.

83. Ibid., 87, 106–9.

84. Alpi, *Robert Siodmak*, 173–75.

85. Sperber and Lax, *Bogart*, 338.

8

Refuge England

Blacklisted American Directors and '50s British Noir

ROBERT MURPHY

> We'll have no more *Grapes of Wrath,* we'll
> have no more *Tobacco Roads.* We'll have
> no more films that show the seamy side
> of American life. We'll have no pictures
> that deal with labor strikes. We'll have no
> pictures that deal with the banker as villain.
>   —Eric Johnston, president of the Motion
>   Picture Association of America

American expatriates blacklisted in Hollywood for their Communist sym-
pathies in the postwar period made a vital contribution to British cinema,
particularly to the development of a British strand of film noir, though their
achievements tended not to be celebrated. In the 1940s and 1950s, most
British films sought distribution in America, and any association with those
who had been blacklisted would seriously damage their commercial prospects.
Give Us This Day (1949), a film depicting the harsh lives of Italian construction
workers in New York during the Depression, directed by Edward Dmytryk
and written by Ben Barzman, was comprehensively excluded from American
cinemas despite winning plaudits at European film festivals. As late as 1959,
Joseph Losey's *Blind Date/Chance Meeting* (cowritten by fellow blacklistees
Barzman and Millard Lampell), which was nominated for a BAFTA award
in Britain, had its chances of success in America blasted by a *Variety* headline
alleging that it was made by "Reds" in partnership with an "ex-Nazi."[1] Bernard

Vorhaus, an American director who made highly imaginative "quota quickies" in England in the 1930s before returning to Hollywood and being denounced as a Communist, pointed out that a "writer using a false name could remain inconspicuous, but it was impossible to direct a film without being noticed to a considerable degree."[2] Unsurprisingly, the majority of expatriates were writers such as Howard Koch, Waldo Salt, Carl Foreman, Donald Ogden Stewart, and Ring Lardner Jr., who were able to work in Britain under aliases. Vorhaus was advised by his solicitor to keep a low profile when he returned to England in 1951, and he renounced filmmaking for a career as a property developer. But four American directors did make significant interventions in British film production: Edward Dmytryk and Jules Dassin in relatively short stays at the end of the 1940s; and Cy Endfield and Joseph Losey over a much longer time-span in the 1950s and 1960s.

Dmytryk, who had directed his first film in 1935, had become RKO's top director after the success of his Ginger Rogers vehicle *Tender Comrade* (1943) and three impressive film noirs—*Farewell My Lovely/Murder My Sweet* (1944), *Cornered* (1946), and *Crossfire* (1947)—all scripted by John Paxton and produced by Adrian Scott. Dassin and Endfield got their big break while working for MGM's shorts department. Dassin's twenty-minute adaptation of Edgar Allan Poe's *The Tell-Tale Heart* (1941) won an Oscar and led to a seven-year contract. He eventually left the studio under a cloud when he refused to direct assignments he considered valueless, but he was able to gain useful experience directing medium-budget studio films.[3] After escaping his contract he made two hard-hitting independently produced films, *Brute Force* (1947) and *The Naked City* (1948), and *Thieves' Highway* (1949) for Darryl Zanuck at Fox; all three films were more closely aligned to his own radical social concerns.

Endfield's break came with a government-commissioned propaganda short dealing with the dangers of inflation. Plans were afoot for it to be given wide distribution, but the U.S. Chamber of Congress declared Endfield's *Inflation* "anti-business"; the substantial print run was canceled, and the film was shelved.[4] Endfield was drafted into the U.S. army, and when he emerged he had to cut a path through the B-movie jungle. A shoestring adaptation of his radio play *The Argyle Secrets* (1948) into an atmospheric film noir led to two "nervous A" films: *The Underworld Story* (1950) and *The Sound of Fury* (1950), which attracted good reviews but little public attention.

Joseph Losey had traveled to Europe and the Soviet Union in the 1930s, worked with Charles Laughton on the London stage, met influential European intellectuals, and come back to command a position of respect in New York radical theater. He kept a wary distance from the already established Orson Welles and Elia Kazan and made his own name with the government-sponsored Living Newspaper Theater. His radio plays attracted the attention of Hollywood; like Dassin and Endfield, he was taken on by MGM. Despite his short *A Gun in His Hand* (1945) being nominated for an Oscar, he made little progress at the studio, but he impressed the influential producer Dory Schary when he organized the Academy Awards ceremony, and maintained his theatrical reputation producing Bertolt Brecht's *The Life of Galileo* in New York and Los Angeles. When Schary became head of production at RKO, he recruited Losey to direct *The Boy with Green Hair* (1948), a message-driven fable stressing the importance of world peace and universal harmony. By the time the film went into production, Howard Hughes had taken over RKO, and Losey's position became untenable. A brief return to MGM yielded little, and he agreed to make *The Lawless/The Dividing Line* (1950) on a very low budget for the exploitation producers William H. Pine and William C. Thomas. Three more congenial independent features followed: *The Prowler* (1950), with a script by the blacklisted Dalton Trumbo, a remake of Fritz Lang's *M* (1950), and an offbeat coming-of-age melodrama, *The Big Night* (1951). None of them attracted much critical or commercial success, but Stanley Kramer was sufficiently impressed by *The Prowler* to offer Losey a three-picture deal.[5] In August 1951, while he was shooting *Stanger on the Prowl* in Italy, Losey was named as a Communist by Leo Townsend, and the Kramer offer was withdrawn. Losey returned to New York in October but could see no future for himself in America unless he was going to name names to the House Un-American Activities Committee (HUAC). In December he arrived in Britain to begin his long exile.

Noir and the City: Dmytryk and Dassin

> "Oh dear!" she exclaimed. "It's sad. Why is it being made in England?" "The blacklist," Sam said. "The director, the writer and I can't work in the U.S. They think we're subversive." "Are you?" Princess Margaret asked, stifling a giggle. . . . Princess Elizabeth listened intently to every word. She turned to Margaret. "We should wish them well."
>
> —Norma Barzman describing a royal visit to the set of *Give Us This Day* at Denham in 1949

Dmytryk's *Crossfire* was critically acclaimed and nominated for five Academy Awards, but its liberal sentiments (an anti-Semitic war veteran murders a Jew who tries to befriend him) attracted the attention of HUAC, and Dmytryk found himself subpoenaed alongside his producer Adrian Scott as one of the Hollywood Ten. The strategy of not cooperating with the committee, pleading the First Amendment, which guarantees Americans the right of free speech, and refusing to answer questions, led to an accusation of contempt of Congress. Two of the Ten appealed this judgment, and sentencing was suspended while the appeal worked its way through the courts. Remarkably, Dmytryk was allowed a passport, valid for a year, on which he traveled to England to make two films.

Dmytryk had been approached by an American independent producer, Rod Geiger, who had befriended Roberto Rossellini while still in the American army and helped him to make *Rome, Open City* (1945) and acted as coproducer on *Paisa* (1946). Having failed to persuade Rossellini to come to America to film Pietro Di Donato's novel *Christ in Concrete,* about the struggle for survival of Italian immigrant construction workers in 1930s New York, he suggested that Dmytryk make it in England in conjunction with the British-based producer Nat Bronsten.[6] To make full use of Dmytryk's talents, Bronsten suggested that while the production was being set up, they make another film based on a jokily macabre novel by the young South African playwright Alec Coppel, *Man about a Dog.* Its plot—a Harley Street psychiatrist plans to murder his wife's lover and dissolve the body in a bathtub filled with acid—had become topical with the trial in March 1949 of John George Haigh, a serial killer who had been using this method to dispose of his numerous victims since 1944.

Obsession/The Hidden Room (1949) turned out to be a surprisingly successful enterprise. Dmytryk deserves credit for the performances he inspired from a cast of actors not known for their versatility. Robert Newton forsakes his eye-rolling villainy (fully demonstrated in David Lean's 1948 version of *Oliver Twist*) for a study in subtlety. Helped by the changes Coppel made to his novel in his screenplay, Newton's Clive Riordan becomes sadder, more poignant, and more likeable. Sally Gray, a showgirl and a gangster's paramour in Alberto Cavalcanti's British noir classic *They Made Me a Fugitive* (1947), brings vulnerability to the aptly named Storm Riordan. Phil Brown, an American actor whose promising career was stifled by the blacklist, is splendidly stoical in dealing with a situation in which his urbane jailor assures him that he will eventually become his murderer. Naunton Wayne, a comic actor whose screen career beyond this film is almost entirely confined to his double act with Basil Radford as the cricket-obsessed Englishmen Charters and Caldicott, combines the best qualities of Holmes and Watson as a seemingly dull but devilishly clever Scotland Yard detective who gets on Clive's trail because of Storm's incurably inquisitive dog.[7]

Dmytryk was eager to work with the same crew on *Christ in Concrete* (now retitled *Give Us This Day*). His cinematographer, Cyril Pennington-Richards, under the guidance of Phil Brown, spent several weeks in New York shooting stills and background footage that could be used to open out what was otherwise an entirely studio-made film. Di Donato's novel had been expanded from a critically well-received short story, but under the sway of literary modernism, he had chosen to write a compendium of poetic allegories rather than a straightforward narrative. Barzman, who had scripted Losey's *The Boy with Green Hair,* took the key event of the novel, the death of Geremio the bricklayer drowned in concrete while working on an unsafe building site, and constructed a story of how poverty and thwarted ambition drove him into such a predicament. Dmytryk, who was awaiting the appeal verdict against the sentence for contempt of Congress, and Barzman, who had moved with his pregnant wife and two small children to London rather than face the next HUAC hearing, saw the film as a means of pushing back the tide against radical filmmaking. Rod Geiger hoped that it would repeat the success of *Rome, Open City* and *Paisa* in the United States as well as Europe. None of them thought that such an intrinsically American story would be barred from being shown in American cinemas.

The beginning, from which the film flashes back, is classic noir—distorted angles, dark shadows, and vertiginous stairwells—as the drunken, desperate Geremio lurches from his wife and family to his mistress. This sets a dark tone for the film, though scenes of happiness—the wedding, the brief honeymoon, the moments when love brings Annuziata and Geremio together—forestall a lapse into misery and despair. Sam Wanamaker's handsome Geremio is a talented individualist—the fastest bricklayer in town—who is reluctantly dragged into communal solidarity. "We are five sticks in a bundle," his band of brothers constantly claims, but Geremio is obviously the kingpin. That such a man should fail to thrive might be an indictment of the American dream, but far from looking "un-American," *Give Us This Day* seems to embody that combination of vibrant community life and striving for individualism that runs through American cinema from Erich von Stroheim to Martin Scorsese.

Dmytryk returned to America in August 1949 and was serving a six-month prison sentence in Mill Point, West Virginia, when *Give Us This Day* won the Best Film award at the Karlovy Vary Film Festival in July 1950. Before he was released, he decided his career was more important than loyalty to comrades he no longer felt much affinity with. He agreed to cooperate with HUAC, confessing his own involvement in Communist activities and naming names—among them Barzman, Losey, and Dassin. Dmytryk—the only one of the Hollywood Ten who was solely a director—thought that unless he appeased HUAC, his career in films was over. But a handful of directors did succeed in defying HUAC and continuing their careers, most notably Dassin, Endfield, and Losey.[8]

*   *   *

The achievement of *Give Us This Day* lies in its re-creation of Depression-era New York at Denham studios. The achievement of Jules Dassin's *Night and the City* lies in its re-creation of postwar London as a noir city, "the city of dreadful night." *Night and the City* is closer to a classic film noir than Dassin's three previous films (*Brute Force, The Naked City,* and *Thieves' Highway*) despite its obviously British story and setting.[9] Dassin and his scriptwriter Jo Eisinger make Harry Fabian, the vicious, unscrupulous pimp at the center of Gerald Kersh's novel, a more sympathetic character, a dreamer, "an artist without an art" whose get-rich-quick schemes bring about his own downfall. As played by Richard Widmark, Harry changes from a Cockney who tells tall tales about his time in America, although he's never been beyond the sound of Bow bells, into a small-time American club-tout. Essentially he's a spiv—one of those colorful, fast-talking characters who, at a time of rationing and shortages, acted as a go-between linking law-abiding but discontented citizens and the criminals who controlled a frighteningly large black-market economy.

The cinematographer Max Greene had worked on dozens of German silent films (as Mutz Greenbaum) before coming to Britain in the 1930s, where he had been responsible for the expressionist shadows in two low-budget British film noirs, *The Green Cockatoo* (1937) and *There Ain't No Justice* (1939). His remarkable chiaroscuro effects in *Night and the City* are integral to Dassin's design for the film. Interiors are equally remarkable: Figler's den, crowded with the accessories he supplies his beggars with to make them appear more pitiful; Bagrag's bar, a dank, unadorned cellar populated by a

Harry Fabian (Richard Widmark), an American hustler in London, in *Night and the City* (1950).

convincingly disreputable clientele; and most impressively, the office haunted by Phil Nosseros (Francis L. Sullivan), the grossly fat nightclub owner—a glass-paneled cave criss-crossed with shadows that become increasingly tangled and weblike as Nosseros oozes frustrated desire for his contemptuously unloving wife (Googie Withers). Exteriors are even more striking. The opening sequence moves quickly from familiar London landmarks to rubble-strewn streets, steep stairs, and sinister alleyways as Harry escapes from a pursuer to the dingy Soho apartment of his girlfriend Mary (Gene Tierney). This opening prefigures the end, an extended sequence in which Harry, his plans gone awry, is hunted down by the underworld boss Kristo. The remorselessness of the chase is set up by an extraordinary thirty-second shot from the back of an open-topped car as Kristo's Italianate chiv-man drives round Piccadilly Circus, pausing to tell street vendors to put out the word that there's a thousand-pound price on Harry's head. Tourists and ordinary Londoners stare at the camera, intrigued but unsmiling.

The Two Versions of *Night and the City*

Two versions of the film were released (and survive). The British version is notably longer, with more of the Gene Tierney/Hugh Marlowe subplot (a crucial part of Kersh's novel) and a less downbeat ending. Presumably Fox decided that if it was to be marketed as a standard noir, Tierney's sentimental role as Harry's long-suffering girlfriend slowed things down too much. But the most distinctive difference is the sound track. Franz Waxman's score for the American version frenetically cranks up the excitement, particularly during the chase sequences. Benjamin Frankel's score for the British version is quieter and more subtle, leaving—in a pre-echo of the jewel robbery in Dassin's *Rififi*—the most dramatic sequence, where Harry is cornered in the Shot Tower, entirely reliant on sound effects. It is very effective.[1]

Note

1. See Andrew Pulver, *Night and the City* (London: British Film Institute, 2010), and the excellent commentaries by Glenn Erickson on the Criterion DVD release of the film (2005) and Paul Duncan on the BFI release (2007). Both Criterion and the BFI include a 2004 interview with Dassin and a useful documentary, featuring the musicologist Christopher Husted.

Harry's long night of the soul begins at twilight (the film is set around midsummer night) on the south bank of the Thames, in the area adjacent to Waterloo Bridge, heavily bombed during the war and being cleared for the 1951

Festival of Britain. As Kristo's thugs close in on him, Harry runs into the Shot Tower, a derelict London eyesore. Like a cornered animal, he displays uncharacteristic ferocity, killing his adversary and escaping with his life to seek shelter with Figler, the beggar-king, before realizing that none of his criminal associates can resist the thousand-pound reward they will gain for betraying him. The final elegiac sequence, shot in early morning light upstream around Hammersmith Bridge, is different in tone from the rest of the film as Harry finally realizes that the game is up, and all he can do is make a futile gesture toward repaying the love and broken promises he has made to the faithful Mary.

George Mills, who went straight from working as assistant director on *Give Us This Day* (and *Obsession*) to *Night and the City*, comments on the very different styles of Dmytryk and Dassin.[10] On *Give Us This Day*, the poetic stylization of Barzman's script and the melodramatic performances give the film an operatic quality, totally unlike the wry Englishness of *Obsession*. Dmytryk, a clever and ingenious director, took his tone from the scripts; thus his own interests and concerns tend to be subsumed by a chameleonlike versatility. Dassin, by contrast, dominates his films: in the case of *Night and City*, invigorating Eisinger's workmanlike script with visual inventiveness and intense virtuoso performances.

An Exile's Life

> From the very beginning I had Home Office and police
> knocking on my door saying "Get out of the country" . . .
> So I sparred with them for two and a half years. I could
> not go anywhere.
>   —Cy Endfield

By 1951, the appeal process had run its course. The Hollywood Ten were packed off to jail, and subpoenas were being served in readiness for a new round of HUAC hearings. Dassin had returned to Hollywood, but he was not allowed in the cutting rooms during the editing of *Night and the City*, and he was sacked from his next film, *Half Angel* (1951), ten days into shooting at the insistence of the star, Loretta Young. An invitation to direct a French noir spoof, *L'ennemi public n° 1* (1953), was withdrawn when the red-baiting trade unionist Roy Brewer warned Zsa Zsa Gabor and the producer Jacques Bar of the consequences of working with Dassin. He eventually found success with an innovative French noir *Rififi* (1955) and continued his career with a number of European films.

The 1952 hearings set off a second wave of exile to Mexico, France, and Britain. Dmytryk and Dassin, regardless of their American troubles, were treated as distinguished visitors—*The Naked City* and *Crossfire* had been nominated for British Academy Awards in 1948. Endfield and Losey, who arrived in 1952, were less well-known.[11] They stayed for much longer and encountered frustration and difficulties, particularly in relation to passports and work permits, though both were able to call on the support of a substantial American expatriate community.

Endfield, who had flirted with Communism in the Depression years but became disenchanted with the party while working in Hollywood in the 1940s, had decided that if he was called to appear before HUAC, he would cooperate. "I was not going to give up my career. Why should I do that for associates that I didn't treasure, for people who I disagreed with?"[12] However, he balked at the seedy rituals involved in being an informer and seized the opportunity to leave the United States while he could still obtain a passport. He arrived in Britain in January 1952 and teamed up with Hannah Weinstein, a New York liberal sympathetic to the blacklistees who had decamped to London (and subsequently Paris), where she produced several film series destined to be shown on British and American television.[13] Endfield directed three pilot episodes of *Colonel March of Scotland Yard,* a series based on the novels of John Dickson Carr and starring Boris Karloff (then living in France) as the head of a fictitious Department of Queer Complaints. They were combined into a feature film, *Colonel March Investigates,* released in 1953 by Eros Films to no great critical acclaim.

Colonel March was followed by *The Limping Man* (1953), a light noir fantasy about an American ex-serviceman (Lloyd Bridges) who returns to Britain to claim his wartime sweetheart. It fits into a cycle of maladjusted-servicemen films stretching from *They Made Me a Fugitive* in 1947 to *The Ship That Died of Shame* in 1955, except that in this case the ex-GI is disturbed only by his dreams, and it is his sweetheart (Moira Lister), a sharpshooting war heroine, who, despite becoming a successful actress, seeks thrills smuggling on her speedboat in an attempt to recapture the excitement of war. Such female restlessness would not be dealt with again until David Hare's *Plenty,* filmed by Fred Schepisi in 1985. Although the plot's implausibility leads to an "it was only a dream" ending, the incidental detail is clearly focused.

Endfield brings a visitor's fascination with the sometimes charming, sometimes sinister aspects of London life. Alan Wheatley and Leslie Philips's wryly comic Scotland Yard detectives reveal themselves as trenchant watchdogs of the nation's safety.[14] The fussily respectable landlady appears to have dark secrets as well as a gauche beatnik daughter. A riverside pub is full of half-friendly, half-frightening characters. The singing French magician's assistant seems indifferent to the news that her ne'er-do-well husband has been murdered, but that's because she knows he is lurking beneath the stage. Bridges and Lister escape from a noisy theater-land party into a neighboring flat and have to pick their way through a soirée gathered together in the gloom to watch a television show.[15] The limping man himself remains a shadowy figure whose motivation for murder is left tantalizingly obscure. These disjointed elements might not dovetail into a coherent film, but *The Limping Man* has a surreal fascination lacking in more neatly tied-up crime thrillers.

Impulse (1954), made for Tempean, the most imaginative of the 1950s B-film companies, is more conventionally noirish, though like *The Limping Man* it is imbued with a dreamlike quality. We are provided with no explanation why a middle-aged American (Arthur Kennedy) is working as an estate agent in a sleepy Home Counties town, though the fact that he has an English wife and a commando-like ability to deal with thugs and crooks suggests that he was stationed in Britain prior to the D-Day landings. Understandably, he is bored, and when the opportunity arises to rescue a pretty nightclub singer and involve himself in her convoluted troubles, he's unable to resist it. Assignations under Hammersmith Bridge, encounters with sleazy coffee-shop owners and corruptible seamen, on top of postcoital breakfasts with the nightclub singer provide him with plenty of thrills, but the lure of the countryside and a forgiving wife prove too strong.

Endfield struggled to maintain a career in Britain. The American embassy in London refused to renew his passport in April 1953, and for two-and-a-half years until they relented, he faced constant harassment from the British authorities over visas and work permits. However, a fruitful relationship with the Polish producer Benjamin Fisz led to two ambitious and expensive films. *The Secret* (1955), based on a play Endfield had directed in London, was shot in Eastmancolor in Brighton. *Child in the House* (1956), adapted from a clever novel by Janet McNeil, is transposed from down-at-heel Belfast to upper-middle-class London. Both films feature noirish rogues (Sam Wanamaker in *The Secret,* Stanley Baker in *Child in the House*) who are redeemed by their relationship with a young girl (Mandy Miller in both films). As with *The Limping Man* and *Impulse,* the propensity toward harmonious resolution is undermined by a gnawing anxiety and discontent. Endfield finally found his métier in *Hell Drivers* (1957), where the noir sensibility is combined with rough, vigorous action.

Raymond Durgnat describes *Give Us This Day* as one of the four great European films about honest toil, alongside *Bitter Rice* (1949), *Le Salaire de la Peur* (1955), and *Gervaise* (1956).[16] *Hell Drivers,* with Stanley Baker as an ex-convict who finds dangerous work driving gravel trucks at high speed down country lanes, could also be ranked here, though as in Henri-Georges Clouzot's film, where desperate men risk their lives with a truckload of nitroglycerin, "honest toil" isn't quite the right term. Unlike *Le Salaire de la Peur,* *Hell Drivers* allows noirish bleakness to be mitigated by daring and courage.

This tendency was to become increasingly apparent in Endfield's subsequent films, *Sea Fury* (1958) and *Jet Storm* (1959). By the time of his great success, *Zulu* (1964), the noirish shadows had disappeared, and heroism and fortitude were triumphant.

Down There

> I was still seeing England with a kind of surprise and
> delight at the contradictions which I saw.
>   —Joseph Losey

Joseph Losey arrived in England in November 1952. He had spent over a year in France and Italy, where he directed *Stranger on the Prowl* (1952), and he briefly returned to New York to confirm that there was no future for him in the United States if he refused to name names to HUAC. After a year spent editing scripts for the notoriously stingy Danziger brothers and Carl Foreman's television series *The Adventures of Aggie* (eventually broadcast in 1956–57), Losey directed his first British film, an adaptation of Maurice Moiseiwitsch's *The Sleeping Tiger.* The unlikely premise of the novel—a psychiatrist per-suades the courts that rather than jailing a seventeen-year-old hoodlum, they should entrust the boy to his care to see if kindness and psychoanalysis can cure him of his criminal tendencies—held little interest for Losey.[17] Nonethe-less, the other strand of the narrative, the affair between the psychiatrist's wife and the young man, fascinated him. In the novel, she is happily married to an attractive husband and is infatuated with a juvenile delinquent with brilliantined hair and an Oedipus complex. Losey and the blacklisted writer Harold Buchman made significant changes to the wife's character, making her an outsider trapped in a cold marriage to a much older man (Alexander Knox, looking more like her father than her husband).[18] Her hostility to the sneering, self-confident, and strikingly attractive youth she's forced to share her house with masks an understandable fascination.

Losey later confessed himself embarrassed by the film's obvious sym-bolism (it climaxes with a car crash through an Esso "Put a Tiger in Your Tank" poster). Compared to *The Prowler,* a more fully achieved film with a sophisticated script by Dalton Trumbo, *The Sleeping Tiger*'s limitations are apparent. But the parallels are striking. In both films a woman married to an older man is seduced by a discontented, manipulative, but physically more attractive outsider. In *The Prowler,* we briefly glimpse the husband as an old man in a dressing gown and hear him as a ghostly presence as he signs off on his late-night radio show. In *The Sleeping Tiger,* Knox's Clive Esmond is a more formidable character, with a judicious mixture of gravitas (which enables him to establish a therapeutic relationship with the young thug) and stubborn self-absorption (which blinds him to the danger that his wife might fall for the younger man's charms).

Dirk Bogarde, waiving his usual high fee after being impressed by Losey's direction of *The Prowler*, is well cast as the louche teenage hoodlum Frank Clements, despite being thirty-two when the film was made. He looks young and dangerous and has none of the puppyish charm of his counterpart in the novel, where the relationship is between a half-formed adolescent and an older woman who revels in his admiration for her. Here he is much more her match: bullying her maid, boastfully carrying out his criminal activities from the shelter of his adopted home, and insolently awaking the sleeping tiger in this emotionally frosty wife. Not surprisingly, she is drawn to the exciting and glamorous bohemian world Frank represents. He allows her a glimpse behind the curtains, an opportunity to explore the dark world beyond respectability's high walls, and it leads not only to infidelity but to death. In this respect, *The Sleeping Tiger* is as salutary a tale as *The Prowler* and light years away from the Moiseiwitsch novel, which ends with cuckolded husband and foolishly unfaithful wife glumly rearranging the furniture of their wrecked marriage.

The Sleeping Tiger was attributed to Victor Hanbury, a modest producer who had not directed a film since the "quota quickie" days of the 1930s.[19] With the problem of the blacklist sidestepped, the canny producers Nat Cohen and Stuart Levy offered Losey the chance to make a series of low-budget films at their small Merton Park studios in South London. *The Intimate Stranger/ Finger of Guilt* (1956) was shot on a smaller budget and a tighter schedule than *The Sleeping Tiger*, though the script, written in conjunction with another Hollywood exile, Howard Koch (the cowriter of *Casablanca*), neatly incorporated their own experience of paranoia and unjust accusation into an intriguing melodrama. In terms of budget, this might be a B film, but Losey was able to attract a talented cast and, at the start of his fruitful collaboration with Richard Macdonald as "design consultant," make judicious use of the studio setting to ensure high production values and convincing performances.

Reggie Wilson (Richard Basehart) is an American director who has been driven out of Hollywood after an affair with the studio boss's wife. He comes to England and, after making a series of B films, marries the British studio boss's daughter and persuades his father-in-law that he should be making more ambitious films.[20] His reputation is threatened when he receives letters from a woman he doesn't know complaining that he has betrayed her by breaking off their affair and marrying another woman to further his career. He makes a clean breast of things with his wife, and together they confront the letter writer. However, she appears so genuine and sincere that his wife begins to doubt Reggie, as does everybody else he tries to convince. He is taken off the big-budget film he was about to start shooting and is on the point of giving up in despair when the girl's impatience and greed expose a sordid conspiracy. The long takes, sometimes with what looks to be improvised dialogue; the performances from Basehart as the increasingly paranoid director and Mary Murphy as his seemingly sweet but wickedly manipulative accuser; the clearly felt significance of the events—false accusation, the nightmare of a canceled production, and the alienation of people hitherto regarded as friends—make it a key film in Losey's oeuvre rather than a routine assignment.

Losey stayed at Merton Park to make *Time without Pity* (1957) for Eros Films.[21] It is an intense and disturbing film, with Michael Redgrave and Leo McKern outbidding each other in melodramatic excess. Critics in Britain disliked the picture, and the Hyam brothers did little to promote it. But in France, when it was revived in 1960 along with the rerelease of *The Boy with Green Hair* and *The Big Night,* it was received with enthusiasm and helped establish Losey as a cult director. Barzman, reluctantly drawn back into collaboration with Losey, adapted his script from Emlyn Williams's *Someone Waiting,* a play about a seedy academic who attempts to wreak vengeance on a businessman who has framed his son for a murder he committed himself.[22] In the play, the boy has already been hanged; in the film, the father (Redgrave), now an alcoholic writer, has twenty-four hours to save his son. Thus the film becomes an increasingly frenzied race against time.

Time without Pity is a seminal film in the revitalization of film noir in new forms. Classic noir protagonists—from Robert Mitchum's Jeff Bailey in *Out of the Past* (1947) to Ralph Meeker's Mike Hammer in *Kiss Me Deadly* (1955)—are often confused and wrongheaded, yet they are never weak and fallible. Even Geremio and Harry Fabian achieve a sort of heroism in death. Redgrave's David Graham, driven on to self-sacrificing success only by his desperation to save a son he has continually let down, remains inadequate. Graham's weakness, however, enables him to recognize the flaws that underlie the murderer's boastful bullying. Losey infiltrates remarkable psychological

The Rich Are Beasts: Robert Stanford (Leo McKern) and victim in *Time without Pity* (1957).

insight into the melodramatic framework. Losey subsequently renounced overt symbolism—exemplified by the scheming secretary's alcoholic mother in her house full of clocks—after he moved to what he considered a more sophisticated style in his collaborations with Harold Pinter. Nevertheless, there is an excitement and intensity here that is lacking in the more abstruse films he made in the 1960s and after.

The motif of somebody denying that they have ever had a passionate relationship with someone, which is the central thread of *The Intimate Stranger,* is also the enigma at the heart of *Blind Date* (1959). In the novel, a slow murder mystery with fascinating postmortem details about Tardieu Spots and how to calculate the time of death, a young man goes to a flat to meet a rich, sophisticated woman with whom he has begun an affair. She fails to turn up; instead, the police call and discover the dead body of a woman. The estimated time of death indicates that he is the murderer. Barzman and another blacklisted writer, Millard Lampell, were called in at short notice to rewrite a script by Eric Ambler, which Losey disliked, and they radically reworked characters and plot. The fledgling reporter becomes Jan Van Rooyer, a young Dutch painter played by the German actor Hardy Kruger; his lover changes from a svelte Hampstead femme fatale to the French wife of a British diplomat who, like Glenda in *The Sleeping Tiger,* seems to have adapted too well to the British upper-middle-class vices of hypocrisy, snobbery, and sexual confusion. Flashbacks to her affair with Jan punctuate his police interrogation and enable us to see her as he does—a repressed, unhappy woman redeemable by love. When she is unmasked at the end, we share Jan's shock, indignation, and sadness that she has jettisoned her chance of happiness and allowed herself to be consumed by bitterness and evil.

Losey, interfering with the script much less than usual, concentrated his creativity on mise-en-scène and performance. The unlikely trio of Hardy Kruger, Micheline Presle, and Stanley Baker (in the first of his four roles for Losey) come together to further Losey's critique of English society. In contrasting scenes of dark and light, Baker's Inspector Morgan's interrogation

Micheline Presle's false Jacqueline, a femme fatale bound by upper-class inhibitions, in *Blind Date/Chance Meeting* (1959).

of Jan in Jacqueline's apartment and a dingy basement in Scotland Yard is relieved by flashbacks that show the developing love affair between Jan and the woman he thinks is Jacqueline. Their encounters—in the Bond Street art gallery where Jan works among art he despises, in the Tate where he awakens Jacqueline's appetite for true art, and in his light-filled studio where he teaches her to draw and makes love to her—are always in daylight and have an air of optimism and energy. An innocent protagonist whose life is thrown into confusion and his view of the world upturned, a femme fatale who attempts to lead him to destruction, and a visual style that presents the world as uncertain and threatening are leavened but hardly lightened by flashbacks to a happiness based on deceit and illusion.

Although the revivification of the blacklist ruined *Blind Date*'s chance of success in the United States, it was well received in Britain, marking a turn for Losey toward a closer integration with British society. The process continued with *The Criminal/The Concrete Jungle* (1960), where, for the first time, Losey turned for his script to a British writer, the young Liverpool-Welsh television playwright Alun Owen.[23] Through Stanley Baker's Soho contacts, he was also able to call on an Anglo-Italian racetrack racketeer, Albert Dimes, for background on the English underworld. Dimes himself had spent little, if any, time in jail, but with a calypso-singing West Indian and a jolly Australian psychopath among his convicts and a seriously disturbed Chief Warder, Losey was obviously not going for unembellished realism.[24] Nevertheless, Richard Macdonald's production design and Robert Krasker's ingenious cinematography makes the studio–re-created prison look real enough, and Losey was the first to show an English prison run by a hierarchy of inmates under the loose and by no means complete control of the warders. Prison is shown as a violent but rigorously organized parallel society, and criminals as an odd mixture of the vulnerable, the calculating, and the cheerfully brutal.

Relatively brief sequences outside the prison—the transition from spartan cell shared with two other men to a luxury flat complete with a sex kitten who "wants to sleep with the great John Bannion," and the quickly planned and executed racetrack robbery followed by even more rapid betrayal and return to prison—are breathtaking in their economy. The prison as photographed by Krasker is a gloomy and dangerous environment, yet it is the bright, cold outside world—where no one can be trusted, and generosity is answered by betrayal—that is really threatening. For the first time, Losey shows an affinity for English locations: the bare, grim streets around the prison, the Wimbledon Common bandstand where the robbery is planned, and the snowy fields where Bannion goes defiantly to meet his maker determined that his secrets die with him give the film an assurance and authenticity that mark it as one of his best.[25]

Fifty Shades of Noir

Dmytryk contributed two important but very different film noirs to British cinema.[26] *Obsession* has been grossly neglected, given how good it is. The ending is much less black than in the novel, but the film has a more resonant chill without the catharsis of a dead victim, a dead villain, and a dead dog. *Give Us This Day,* after its long slumber in the museum of lost films, has now received recognition. Peter Bondanella describes it as a "masterpiece" and praises its "tragic grandeur and complexity worthy of great drama"; Erica Sheen attempts to situate the film in a context that embraces Rossellini and Italian neorealism, and the defeat of the Italian American radical tradition in New York in the late 1940s.[27]

Night and the City is the peak of Dassin's noir achievements, though for a long time it was overshadowed by the more showily accessible *Rififi* (1955), one of the few foreign-language films to be dubbed into English and given a wide-circuit release in Britain. Informing and betrayal are a constant subtext in both films. The French elements in *Rififi*—its similarity to Jacques Becker's *Touchez pas au Grisbi* (1953) and the films of Jean-Pierre Melville—has led to it being classified as a French film. *Night and the City,* by contrast, has become a key component of American film noir, even suffering the indignity of a New York–set remake in 1992. The British elements have tended to be submerged as it has risen up the pantheon of American film noir, but Kersh's remarkable story and characters, the performances of the mainly British cast, particularly Googie Withers and Francis L. Sullivan, and the bomb-scarred London setting suggest that it should be regarded as a British film, a fitting companion for Carol Reed's *The Third Man* (1949), the Boulting brothers' *Brighton Rock* (1948), and Cavalcanti's *They Made Me a Fugitive.*

Endfield's *The Limping Man* has a circular dream structure that leads to a benign ending, but its bizarre logic, fragmentary narrative, and the plight of an innocent man involved in dangerous events over which he has no control mark it as noir. *Impulse,* too, although it casts off its dark shadows without much more than a salutary shrug, is a journey into the noirish nightmare. Endfield is adept at using noir style, albeit his outlook, even when struggling against persecution, is essentially sanguine.[28] Losey, permanently discontented, edgy, and ambitious, was less eager to make his peace with the world, and noir became a fitting expression for his unsunny view of the world. The bitter sensibility that comes from Losey's own struggle with dark forces finds its fullest expression in this group of modest British films. Despite the compromising nature of their production, they are as an effective vehicle for his concerns as the tricksy modernism of the Pinter collaborations and the sparse, bleak Bressonian minimalism of *Secret Ceremony* (1968) and *Mr. Klein* (1976).

What marks all these films is the way in which directorial panache enhances stories that could be tendentious, dull, or absurd in less capable hands. With the exception of Dassin's *Night and the City,* none of the films fits the mold of American film noir. Rather, they are noir-inflected melodramas, where the troubled view of the world held by their persecuted directors sends out ripples of disturbance in the calm waters of British cinema. However, if they bring American intensity and energy into a cinema often characterized by restraint and understatement, they also make good use of British locations, British art directors and cinematographers, and British actors. America's loss was Britain's gain.

Notes

1. Qtd. in David Caute, *Joseph Losey: A Revenge on Life* (London: Faber and Faber, 1994), 135.

2. Bernard Vorhaus, *Saved from Oblivion* (Lanham, Md.: Scarecrow Press, 2000), 122.

3. See Colin McArthur, *Underworld USA* (London: Secker and Warburg, 1972), 93–97, for a positive reassessment of Dassin's MGM contract films.

4. See Brian Neve, "*Inflation* (1943) and the Blacklist: The Disrupted Career of Cy Endfield," *Historical Journal of Radio, Film and Television* 30.4 (December 2010): 515–28.

5. The three films mentioned are *High Noon* (dir. Fred Zinnemann, 1952), *The Four-Poster* (dir. Irving Reis, 1952), and *The Wild One* (dir. Laslo Benedek, 1953). See Tony Rayns and Patrick Eason, "Interview with Joseph Losey," *Cinema* 3 (June 1969): 18.

6. Not much is known about Bronsten, who was responsible for two important British noirs, *They Made Me a Fugitive* and Lance Comfort's *Silent Dust* (1949), and the mill-owning saga *The Master of Bankdom* (1947). Dmytryk thought Bronsten had made his money as a "plastics engineer" during the war and had "gotten into films for the sole purpose of advancing his girlfriend's career." She was a Russian opera singer called Marushka, but she doesn't seem to appear in any of Bronsten's films. See Edward Dmytryk, *It's a Hell of a Life but Not a Bad Living: A Hollywood Memoir* (New York: Times Books, 1978), 112.

7. Charters and Caldicott first appeared in Alfred Hitchcock's *The Lady Vanishes* (1938).

8. John Berry should also be included, but he spent most of his exile in France, along with several others, including the Barzmans and Jules Dassin. See Rebecca Prime, "The Old Bogey: The Hollywood Blacklist in Europe," *Film History* 20.4 (2008): 474–86.

9. On Dassin and film noir, see Tom Ryall, "Jules Dassin," in *Film Noir: The Directors,* ed. Alain Silver and James Ursini (Pompton Plains, N.J.: Limelight Editions, 2012), 39–51.

10. *Film Industry* 7.54 (August 25, 1949): 9.

11. *The Sound of Fury* was nominated for a British Academy Award in 1951, but the ceremony was canceled because of a clash with the funeral of King George VI. The prize went to *La Ronde.* See Brian Neve, *The Many Lives of Cy Endfield* (Madison: University of Wisconsin Press, forthcoming).

12. Brian Neve, "An Interview with Cy Endfield," *Film Studies* 7 (Winter 2005): 119.

13. See Dave Mann, "Epicurean Disdain and the Rhetoric of Defiance: *Colonel March of Scotland Yard*," *Scope,* June 11, 2008, http://www.scope.nottingham.ac.uk/article.php?issue=11&id=1021&section=article&q=cult.

Weinstein's biggest success was *The Adventures of Robin Hood* (1955–58), which benefitted from intelligent, sophisticated, and mildly subversive scripts by blacklisted writers, including Howard Koch, Waldo Salt, Ring Lardner Jr., and Donald Ogden Stewart (all writing under aliases).

14. *The Limping Man* provided Leslie Philips with his first proper part. It set his persona for the next fifty years. Alan Wheatley was to reappear shortly as the Sherriff of Nottingham in *The Adventures of Robin Hood.*

15. In 1953, a television set was still a luxury enjoyed only by a tiny minority in Britain.

16. Raymond Durgnat, *A Mirror for England* (London: Faber and Faber, 1970), 125.

17. Frank Clements, the seventeen-year-old delinquent from a respectable middle-class home, looks to be inspired by Christopher Craig, the sixteen-year-old from a similar background committed to life imprisonment for shooting a policeman in 1952; his slightly older and seemingly innocent working-class accomplice Derek Bentley was hanged.

18. As Leo Davis, Harold Buchman had supplied the scripts for the three stories of Endfield's *Colonel March Investigates.* Alexis Smith, like Knox a Canadian, gives a subtle performance as the wife.

19. Endfield reached a similar agreement with the documentary maker Charles de la Tour (the father of the actors Frances and Andy de la Tour), who is credited with the direction of *The Limping Man* and *Impulse.*

20. The parallels with Losey's life are amusing but inexact. Jack Moss, whose wife, Louise, Losey met in 1942 and married in 1944, was Orson Welles's production manager rather than Losey's boss, and hitching up with the beautiful and popular Louise helped rather than hindered his career.

21. Eros was a distribution company set up by Phil and Sid Hyams, London-Jewish exhibitors who had been responsible for building several of London's biggest cinemas in the 1930s. Eros also backed most of Endfield's films prior to his deal with Rank over *Hell Drivers.*

22. Emlyn Williams is important to British film noir. He plays "Shortie" Matthews in the first important British noir, *They Drive by Night* (1938), as well as a memorably sinister villain in Jack Cardiff's *Beyond This Place* (1959). In his most famous play, *Night Must Fall* (filmed in 1937 by Richard Thorpe and 1964 by Karel Reisz), the murderer carries around the head of a previous victim in a hatbox.

23. *The Criminal* already had a script by Hammer's resident writer, Jimmy Sangster. Losey didn't like it and was able to commission a new one by Alun Owen, who would go on to write the script for *A Hard Day's Night* (1964).

24. Dimes was bound over for three years for his involvement in the affray that led to the murder of a Jewish nightclub doorman, "Little Hubby" Distelman, in 1941. His more recent involvement in "The Battle of Frith Street" of 1956 had resulted in acquittal. See Robert Murphy, *Smash and Grab* (London: Faber and Faber, 1993).

25. Losey told Michel Ciment that the budget was around sixty thousand pounds, or $180,000, though this seems unrealistically low. Ciment, *Conversations with Losey* (London: Methven, 1985), 186.

26. Dmytryk contributed another two noirish films to British cinema. *So Well Remembered* (1947), made as a collaboration between the Rank Organisation and RKO, is a small-town family saga, but it has an evil femme fatale (Martha Scott) who murders her father and causes the death of her son. It can also be seen as a companion piece to *Give Us This Day* (which Rank also backed) in its social-reform agenda. *The End of the Affair,* which Dmytryk returned to Britain to make in 1954, is an explicitly noirish-styled

adaptation of Graham Greene's gloomy love story, drawing heavily on atmospheric lighting and guilt-ridden voiceovers.

27. Peter Bondanella, *Hollywood Italians: Dagos, Palookas, Romeos, Wise Guys, and Sopranos* (New York: Continuum, 2004), 30; Erica Sheen, "Un-American: Dmytryk, Rossellini, and *Christ in Concrete,*" *Film Studies* 7 (Winter 2005): 32–42.

28. The exception among Endfield's films is *The Sound of Fury,* which, with its lynch-mob ending, is even more of a working-class tragedy than *Give Us This Day.*

9

A Little Larceny

Labor, Leisure, and Loyalty in the '50s Noir Heist Film

MARK OSTEEN

"None of these men are criminals in the usual sense; they've all got jobs, they all live seemingly normal, decent lives. But they got their problems, and they've all got a little larceny in 'em." With these words, Johnny Clay (Sterling Hayden) describes the crew he has assembled to pull off a racetrack robbery in Stanley Kubrick's *The Killing* (1956). A milquetoast cashier with a wayward wife, a cop in debt to a gangster, a lonely bookkeeper, a farmer, a chess-club manager, and a bartender married to an invalid: such ordinary men with "problems" populate the gangs in many 1950s heist noirs. These films' representation of criminals as regular, if quietly desperate, Joe Lunchboxes encourages viewers to root for them. Yet that same humanity—displayed in foibles such as boastfulness, an obsession with young girls, and racial prejudice—also dooms them. As *The Asphalt Jungle*'s (1950) mastermind Doc Riedenschneider (Sam Jaffe) puts it, he and the others "work for our vice."

But they do work. Heist films emphasize the craftsmanship of the participants, many of whom disguise themselves as blue-collar workers—sewer men, flower deliverers, truck drivers, hat-factory employees—as they execute their crimes. These are the same trades that these men might follow if they weren't criminals. Their alternative to work is . . . work—albeit for higher wages. It's not an accident that these elaborate robberies are referred to as "jobs." This fact also helps to explain a recurrent pattern in heist movies: the robberies go smoothly while the men are on the job, but rapidly unravel as soon they leave the work site.

The gangs even imitate specific aspects of the twentieth-century work world. For instance, many participants are selected for their specialized skills. Such a division of labor translates Fordist factory models to the underworld, and with the same goal: dividing tasks to minimize risk and to make the best use of resources.[1] Further, heist gangs' obsessive attention to timing exemplifies Taylorist principles of scientific management, which had by midcentury "come to dominate managerial theory and practice."[2] These tenets include separating execution from planning, replacing rule-of-thumb estimates with precise measurements, and using time and motion studies to produce optimum performance.[3] The gangs successfully use these principles, but the films also show how the same principles tend to erase workers' individuality and engender the types of alienation that Karl Marx so pungently described.[4] As critics of Taylorism observed, its specialization creates a class system that divides labor from management, brawn from brains.[5] The films thus not only mirror the noncinematic working world (which was filled with labor agitation, caused in part by rigidly applied Taylorist principles); they also reveal how organizations that aim to undermine lawful society end up imitating it.

Because each specialist uses his skills to advance the larger goal, a heist requires teamwork.[6] In that regard, the job is also a game. It is no surprise, then, that tropes of sport or gambling appear in every 1950s heist film: the title crime in *Armored Car Robbery* (1950) takes place outside Wrigley Field; *The Killing* is set at a racetrack; the heisters in *Kansas City Confidential* (1952) are identified by four torn playing cards; the college boys in *5 against the House* (1955) try to rob Harold's Casino, and so on. The heist itself—in this light, not a "job" but a "caper"—becomes a risky bet, a race against time. Crime is depicted as merely a higher-stakes version of everyone else's activities, a shortcut to the American dream of upward mobility through enterprise—albeit one that relies on deception. What does one wear when playing games or tricks? A uniform or costume. Hence the genre's recurrent masks and disguises, from the gas masks in *Criss Cross* (1949) to the students' Wild West outfits in *5 against the House,* suggest that the criminals are not working but playing. The fact that the robbers never get their loot thus derives both from the requirements of the Production Code (according to which crime must be punished) and from the suspicion that these robbers, though disguised as workers, are (according to the ethos of the heavily unionized 1950s) really no better than scabs. I propose that the representation of heist gangs as at once workers and players registers uncertainties about the range and limitations of labor and leisure in the 1950s, a time when Americans possessed more leisure time than ever before. In addition, because these criminal capers are usually exclusively male enterprises in which women are at best spectators or helpers, and more often interlopers or distractions, the films also dramatize evolving ideas about masculinity and its relation to work and play—themes also reflected in important 1950s novels and films such as *The Man in the Gray Flannel Suit* (novel: 1955; film: 1956) and *Patterns* (1956).

Nor is it an accident that the first true heist movies appeared in 1950, between the first and second round of House Un-American Activities Committee (HUAC) hearings. The films' secret schemes and multiple betrayals reflect the paranoia that pervaded Hollywood in these years, and their many informers and compromised cops embody the ubiquitous feeling (not only in Hollywood) that no one could be trusted, that anyone might turn out to be a Communist, or that a former associate might rat you out. As J. P. Telotte has observed, multiple double crosses are the "ultimate law" of these films.[7] In this way, 1950s heist films address the erosion of community both inside and outside of Hollywood. Collective action, they suggest, is possible only in the underworld, and even there it is fleeting and unreliable. The genre, in short, opens a window onto contemporary attitudes about labor, leisure, and loyalty through stories about elaborate criminal projects.

Precursors

The true heist picture, which places a meticulously planned, collectively executed robbery at its center, emerged as a significant film-noir subgenre after 1950. But two earlier films, both directed by Robert Siodmak, introduce its themes and tropes. The first noir heist is the Prentiss Hat Factory job engineered by Big Jim Colfax (Albert Dekker) in *The Killers* (1946). In one of this innovative film's eleven flashbacks—this one narrated by Charleston (Vince Barnett), the ex-cellmate of protagonist Ole "Swede" Anderson (Burt Lancaster)—we witness the initial meeting, where we learn of Swede's continuing infatuation with Colfax's girlfriend, Kitty Collins (Ava Gardner), see the mistrust among the gang members, and note the demurral of Charleston, who finds the plan too risky and advises Ole against participating.

Swede threatens Colfax after the boss treats Kitty roughly; Colfax stops him with, "The job comes first. . . . But afterwards we'll have business together." The sense that the heist is serious business is bolstered during the robbery sequence, which is enacted in the only flashback not narrated by a character. It is instead read from an old newspaper story by insurance investigator Jim Reardon's boss, Kenyon (Donald MacBride). His neutral narration functions as an aural equivalent of the gang members' stoic facelessness during the job: dressed as employees and carrying lunchboxes, the bandits are indistinguishable from the workers. Siodmak and cinematographer Woody Bredell present the heist in an ingeniously executed sequence shot. After a crane shot swoops down over the men entering the factory,

Which ones are the robbers? Gang leader Big Jim Colfax (Albert Dekker, far left) looks over his shoulder at Dum Dum (Jack Lambert, far right), as they enter the Prentiss Hat Factory in *The Killers* (1946).

the camera moves left as they enter and rob the payroll office, tracking them (without a cut) as they follow a truck through the gates (the camera moves to the truck before the robbers do) and escape after a gun battle. Both sequence and robbery are "performed . . . with detailed precision," as Kenyon's voiceover intones: the filmmakers mirror the criminals. As long as the men are inside the plant, the job goes beautifully. But afterward, led to believe by Kitty that he is being double-crossed, Swede steals the money from Colfax and company. Later, Swede is double-crossed by Kitty, who robs him and returns the money to Colfax—a double betrayal that ultimately leads to Swede's death.

Similar treacheries pervade the aptly titled *Criss Cross,* also starring Burt Lancaster, who, as Steve Thompson, is lured by the femme fatale Anna (Yvonne De Carlo) into participating in an armored-truck robbery. Much of the film unfolds in flashback as Steve, driving the truck to its rendezvous with the gang, traces the winding road of memory to the current moment. He recalls how the leader, Slim Dundee (Dan Duryea), recruited Finchley (Alan Napier), a chess player with a foreign accent and a drinking problem, to plan the robbery. It's Finchley's idea to have the robbers pose as sewer workers and to use an ice-cream truck as a decoy.

The phony sewer workers set off a bomb in a manhole; during the smoke-filled aftermath, the robbers don grotesque, troll-like gas masks. In the smoke it's difficult to tell the good guys from the bad—precisely Steve's problem. Torn between Anna and her shady cohorts and his old friend Pete, a police detective, he is the quintessential divided noir protagonist, and one of many noir characters who finds his legit job unsatisfying.[8] As the "inside man" during the heist, he is simultaneously working for and against his company. Hoping to protect "Pop," his aging fellow employee, Steve had insisted that there be no shooting, but that stipulation is quickly forgotten in the chaos. Once Pop is wounded, an angry Steve—who does not wear a mask—turns coat and begins to fight the robbers. Shot during the holdup, he awakens in the hospital, his left arm (the sinister side) in a cast, to learn that he has been hailed in the newspapers as a hero. He is—and he is not: he has criss-crossed himself. Double crosses proliferate after Steve eludes his would-be assassin and tracks Anna to her hideout, where she betrays him again before Slim kills them both.

Although both movies adumbrate later heist films' blurring of the lines between labor and crime, these early pictures are concerned more with individual guilt than with social analysis. Later heist movies concentrate more on group dynamics and collective action to expose the period's evolving definitions of labor, leisure, and loyalty. In fact, we can pinpoint the birth date of the true heist film: June 8, 1950.[9] That day marked the release of John Huston's *The Asphalt Jungle* and Richard Fleischer's *Armored Car Robbery*, two films that form the dexter and sinister arms of the genre.

Dexter and Sinister

In *The Asphalt Jungle,* corrupt lawyer Alonzo Emmerich (Louis Calhern) hears his wife confess her fears. "When I think about those awful people you come in contact with, downright criminals, I get scared," she tells him. "Oh, there's nothing so different about them," he suavely replies. "After all, crime is only a left-handed form of human endeavor." A dissolve superimposes his face over that of Dix Handley (Sterling Hayden), a "downright criminal" who, with Emmerich's backing, has helped to pull off a jewelry-store burglary. The wealthy lawyer and the hood are two of a kind, except that Dix is more honorable. If Emmerich's words strike us as a weak excuse for his involvement, they nevertheless explain the 1950s heist film's concentration on "seemingly normal, decent" men who turn to crime as an alternate commercial enterprise. Released in the wake of the initial HUAC hearings, Huston's film also dissects the ethics of secrecy and provides a template for the caper films that followed.

Like most noir heist gangs, Doc Riedenschneider's crew exemplifies the traits of a secret society, as brilliantly analyzed by the early twentieth-century sociologist Georg Simmel. Such groups, he writes, create a "second world alongside the manifest world"—a "city under the city," as the film has it.[10] The secret endows each member with "inner property" (331)—an enormous boon for lower- or working-class citizens who own little else of value. Yet a secret inevitably contains a "tension that is dissolved in the moment of its revelation" (333): the phenomenon created to prevent betrayal also produces its likelihood. Simmel further suggests that "the secret society emerges everywhere as the counterpart of despotism and police restriction" (347). Thus, as HUAC cracked down on Hollywood and the red scare swept through America, subversive groups and "un-American" ideas were pushed underground. Heist pictures emerged as a vehicle to dramatize alternative collective action and to question the status quo at a moment when direct challenges to capitalism and law and order had become taboo. Unfortunately, as Simmel observes, secret societies usually end up imitating the structures and values of the society they aim to repudiate (360). And so these gangs mirror the flaws of the legitimate work world: as they fall apart, their solidarity is supplanted by greed, loyalty by betrayal, teamwork by retribution.

Early in Huston's film, when Dix complains to his friend Gus (James Whitmore) that owing money to the slimy bookie, Cobby (Marc Lawrence), damages his "self-respect," Gus lends him a thousand dollars; a call to their friend Louie (Anthony Caruso) yields another thousand. Soon Dix is visited by Doll Conovan (Jean Hagen), who has lost her job and apartment; he agrees to put her up at his place, no strings attached. These "first-class men" (to use Taylor's term for reliable workers) are clearly actuated by humane values such as loyalty and generosity.[11] Yet they are also trapped: Gus in his seedy diner, Louie in his cramped apartment, Dix by his gambling addiction. They are thus ripe for the promise of quick money.

A million dollars in jewelry is waiting to be taken from Belletiere's; all Doc requires are the right men and some seed money. Because "men get greedy," he explains to Emmerich, the "helpers"—a "boxman" (safecracker), driver, and "hooligan"—will each receive a flat fee rather than a cut of the take. Reynold Humphries comments that this scene resembles a corporate board meeting "from which the workers and their representatives have been excluded": the proletariat are neither involved in the planning nor partake of the profits.[12] As mere "functional units" in what Fran Mason calls a "Fordist division of labor,"[13] the boxman (Louie), driver (Gus), and hooligan (Dix)—their labels indicate their low status—are alienated workers. But Dix is not really a hooligan; what drives him is not greed but a nostalgic dream of returning to Hickory Wood, his ancestral Kentucky farm, which nurtured the love of

Doc (Sam Jaffe) explains the heist scheme to (from left) Dix (Sterling Hayden), Louie (Anthony Caruso), and Gus (James Whitmore) in *The Asphalt Jungle* (1950). Single-source overhead lighting casts shadows on the men's faces and doubts on their prospects.

horses that has been warped into a gambling problem. Though self-deluded, Dix is generous and loyal; that's why Doll, who "never had a proper home," loves him.

As Doc outlines his painstakingly conceived plan to his crew, the single-source overhead lighting casts shadows on the men's faces and doubts on their success. Yet once they enter Belletiere's, Louie's skill and Doc's management put the jewels in their hands. Alas, a guard, alerted by nearby alarms, interrupts their departure. Dix punches him; the man's gun falls and shoots Louie in the gut. With this mishap, the scheme begins to crumble. In fact, as Simmel would predict, the gang's solidarity has started to unravel earlier, its loose thread being Emmerich, who plans to double-cross the others, grab the jewels, and disappear. His scheme fails when Doc and Dix fail to believe his cover story and kill his co-conspirator, the private eye Brannom, who wounds Dix in the struggle.[14] Things go further downhill from there: Emmerich kills himself, Louie dies from his wounds, and Cobby—played by Marc Lawrence, who testified before HUAC not long after the film was released—turns stool pigeon, leading to Gus's arrest. So much for solidarity.

That leaves only Dix and Doc, who has the jewels but no way to turn them into money. Doc blames greed for the plan's failure, but greed isn't *his* chief vice; it's a different deadly sin—lust. He ends up being nabbed because he can't tear his eyes away from a dancing teenaged girl. He worked for his vice, but his vice didn't pay. As for Dix, Police Commissioner Hardy (John McIntire) describes him as "a man without human feeling or human mercy." Yet we have already witnessed Dix's humanity, and his final, poignant moments further undercut Hardy's pronouncement. Despite not having "enough blood left in him to keep a chicken alive," he makes it back to Hickory Wood, only to collapse and die in a pasture, nuzzled by a mare and her colt. Like Louie and Gus, Dix is the victim of an urban jungle where those lacking education or resources inevitably end up as prey. But despite being disenfranchised and desperate, the film's criminals are more honorable than the jaded Emmerich or the film's corrupt cop, Lieutenant Ditrich, who have besmirched Dix's vision of an unspoiled America.

Looming in the background are the HUAC hearings. After the first round, in October 1947, Huston, along with several other Hollywood liberals, formed the Committee for the First Amendment (CFA) to defend the subpoenaed radicals, some of whom were later jailed as belonging to the Hollywood Ten. But the CFA rapidly collapsed after a wave of negative publicity, and in November, studio heads signed the Waldorf Statement, which instigated the blacklist.[15] *The Asphalt Jungle* thus records Huston's loss of faith in collective action. Like the Hollywood Left and the unions whose agitation precipitated the right-wing crackdown, the heist gang has power as a group, but mistrust and pressure from fearmongers destroy them. Art also adumbrates life: soon after the film's release, Hayden and Lawrence gave the names of ex-Communist associates to HUAC rather than sacrifice their careers.[16]

Whereas Huston's film empathizes with the gang, *Armored Car Robbery* favors the police, led by Lieutenant Cordell (Charles McGraw). Like many pseudo-documentary noirs, it highlights the all-encompassing power of law-enforcement technologies. Aware of that power, criminal mastermind Dave Purvis (chillingly enacted by William Talman) copies the cops: at the film's opening, he sends a fake distress call to determine how long the police take to arrive at Wrigley Field (then the home of Los Angeles' minor-league base-ball club), where he plans to rob an armored car of half a million dollars. As he holds his stopwatch, the radio announcer provides play-by-play. Purvis is smart, but he is also a cold-blooded psychopath, and his minions are an unimpressive lot: the hapless promoter Benny McBride (Douglas Fowley), whose burlesque dancer wife, Yvonne (Adele Jergens) is cuckolding him with Purvis; and Al Mapes (Steve Brodie) and Ace Foster (Gene Evans), career criminals. The odds for success don't look too swell, but Purvis, who boasts a clean record ("not even a parking ticket") and who pulled off a big heist in Chicago, improves them; fittingly, he'll get half of the loot.

Diagramming the plan on a window shade, Purvis explains that they must complete the job within three minutes—before the police have time to get there. During the heist, he and Benny dress in coveralls, and Purvis carries a lunchbox. In fact, Purvis plays many roles: if earlier he acted as a police dispatcher, now he serves as third-base coach, relaying wordless signs (a tug of the cap, a touch of the cheek) to the gang as Ace drives up in an old jalopy to divert the guards' attention. In the background the crowd roars, as if cheering on the robbery team. Taylorist principles seem to prevail as the men toss a smoke bomb, don gas masks, and Purvis clicks his stopwatch. But his management is flawed: the police arrive before they have finished; Cordell's partner is killed and Benny wounded.

Dave Purvis (William Talman) plays third-base coach, sending his team the sign to steal in *Armored Car Robbery* (1950).

Now Fleischer cuts back and forth between Purvis and Cordell to coun-
terpoint the latter's humanity with the former's inhumanity. Whereas Cordell
grieves for his partner, Purvis won't take Benny to a doctor—"we're wasting
time," he snarls. He does promise to hand Benny's share to Yvonne—which
only means that he'll get Benny's money as well as his wife. After the gang
successfully eludes a roadblock by passing as oil-field workers, Ace is shot
and captured. Purvis doesn't care: now there's more moolah for him, and
more "time to spend it." But even he has a weak spot: Yvonne. After the
police learn that the lipstick on Purvis's collar is "theatrical," Cordell and his
new partner, Ryan, "kill time" at her burlesque theater and collar Mapes,
who has shown up looking for his cut. Mapes quickly folds under interrogation—no solidarity here—but mostly seems dismayed that his labor will go
unremunerated, protesting, "I earned that dough fair and square!"

The cops' next play is to catch Yvonne "off base." How? Bug her room,
and "force her hand" by having Ryan masquerade as Mapes (this time, the
cop is in disguise). The ruse doesn't fool Purvis, but he can't elude the police,
who have his car bugged, so that when he forces Ryan to drive to the airport,
the cops are on his heels. An attempt to charter a private plane fails when
the pilot can't take off, after which the fleeing Purvis is run over by a plane,
the coveted loot left to blow across the tarmac.

With his icy demeanor and obsession with time, Purvis (as his name indicates) represents a perversion of the police's technological efficiency. At
once surly coach and soulless factory supervisor, Purvis stands for the sinister
sides of labor and leisure, particularly the worst traits of Taylorism, which,
critics claimed, fostered competition rather than cooperation.[17] He is the evil
counterpart of Cordell's righteous male authority. The only 1950s heist noir
to evince no sympathy for its bandits, *Armored Car Robbery* suggests that,
like ex-Communists, crooks will always betray each other when pressed. For
many of today's viewers, however, the police's Taylorist omniscience may
seem as chilling as Purvis's heartless automatism.

Games of Chance

At 9:58 A.M., a man in coveralls and cap parks his florist's van between a bank
and a flower shop. While he is inside, an armored truck parks in front of his van.
The florist's man picks up his flowers and drives off. Seconds later, four masked
men in coveralls and caps park in the vacated spot in an identical florist's van;
within fifteen seconds they have knocked out the guards, grabbed several bags
of money, and escaped with the take. By 10:02 it's all over: an efficient heist,
superbly planned by embittered ex-cop Tim Foster (Preston Foster), who, like
Dave Purvis, has spent days timing entrances and exits down to the second.

But why do the robbers leave their masks on after the job is finished? Because Foster has shrewdly determined that only he will know the others' identities. His control of knowledge gives him a "pat hand," a metaphor that is reinforced when he reveals how the members will recognize each other later: each receives a torn playing card—kings, all.[18] However, because we have seen the masked Foster interview each man in the same chair, looming over each like a punitive (foster) father, we share his knowledge of these miscreants: nervous, chain-smoking Pete Harris (Jack Elam); cop killer Boyd Kane (Neville Brand); weaselly lothario Tony Romano (Lee Van Cleef).[19]

Such tropes of gambling and sports pervade Phil Karlson's *Kansas City Confidential*. But there is a wild card: Joe Rolfe (John Payne), the sap who drove the real florist's van and is fingered for the crime before being released. Out of work and embittered, he tracks the crooks to El Borados, Mexico, where they will meet to split up the money.[20] Along the way he finds Harris at a dice table and forces himself into the scheme, hoping to use Harris as a "bird-dog to point the way." But after Harris is killed at the airport (while holding the King of Spades), hunting gives way to fishing, with Rolfe, now impersonating Harris, as both bait and angler. He makes his way to El Borados, where Romano and Kane are "on the hook" as they await their leader, unaware that one of the fishermen they've met is the mastermind. Knowing that the money they stole is marked and can't be spent, Foster plans to set up the others to be arrested, then pocket the three-hundred-thousand-dollar reward for apprehending them.

Like Steve Thompson, Rolfe is a divided character, a veteran and ex-con with a grudge and a violent streak, but inside a "normal, decent" guy who might be tamed by the right woman. That woman is Foster's daughter, Helen (Coleen Gray), a charming law student who unearths the good side of "Pete." Although she asserts to Rolfe that "people rarely look like what they are," she fails to penetrate his disguise. But Helen is what she seems, and her authentic goodness represents the humanity and rule of law that her father and Rolfe—the cop who has become a criminal and the ex-con playing investigator—have forgotten. She resurrects the gentle dad buried in Foster and, with a fortuitous entrance, saves Rolfe, after Romano and Kane determine that he isn't Harris (Kane served time with the real Pete).

In the film's climax, Foster, still incognito, drives the other three to his fishing boat in a panel truck that resembles their florist's van. The others aren't really planning to fish, but Foster is, and these men are the bait. Once on board, Rolfe proposes to Romano that they cut Kane out; Romano kills Kane; Romano and Foster are shot in the ensuing struggle. With his dying words, Foster absolves Rolfe and gives his blessing to Joe and Helen's union. True to his name, he has acted as Rolfe's foster father, in the process redeeming his "son" and himself.

5 against the House

Gaming is prominent in Phil Karlson's second heist film, *5 against the House*, in which four college students (and one girlfriend) scheme to rob Harold's Casino in Reno. Early in the film, the students—Al, a Korean War veteran (Guy Madison); Brick (Brian Keith), his buddy, who suffers from post-traumatic stress disorder; Ronnie (Kerwin Mathews), a brilliant dilettante; and jokester Roy (Alvy Moore)—visit Harold's. Although Ronnie notes the mirrors and observation posts (and witnesses a would-be robber being arrested), the visit plants a seed in his mind: to plan the "perfect crime."

These are students, not workers, so their motives are different from those of older heisters. Brick, who suffers from violent rages and feels the "edge-off-of-everything blues," is aimless and bored. The spoiled Ronnie just wants "to be first at something" and longs to test his manly intelligence with this "field experiment in psychology" (it's "the best idea since the bikini bathing suit!"). Al, acting as a big brother to Brick (who saved his life in Korea), isn't even aware that a heist is planned. For some reason, he thinks a return trip to Reno will solidify his relationship with lounge singer Kay (Kim Novak). On the drive to Reno, Brick divulges the plan to Al and at gunpoint forces him to comply. Ronnie had conceived the heist as simply a "stunt" and planned to give the money back. Brick's interference transforms it from an intellectual exercise to a battle.

Because it's Jamboree time in Reno, the students don ludicrous Wild West costumes and beards to blend with the similarly dressed crowd (the disguises also suggest that the scheme copies the Western movies that have shaped their ideas of valor). Among the more ingenious (and implausible) elements in their plan is to place a tape recorder within a mock money cart; it plays threatening prerecorded phrases to convince casino employee Eric Berg (William Conrad) that a very small man is hidden inside. But Ronnie neglected to prepare for the possibility that Eric wouldn't cooperate, and when Berg slides the cart downstairs instead of out the door to the getaway vehicle, the plan collapses. Brick flees to a parking garage, where Al (his costume now suitable for his role as self-appointed sheriff) persuades his friend to give himself up. This anticlimactic ending (no one gets hurt, and no one mentions jail) reinforces the sense that the heist is just a game, after all. If in other heist films the robbery is a job, here it resembles nothing so much as a class project.

Foster's secret society, as Simmel predicts, founders because the precautions designed to ensure loyalty also erode it: the cards and masks create kernels of tension that erupt in betrayal. This theme implicitly evokes the HUAC hearings, but they are alluded to more directly when Helen asks Rolfe about his "friends." He responds, "If you were my attorney, how would you advise me to answer?" Reply: "I'd tell you not to answer at all . . . it might incriminate you." Several witnesses before HUAC (whose hearings were going on at this time) similarly invoked the Fifth Amendment, thereby avoiding jail but getting themselves blacklisted. Karlson's film raises the same questions the hearings summoned: can a person (whether he be a fake gangster or an ex-Communist) change? Is informing on disreputable associates a duty or a betrayal? The film provides no answers but suggests that trust is necessary for both romantic and business success.

Men at Work

Johnny Clay believes that choosing "normal, decent" men for his audacious racetrack robbery will help them elude the police: who will suspect these ordinary Mikes and Georges?[21] But while the major participants in *The Killing*'s heist are amateurs at crime, pros perform key ancillary jobs: Nikki (Timothy Carey), a teeth-gritting hit man, is hired to shoot the favored horse and trigger a diversion; Maurice (Kola Kwariani), a tough chess-club manager, must start a fight to create a second distraction at the bar. As in *Asphalt*, these secondary players receive a flat fee rather than a cut of the take. The primary players must do something tougher: become like machines, for Clay has timed the plan down to the minute, so that each man must follow the template or ruin the scheme. *The Killing*'s unique structure, which recounts the same events from several different angles, in overlapping flashbacks, mirrors the clockwork precision of the robbery, which James Naremore describes as "almost military."[22] More to the point, Clay's orchestration (he carries his submachine gun in a guitar case) exemplifies several Taylorist principles: fragmenting jobs to minimize skill requirements; separating execution from planning; dividing direct labor (the amateurs) from indirect labor (the pros); conducting time and motion studies to ensure optimum performance; paying according to result.[23] Indeed, cashier George Peatty (Elisha Cook Jr.) and bartender Mike O'Reilly (Joe Sawyer) are performing their regular jobs at the racetrack as the heist proceeds, further eliding boundaries between labor and caper. However, their workplace is for most people a playground. Hence, more than other heist films, *The Killing* suggests that criminality is merely a "left-handed form" of leisure in which bettors hope to make a killing.

If each member is alike in having a "little larceny" in him, each one stoops to stealing for a different reason: the pathetic Peatty longs to placate his promiscuous wife, Sherry (Marie Windsor); Marvin Unger (Jay C. Flippen) wants to impress, and maybe possess, Johnny by furnishing seed money; O'Reilly hopes to help his ill spouse; cop Randy Kennan (Ted de Corsia) is under the gun for a gambling debt. Each man "works for [his] vice." Their human needs and flaws encourage us to root for these desperate characters and become complicit in their criminality, but they also make us feel superior to them and, perhaps, hope that they fail. As Maurice explains to Johnny (in an impenetrable accent), "The gangster and the artist are alike in the eyes of the masses. They're admired and hero-worshipped, but there is always present an underlying wish to see them destroyed at the height of their glory." Maurice's statement not only explains our ambivalence; it also underlines the sense that the film's characters court self-parody, that many of them (particularly Nikki and Val [Vince Edwards], Sherry's paramour, who plots to steal the take) have modeled themselves on movie gangsters—as implied by the row of "bad guy" shooting targets among which Clay outlines Nikki's job.

Johnny's part, however, is truly a performance, as indicated by his grotesque clown mask, a disguise that fits the heist genre's masquerade motif as well as the film's darkly comic tone and trope of clowning. Thus, for example, after the gang catches Sherry eavesdropping on their meeting, Kennan ("a funny kind of cop," according to Johnny) sarcastically advises George to "sing us a chorus from *Pagliacci*"—an opera about a clown. But the real joke is on the gang for, despite Johnny's punctilious planning (and the heist's incredible success), he makes stupid mistakes. One of them is trusting George even after they have caught Sherry snooping. Consequently, as the men wait for Johnny to arrive with the loot, Val and his associate intervene. Peatty starts a gunfight in which everyone but himself is killed. He then returns to his apartment to confront Sherry, and, as their parrot sardonically protests ("ain't fair, ain't fair!"), he shoots her. Dying, she describes the whole affair as "a bad joke without a punch line." But there is a punch line—and it's one of the most ironic moments in the entire noir canon (albeit borrowed from *Armored Car Robbery*). It follows from another of Johnny's foolish decisions: to buy a cheap suitcase with a broken lock to carry the loot. After airline employees refuse to let him carry the bag onboard (lesson: never let them check your luggage), he and his girlfriend, Fay (Coleen Gray), watch helplessly as an overladen baggage cart swerves to miss an errant poodle. The suitcase tumbles to the ground, scattering the ill-gotten gains across the runway. Ain't fair![24]

The Killing also introduces Kubrick's signature theme: that human creations, no matter how sophisticated, are as fallible as their creators and may overwhelm them.[25] He displays this theme via story, mise-en-scène, and set design. For example, although Clay moves from room to room while discussing his "normal, decent" men (the camera freely moving through walls), bars predominate elsewhere, suggesting the characters' entrapment and adumbrating their fate.[26] His scientific management fails because, as critics of Taylorism had begun pointing out at this time, men are not machines and resent being treated as mere factors of production.[27] They are, rather, impelled (or pursued) by human drives, addictions, and emotions. One of these is sex, and it's what dooms the caper: George wants Sherry, but she wants Val. In providing the insecure George with enormous "inner property," the heist plan sows the seeds of betrayal. Yet if the story's sardonic tone seems apolitical and quintessentially Kubrickian, the Sherry-George subplot also alludes to HUAC and the blacklist (still in effect in 1956). Unable to keep his mouth shut, George, like many ex-Communists, betrays his friends. On the one hand, Peatty represents those (like Hayden) who named friends and associates; on the other hand, he exemplifies the pervasive feeling that nobody can be trusted, that even a humble cashier (or cop) might be a suspicious character—or even a Red.

There is also an informer in Jules Dassin's 1955 heist film, *Rififi*. Ironically, he is played by Dassin himself, who had fled the United States to *avoid* testifying before HUAC! Dassin's role as Cesar, the crafty Milanese safecracker who, under duress, discloses the location of stolen jewels to a rival gang, places the Hollywood blacklist in the film's immediate background. *Rififi* was Dassin's first post-exile film; though set in France and cast with French actors, its criminal characters, gritty black-and-white cinematography, and betrayal-packed story bear the noir stamp.[28]

Rififi also follows the noir-heist template, while spending more time on the planning and robbery than do American heist pictures. We are introduced to the leader, Tony (Jean Servais), at a card game, but for the most part these robbers—Cesar, Jo (Carl Möhner, whose son, Tonio [Dominique Maurin], is Tony's godson), and Mario (Robert Manuel)—are definitely men at work. Their job: rob a safe full of jewels from Mappin and Webb, a heavily guarded store with an apartment on the floor above it. The crew carefully cases the place, timing its opening with a stopwatch and memorizing the location of every other building on the block. After Cesar checks out the store's alarm, the heisters buy an identical one to test its capabilities, learning how to muffle with fire-extinguisher foam the vibrations that set it off.

During the brilliantly directed heist sequence, the men exchange no words. We hear only the creaking of shoes, stray street sounds, and the muted blows of the hammer with which they remove the floorboards above the store.[29] Jo, who does most of the physical labor, is clad in casual work clothes; the others wear suits—fitting garments for a mastermind (Tony), expert craftsman (Cesar), and impresario (Mario). But the entire sequence is, as Philip Watts has commented, "an ode to work."[30] Hence, even Tony must laboriously descend on a rope to deploy the fire extinguisher on the alarm. Then Cesar drills holes in the safe to open it without explosives. These men may be as decent as Clay's crew (we witness Tony's fierce loyalty to Jo, for example), but they're not amateurs. As in *The Killing*, the filmmakers parallel their work with the criminals': not only does the director play a safecracker, but the film indicates that both jobs require professionals who plan carefully and marshal diverse skills and talents.

Everything goes beautifully while the men are on the job, but soon afterward their human weaknesses spoil things. Tony, who shockingly beats up his ex-girlfriend, Mado, early in the film, has a terrible temper and a penchant for revenge. Jo's family loyalties conflict with his criminal activities, and Cesar has an uncontrolled libido. Consequently, after the successful heist ("The biggest take since the Sabine women!" a newsboy shouts), Cesar can't resist giving an expensive ring to his girlfriend. The Grutters, rival gangsters who own L'Age d'Or nightclub, learn about the gift and torture Cesar until he divulges the jewels' location, which leads to the deaths of Mario and his girlfriend. When Tony learns what Cesar has done, he confronts the bound safecracker. "I really liked you, Macaroni," he admits, but "you know the rules." In this game, cheaters pay the ultimate penalty. Exiled because of the blacklist, Dassin plays the informer he refused to become in real life.[31]

Despite Cesar's disclosure, the Grutters don't find the jewels, so they kidnap Tonio, hoping to exchange him for the treasure. Tony tracks them to a construction site outside Paris, kills two Grutters, and rescues Tonio. But unaware that Tony has already found his son, Jo arrives at the site with a suitcase full of cash (a fence has paid them for the jewels) and is killed by Pierre. Returning to the site, Tony kills Pierre Grutter but is wounded himself and can barely remain conscious on the drive back to the city. Meanwhile, Tonio, wearing a cowboy outfit, stands on the car seat waving his toy gun around. From his point of view, the camera swirls and tilts until Tony passes out and wrecks the auto. Tony's thirst for revenge and Jo's family allegiances have finished what Cesar began. Moreover, the doubling of Tony and Tonio implies that, despite his dissipation and world-weary demeanor, the man is at heart a kid playing cowboys and Indians. The film's title, taken from a song performed at L'Age d'Or, implies as much. "Rififi" is "the lingo of the streetwise / the battle cry of real tough guys / . . . all it means is 'rough 'n' tumble.'" A word for rough sex or a rumble, "rififi" is what wayward lads do for fun. This film's robbers, then, are as much boys at play as men at work.

The Gold Rush

In a driving rain, a group of ponchoed men—the gray stockings over their faces making them appear ghostly—rob a train of three million dollars in gold bullion. Like the *Rififi* crew, the bandits in *Plunder Road* (1957) say nothing during the job (although we hear voiceovers giving us their thoughts). The heist is swift and efficient: the men's costumes seem to have turned them into the robots so prized by Taylorism. Indeed, their spectral appearance invokes the anonymity of modern money. That is, twentieth-century money has no material foundation but is pure sign, its value deriving from interpersonal trust and faith in the political system that ratifies it. These faceless men (whom we barely come to know in the course of the film) also epitomize the social exchanges that dematerialized money promotes. As Simmel speculates, modern money, with its compressibility, abstractness and "effect-at-a-distance," encourages an alienation that fosters secret societies (335). In contrast, gold is a vestige of an obsolete economic regime in which value was thought to inhere in the weight of metal. As Jean-Joseph Goux reminds us, money incorporates three aspects: it serves as a measure of value (its "archetypal" or "imaginary" function); functions as medium of exchange and circulation (a symbolic or token function); and comprises a physical store and means of payment (a real function).[32] This last function has waned as metallic money has been supplanted by paper, and now electronic, currency. These distinctions are more than theoretical; they play a major role in *Plunder Road,* for it is the very materiality (the "real" aspect) of the stolen gold that foils the men's carefully laid scheme.

The crew divides the gold into three trucks, aiming to drive it to Los Angeles. During the trips we are introduced to the bandits: in a tanker are mastermind Eddie Harris (Gene Raymond) and Frankie, a former race-car driver (Steven Ritch, who also wrote the screenplay); at the wheel of a moving van is Roly Adams (Stafford Repp); an ABC rental truck contains ex-stuntman Munson (Wayne Morris) and Skeets (Elisha Cook Jr.), a lifelong crook who plans to send his son to college and move to Rio with the dough. The men remain on the job for much of the film, but their work is also a game: a race against time for the robbers and an entertaining chase for the "normal, decent" folks who follow the story in the media. For example, when Skeets and Munson stop for gas, the attendant mentions the robbery and sadly notes that crooks today have no chance "with radio and all that science against them." Later, Eddie and Frankie pull into a diner, where a waitress and her customers discuss what they would do with that much money. It's clear that these law-abiding folks have "a little larceny" in them. As Maurice declared in *The Killing,* criminals are subject to both schadenfreude and admiration; part of that admiration derives from the belief that the police are too powerful—a perception that the film, with its constant radio reports and ubiquitous cops, dramatizes.

Roly is captured after he halts at a roadblock, where the troopers hear his radio tuned to police frequencies and assume he is a criminal. Munson and

Skeets stop at a weigh station, where their truck is determined to be 4,500 pounds overweight; the extra tonnage gives them away. The very materiality of the gold they have stolen—its "real" aspect—topples their scheme. Only Eddie and Frankie reach Los Angeles, where they carry out one of the most ingenious gambits in the heist genre. Given access to a foundry (Eddie's girlfriend works for the company), the men smelt down the bullion and transform it into a car bumper. After attaching it to their fancy Cadillac (chrome plating disguising the gold), they change clothes and drive toward the pier, where they'll board a ship to Europe. It's as if the men have *become* gold: Frankie exults that he "feels like a million," and their new attire—open shirts and casual jackets—suits their new identities as men of leisure, a different species from all those people who, Eddie sneers, "work for a living." But while they may be special, their car is not; it's just another auto on the freeway, all as identical as dollar bills, all caught in an L.A. traffic jam. The Caddy becomes special again only when it is rear-ended by a distracted driver, and the police discover the golden bumper. A panicked Frankie pulls a gun and gets killed; Eddie jumps from an overpass but falls beneath a car. He is now fully anchored to materiality. "Normal, decent" motorists stop and gawk, whether in celebration or lamentation we can't be sure. The freeway that promised to emancipate them is really a grave, just as the gold that symbolized their liberation ultimately traps them. Eddie's scientific management is no match for the police's superior manpower and technology.

Take Your Pick

No one squeals in *Plunder Road*. As the blacklist faded, the figure of the informer became less salient. Yet the blacklist plays a part in an even later heist film (one often called the last noir of the classic period), Robert Wise's 1959 *Odds against Tomorrow*. Although the crisp screenplay for this tale of three men trying to rob a bank is credited to the African American novelist John O. Killens, it was actually written by the blacklisted radical writer-director Abraham Polonsky.[33] Yet if betrayal is a principal theme in *Odds,* the film is less concerned with blacklisting than with blackness—and whiteness.

Again an embittered ex-cop (he "wouldn't talk" and got a year for contempt, like an "unfriendly" HUAC witness), this time one Dave Burke (Ed Begley) organizes the scheme: to rob a bank in small-town Melton. He recruits Earle Slater (Robert Ryan), an ex-con and veteran hoping to restore his lost masculinity. Not only does his wife, Lorry (Shelley Winters), support him; he seethes with rage and simmers with suppressed sexual energy. To visualize Slater's confinement, Wise frequently films him in doorways or at low angles so that his head seems to bump against the ceiling. One night when Lorry is out, a neighbor, Helen (Gloria Grahame), seduces Slater by asking him how it felt to kill someone. He admits that he found it pleasurable, that it made him feel free. Helen too finds murder exciting: she belongs to those "masses" who worship the criminal. Burke—practicing the empathetic, Mayoist management style that succeeded Taylorism—also seduces Slater by assuring him that this is only a "one-time job," just "one roll of the dice."

The second recruit, African American jazz musician Johnny Ingram (Harry Belafonte), seems Slater's opposite, as suggested in the opening sequences, in which Slater and Ingram encounter the same black children and elevator operator outside Burke's apartment. Whereas Slater is grim and surly, the dapper Ingram is friendly and outgoing. Ingram eventually signs on to the plan. But why would this man—not just a "normal, decent" guy but a suave, handsome singer—be interested in a risky robbery? We soon get our answer: although he has a flashy car and an adorable daughter, Ingram is a gambling addict who owes alimony to his ex-wife and $7,500 that he can't pay back to a mobster named Bacco. On an outing to the park with his daughter, Ingram spends the day dodging gangsters and calling about his bets while the little girl rides merry-go-round horses. Ingram, we see, is trapped on his own horse-driven merry-go-round. He too is angry, cursing out his ex-wife after he interrupts her PTA meeting with some white parents and, after Bacco gives him an ultimatum, getting drunk at the club and ruining Mae Barnes's performance of "All Men Are Evil." The recruits are two of a kind—desperate and resentful—and Burke is an equal-opportunity employer.[34]

Some of Ingram's anger is the understandable frustration of a black man in a racist society. That society is embodied in Slater, who balks when he learns that the other member of the gang is a "nigger" (he utters this word while casing the Melton bank, his face scored with shadows). Indeed, their entire plan is based on the alleged inability of white people to tell apart two dissimilar black men. Burke has learned that an African American counter-man, Charlie, brings sandwiches and coffee to the bank employees after hours on Fridays. Ingram will don cap and white jacket to masquerade as Charlie; once the guard opens the door, the thieves will dash in and steal the cash.

Burke has planned meticulously: he knows almost two hundred thousand dollars in untraceable cash is available every Friday, knows what time Charlie arrives, and knows where the police will be. But Slater and Ingram never trust each other: at the beginning of the job, Slater refuses to give the getaway car's keys to Ingram (who is supposed to drive) and instead hands them to Burke. So when the caper begins to go foul—they take too long in the bank, a cop stops to talk to a mailman and spots the masked men leaving—and Burke is shot, they can't escape. The dream of a big score forgotten, Slater and Ingram face off in a gun battle at an oil refinery that ends in a conflagration. Finding their charred bodies, a rescue worker asks, "Which is which?" Answer: "Take your pick." Slater's boiling racism is to blame, but so is Ingram's burning resentment. Though Ingram seems more normal and decent than the repellent Slater, the two are ultimately the same. Wise's message couldn't be more pointed: racism leads to what Langston Hughes predicted when he asked what happens to a dream deferred: "Does it dry up like a raisin in the sun? / Or fester like a sore—. . . or does it explode?"[35] Interracial collective action may be possible (we see it in Mrs. Ingram's PTA meeting), but only when it is built on a foundation of trust. *Odds* suggests that racism and red-baiting spring from the same sources, ones that Polonsky knew all too well: hatred and fear.

Although Taylorism was succeeded by more humane management styles, and the blacklist eventually ended (Dalton Trumbo's screenwriting credit for Kubrick's 1960 *Spartacus* being one of the killing blows), the heist film's insights endure: that secret societies engender bonds of loyalty that fray when a goal is accomplished; that collective endeavors—whether they be manufacturing, crime, athletics, or politics—require a suspension of the American ethos of individualism; that, given humans' seemingly irrepressible desire to compete rather than collaborate, collectivity is nearly impossible to sustain.

In blurring the lines between labor and leisure, heist gangs reflect a shift in norms and a profound ambivalence. On the one hand, they suggest that activities like gambling corrode the hallowed American belief that only hard work brings success: that real men don't play. Yet they also criticize management styles that dehumanize workers, and expose a powerful attraction to male-oriented collective leisure pastimes such as sports and gambling. The heist picture thus exposes seams in midcentury mores: why else do "normal, decent" people choose crime over work, root for criminals, or watch these movies? In an era that ostensibly prized law and order, the heist picture dramatizes a hidden desire to buck the system, to make a big score, to get something for nothing. In critiquing the mechanization of labor, the 1950s heist film reminds us that robbers, like workers, are human beings, and thereby pleads for a more humane balance between individuality and collectivity, work and play.

Notes

1. Fordism (named after its major proponent, Henry Ford) seeks to "achieve higher productivity by standardizing the output, using conveyor assembly lines, and breaking the work into small, deskilled tasks." Fordism "emphasizes minimization of costs instead of maximization of profit." "Fordism," BusinessDictionary.com, accessed August 21, 2012, http://www.businessdictionary.com/definition/Fordism.html.

2. Stephen P. Waring, *Taylorism Transformed: Scientific Management Theory since 1945* (Chapel Hill: University of North Carolina Press, 1991), 9. Taylor himself believed that his principles were "applicable to all kinds of human activities," which seem to include

crime. See Frederick W. Taylor, *The Principles of Scientific Management* (New York: Harper and Row, 1911), 7.

3. Taylorism "breaks every action, job, or task into small and simple segments which can be easily analyzed and taught." "Taylorism," BusinessDictionary.com, accessed August 21, 2012, http://www.businessdictionary.com/definition/Taylorism.html. As Edward Dimendberg notes, "[T]emporal exactitude is to the caper film what scientific management is to the assembly line." Edward Dimendberg, *Film Noir and the Spaces of Modernity* (Cambridge, Mass.: Harvard University Press, 2004), 200.

4. Karl Marx, "Economic and Philosophical Manuscripts of 1844," in *The Marx-Engels Reader,* ed. Robert Tucker, trans. Martin Milligan (New York: Norton, 1978), 72–77. Critiques of Taylorism became widespread by the middle of the twentieth century, many of them focusing on such mechanization.

5. Waring, *Taylorism Transformed,* 7.

6. Stuart Kaminsky points out that heist movies derive from stories of "communal quests requiring cooperation of men with special powers." Stuart Kaminsky, *American Film Genres* (New York: Dell, 1974), 101. The "special group" structure also grew from the platoon film that became popular during World War II. Like the heist film, the platoon film involves a set of characters charged with a mission in which specialists and eccentrics come together for group action.

7. J. P. Telotte, "Fatal Capers: Strategy and Enigma in *Film Noir,*" *Journal of Popular Film and Television* 23 (1996): 165.

8. See Jack Shadoian, *Dreams and Dead Ends: The American Gangster Film,* 2d ed. (New York: Oxford University Press, 2003), 309. Shadoian also provides a capsule portrait of Finchley (312).

9. These dates are given in Alain Silver and Elizabeth Ward, eds., *Film Noir: An Encyclopedic Reference to the American Style,* 3d ed. (Woodstock, N.Y.: Overlook Press, 1992), 13, 14.

10. Georg Simmel, *The Sociology of Georg Simmel,* ed. and trans. Kurt H. Wolff (Glencoe, Ill.: Free Press, 1950), 330. Subsequent references are cited by page number parenthetically in the text.

11. See Daniel A. Wren, *The Evolution of Management Thought,* 4th ed. (New York: John Wiley and Sons, 1994), 112.

12. Reynold Humphries, "The Politics of Crime and the Crime of Politics: Postwar Noir, the Liberal Consensus and the Hollywood Left," in *Film Noir Reader 4,* ed. Alain Silver and James Ursini (Pompton Plains, N.J.: Amadeus Press/Limelight Editions, 2004), 237.

13. Fran Mason, *American Gangster Cinema: From* Little Caesar *to* Pulp Fiction (London: Palgrave Macmillan, 2002), 99.

14. Here the story dramatizes what midcentury critics of Taylorism were saying: that it creates "conflicts between workers and managers" (Waring, *Taylorism Transformed,* 7).

15. The most thorough account of the hearings and aftermath remains Larry Ceplair and Steven Englund, *The Inquisition in Hollywood: Politics in the Film Community, 1930–1960* (Berkeley: University of California Press, 1983), 254–98.

16. Tormented by guilt, Hayden spent his later years apologizing and condemning the blacklist. See Ceplair and Englund, *Inquisition in Hollywood,* 364, 391; and Victor Navasky, *Naming Names* (New York: Viking Press, 1980), 129–30. In the latter, Hayden tersely summarizes the predicament of all the witnesses: "Cooperate and I'm a stool pigeon. Shut my mouth and I'm a pariah" (130). Lawrence told Lee Server that testifying was "like a

stab in the back. You're still breathing, but you . . . can't get the thing out of your back."
See Lee Server, "Marc Lawrence: The Last Gangster," in *The Big Book of Noir,* ed. Lee
Server, Ed Gorman, and Martin H. Greenberg (New York: Carroll and Graf, 1998), 53.

17. Waring, *Taylorism Transformed,* 25. Taylor stressed that his principles require and
promote "cooperation, not individualism," but they seldom worked that way in practice
(*Principles of Scientific Management,* 140).

18. Simmel cites an historical precedent for this gambit. The Omladina, a Czech secret
society, divided itself into cells called "thumbs" and "fingers"; each thumb would choose
fingers, who would then choose another thumb, and so on. "The first thumb knew all
the thumbs, but they did not know each other." Simmel, *Sociology of Georg Simmel,* 357.

19. This film has the distinction of bringing together, for the only time, these three
terrific character actors, each famous for portraying heavies. Karlson and cinematographer George Diskant heighten these characters' ugliness with frequent Eisensteinian
close-ups of their constantly sweating faces.

20. Rolfe fits Shadoian's description of Karlson's typical protagonists, who "stagger
dully about as life's punching bags, until they can't take it anymore and go haywire"
(Shadoian, *Dreams and Dead Ends,* 196).

21. James Howard, in the *Stanley Kubrick Companion* (London: Batsford 1999), 46–47,
speculates that Hayden was cast as Clay partly because of his performance in *The
Asphalt Jungle.*

22. James Naremore, *On Kubrick* (London: British Film Institute, 2007), 77. The
source novel, Lionel White's 1954 *Clean Break,* employs a similar structure. See Lionel
White, *The Killing [Clean Break]* (n.p.: Black Mask Books, 2008).

23. Clay's management style, however, is closer to that of George Elton Mayo's
"corporatists," who sought to imitate "orchestra conductors, samurai masters, parents,
teachers, and therapists," than to Taylor's scientist/dictators. Waring, *Taylorism Transformed,* 193.

24. In the source novel, Peatty tracks Clay to the airport and shoots him there. White,
The Killing, 173.

25. Viz: the madness of Hal, the supercomputer in *2001: A Space Odyssey,* or the
Ludovico treatment by which the government transforms Alex into a Pavlovian crea-
ture in *A Clockwork Orange,* or the Doomsday Machine that destroys humanity in *Dr.
Strangelove.* Now there's a punch line!

26. David Hughes, *The Complete Kubrick* (London: Virgin Publishing, 2000), 41–42.

27. Waring, *Taylorism Transformed,* 12, 7.

28. Dassin had directed several significant noirs in the United States, including the
prison melodrama *Brute Force* (1947), the quasi-neorealist procedural *The Naked City*
(1948), and the leftist trucking tale *Thieves' Highway* (1949). For a discussion of these
films in light of Dassin's politics, see my *Nightmare Alley: Film Noir and the American
Dream* (Baltimore: Johns Hopkins University Press, 2013), 225–28.

29. Philip Watts observes that the silence during the heist sequence invokes Dassin's
own personal history, which involved "silences produced when governments become
intent upon compelling citizens . . . to speak, to reveal their secrets." See Philip Watts,
"*Rififi* and the Politics of Silence," *L'Esprit Créateur* 51.3 (2011): 47.

30. Ibid., 49.

31. In an interview on the European DVD of *Rififi,* Dassin states that during Cesar's
death scene he was thinking of "friends who in a bad moment during the McCarthy era
betrayed other friends" (qtd. in ibid., 54).

32. Jean-Joseph Goux, *Symbolic Economies: After Marx and Freud*, trans. Jennifer Curtiss Gage (Ithaca, N.Y.: Cornell University Press, 1990), 47–48; Jean-Joseph Goux, "Ideality, Symbolicity, and Reality in Postmodern Capitalism," in *Postmodernism, Economics, and Knowledge*, ed. Stephen Cullenberg, Jack Amariglio, and David F. Ruccio (London: Routledge, 2001), 166–67.

33. Polonsky had written the terrific boxing noir *Body and Soul* and directed the poetic gangland tale *Force of Evil* in the 1940s before HUAC swooped in.

34. Belafonte, who produced the film for his own company, HarBel, insisted that Ingram be depicted as a flawed character. In the source novel, Ingram is not a musician but a professional gambler. See William P. McGiven, *Odds against Tomorrow* (1957; reprint, London: Xanadu Press, 1991). Much of the novel's action takes place after the robbery, as Slater and Ingram, holed up in a farmhouse, eventually achieve a rapprochement. For more on the musical aspects of the film, see Osteen, *Nightmare Alley*, 172–74.

35. Langston Hughes, "Harlem [2]," *Montage of a Dream Deferred*, in *The Collected Poems of Langston Hughes*, ed. Arnold Rampersad (New York: Vintage, 1994), 426.

10

Periodizing Classic Noir

From Stranger on the Third Floor to the "Thrillers of Tomorrow"

ROBERT MIKLITSCH

> Don't know much about history,
> [. . .]
> Don't know much about the French I took.
> —Sam Cooke, "Wonderful World"

The question "What is film noir?" has haunted critics, if not fans, almost from the moment the "genre" became an object of study. There are numerous ways to approach this issue or tissue (genre, formal elements, thematic motifs, production cycles, etc.), but one popular angle has been historical, as in: When did the classic or "historical" period of American film noir begin and end?[1]

The problem, of course, with this periodic approach is that it begs the question, since to pinpoint the advent and end of classic noir presupposes some determinate knowledge about its essence or identity—about what it is. Although it's at this point that many viewers throw up their hands and invoke Justice Potter Stewart's famous opinion about hardcore pornography ("I know it when I see it"), in what follows I use three recent studies—Jennifer Fay and Justus Nieland's *Film Noir: Hard-Boiled Modernity and the Cultures of Globalization* (2010), Jonathan Auerbach's *Dark Borders: Film Noir and American Citizenship* (2011), and Shannon Clute and Richard L. Edwards's *The Maltese Touch of Evil: Film Noir and Potential Criticism* (2011)—as prompts to reflect upon the periodization of classic American noir. I pay special attention to the so-called demise of the classical era by way of Robert Wise's *Odds against Tomorrow* (1959), an unusually rich text that points both forward and backward: backward to 1940s postwar "social problem" noirs such as *Crossfire* (1947) and forward, as a "thriller of tomorrow," to the 1960s neo-noir and beyond.[2]

Alpha: A Panorama of (Un-) American Film Noir, 1941–58

"Toward a Definition of Film Noir," chapter 2 of Raymond Borde and Étienne Chaumeton's *A Panorama of American Film Noir, 1941–1953*, begins: "Film noir is *for us*: that is to say, for Western and American audiences of the 1950s. It responds to a certain kind of emotional resonance as singular in time as it is in space."[3] In the introduction to their study, Borde and Chaumeton signal their debt to Nino Frank's pioneering review "Un Noveau genre 'policier'" ("Nino Frank, one of the first to speak of 'film noir'"[4]) as well as their difference from him, noting that Frank's criticism "lacked, it has to be said, the necessary distance."[5]

While it's unclear whether this distance is a function of time or perspective, Borde and Chaumeton's 1979 "postface" commences by memorializing the death of classic noir and, in the process, endorsing their own periodization of the genre: "Nineteen-fifty-five. An era draws to a close. Film noir has fulfilled its role, which was to create a particular sense of malaise and to transmit a social critique of the United States."[6] In addition to ascribing to the genre a specific affect and political intent that may or may not be true, this characterization possesses an odd teleological ring, as if Film Noir were a character with a classic Hollywood arc. From whence, one wonders, does this characterization come?

To answer this question, it's useful to return to what Borde and Chaumeton consider the "first great work," *The Maltese Falcon.*[7] Although John Huston's film was released in the United States in 1941 at the beginning of World War II, it was not screened in Paris until the summer of 1946, when France was emerging from *les années noires*—"the dark years of the occupation."[8] Given the bleak postwar climate, it's no surprise that critics, who were part of a new, frequently left "film culture of ciné clubs, cinémathéques, and weekly and monthly film journals" that encouraged "sophisticated reflection and debate,"[9] enthusiastically responded to American films emblazoned with "ambiguity" and "contradiction," "ambivalence" and "equivocation."[10]

This sympathetic or "progressive" view of film noir, which reversed the negative valence of the term that had circulated in the right-wing "politicized cultural journalism" of the *avant-guerre* or prewar Paris,[11] is not, however, the whole story. Glossing the opening of Borde and Chaumeton's "Toward a Definition of Film Noir" ("Film noir is *for us*"), Marc Vernet argues that the "notion of film noir, for them, was meaningful only for French spectators cut off from the American cinema during the war years and discovered during the summer of 1946, under the impetus of the Blum-Byrnes accords."[12] Since these accords "reopened the French market to American cinema," film noir should be placed, according to Vernet, "under the sign of the American invasion."[13]

You do not have to be a literary detective to sniff out the ambiguity of the last loaded locution. The initial French reception of film noir was itself predicated on a paradoxical structure of feeling: "On the one hand, [the United States] permitted victory in the struggle against Nazism and offers the image of a people whose standard of living is sharply superior to that of the French, who until at least 1955 were caught in an economy of scarcity inherited from the war. . . . [O]n the other hand, the United States is an imperialist menace that threatens to impose upon France values and a culture that are not its own."[14] The second, anti-imperialist formation captures the French apprehension about what would later be called "marshallization" or "coca-colonization."[15] For example, Henri-François Rey titled his 1948 review of the "captive" cinema of *Double Indemnity* (1944), *The Woman in the Window* (1945), and *Scarlet Street* (1945) "Hollywood Makes Myths Like Ford Makes Cars."[16] (Rey's review appeared in *L'Écran français,* the same Communist journal that published Frank's "A New Genre of 'Police Film.'") And Louis Aragon, lamenting the temporary substitution of a Ford automobile for a sculpture that paid homage to Victor Hugo, opined, "The Yankee, more arrogant than the Nazi iconoclast, substitutes the machine for the poet, Coca-Cola for poetry."[17]

Rey's and Aragon's perspective is reflected in Jean-Pierre Chartier's "The Americans Are Making Dark Films Too," which, like Frank's review, appeared in the fall of 1946 but is conspicuously absent from Borde and Chaumeton's study. (Chartier's review was published in *Revue du cinéma,* which Jean-George Auriol had relaunched after the war in order to "combat the nationalist praise heaped on the *cinéma de qualité*" associated with René Clair and Marcel Carné.[18]) About Chartier's disenchanted response to American "dark films," Fay and Nieland write, "Where Frank finds in film noir a cynical vitality upon which French intellectuals might improve, one senses in Chartier's review that the 'murky, dreamlike visual style' of noir . . . augurs a new genre of 'fatal, inner evil' that Paris might do well to repel."[19] A moralist and humanist, Chartier was deeply pessimistic about the flagrant "pessimism and disgust for humanity" on display in *Double Indemnity* and *Murder, My Sweet* (1944).[20] Unlike the "French school of film noir" represented by Carné's *Le Quai des brumes* (1938) and *Hôtel du Nord* (1938), which are brightened by "hints of revolt" and where "implicit social reform opens the door to hope,"[21] American noir, for Chartier, was a dead end or blind alley.

Cut to 1955 and Robert Aldrich's *Kiss Me Deadly,* which Borde and Chaumeton call the "flip side" of the inaugural film of the noir series, *The Maltese Falcon*: "Between 1941 and 1955, between the eve of the war and the advent of the consumer society, the tone has changed."[22] Although Borde and Chaumeton do not establish a causal relation between the *société de consummation* and the new "despairing" tone of *Kiss Me Deadly,*[23] there appears to be a not-so-subterranean connection between the two events. One way to understand this tonal change is to note, as Vernet does, that by 1955 the French had recovered from the postwar "economy of scarcity" and entered the "age of affluence." So, commenting on the role of modern art in *Kiss Me Deadly,* personified by the mysterious art collector, Mr. Mist of the Modern Gallery of Art (Mist, alluding to the Great Whatsit, tells Velda [Maxine Cooper], there's "new art in the world"), Jonathan Auerbach avers that modernism in Aldrich's film has "become commodified into a series of hollow gestures—mere affectation drained of any affect beyond fear."[24] Accordingly, while the private investigators played by Humphrey Bogart in *The Maltese Falcon* and Robert Mitchum in *Out of the Past* (1947) are undeniably cool, Mike Hammer's coolness as performed by Ralph Meeker is "consistently

Thrills + Suspense = Box Office: *Variety* ad for the original release of *Kiss Me Deadly* (1955).

linked throughout the movie to commodities and consumerism."[25] With his Jag roadster ("Va-va-voom!") and swank midcentury apartment complete with TV, cocktail stand, and reel-to-reel tape recorder/answering machine, Hammer is the fifties "dick" as playboy of the Western world.

There is, however, a world of difference between Hammer and the film's take on his prickly, What's-in-it-for-me? character. "Aldrich does not hide his contempt for his film hero," Roger Tailleur noticed in *Positif* in May 1956.[26] Although censorship in the form of the Production Code Administration is no doubt partly responsible for this difference, the director Aldrich and the screenwriter A. I. Bezzerides were able to transmute the lead of Mickey Spillane's prose, what Richard Maltby calls "commodified trash,"[27] into gold. In "Evolution of the Thriller," which appeared in the Christmas 1955 edition of *Cahiers du cinéma*, Claude Chabrol was among the first to advance the latter argument, writing that the filmmakers had taken "threadbare and lackluster fabric and splendidly rewoven it into rich patterns of the most enigmatic arabesques."[28]

Together with François Truffaut, who considered *Kiss Me Deadly* the "most original American film since *The Lady from Shanghai* [1948]," and Jacques Rivette, who heralded Aldrich as "evidence of the arrival of the auteur in Hollywood," Chabrol was instrumental in the canonization of *Kiss Me Deadly.*[29] The transactional nature of this process is epitomized by Aldrich's own reappropriation of Borde and Chaumeton's "original" appropriation of American film noir. I'm referring to the now-famous photograph of the sun-glassed Aldrich on the set of *Attack!* (1956), holding a copy of *A Panorama of American Film Noir.* Although this photo may not be a "smoking gun," it points up a series of complex border crossings that has discursively constituted the genre since its inception.[30]

Like Fay and Nieland, who advocate for a dialectical understanding of "noir's ambiguous modernity," Auerbach is alert to the "affirmative" aspect of late modernity manifest in *Kiss Me Deadly.*[31] The key here is the "specific sense of malaise" that Borde and Chaumeton seize on in their study and allude to in their 1979 valedictory remarks on the "vocation" of classic noir.[32] This sense or sensibility—what Auerbach calls the "uncanny in the un-American"[33]—is the verso of American-style cosmopolitanism and globalization that Fay and Nieland trace in their book, disclosing a central "affective dimension of the Cold War": the anxiety and insecurity, alienation and resentment, about "who belongs in the United States and who does not."[34]

In *Kiss Me Deadly,* this contested issue has mutated from the hysteria and paranoia about an especially "unhomely," because foreign and domestic, enemy—"Reds under the beds"—to a more generalized, free-floating fear: the Great Whatsit. "Manhattan Project. Los Alamos. Trinity." This sublime object of desire is never completely decrypted in the course of *Kiss Me Deadly* (it simply blows up, like an atomic bomb, in the characters' and our faces at the end), but it's a perfect metaphor for the genre. It's also a perfect example of what Clute and Edwards refer to as auto-exegesis, the way in which film noirs—"through calculated intertextual borrowings and self-conscious humor"—"read themselves."[35]

The title of Clute and Edwards's study, *The Maltese Touch of Evil*, raises provocative questions about periodization and approach as well as genre and audience. In fact, the title, according to the authors, is intended as a "provocation," a "challenge to existing orthodoxies of noir historiography" and an instance of the "recombinant logic" of film noir.[36] With its mashup of *The Maltese Falcon* and *Touch of Evil* (1958), *The Maltese Touch of Evil* not only hints that there's no "clean beginning or end" to the history of film noir but that the genre is not so much a canon or corpus as an exquisite cadaver.[37]

While Clute and Edwards's preferred methodology, Oulipianism, is decidedly antisurrealist, the fact that it derives from a "collegial group of writers and mathematicians associated with the Collège de 'Pataphysique'" is yet another example of the French connection that's so central to the discursive history of American film noir. Indeed, inasmuch as the authors' approach is based on their podcast, *Out of the Past: Investigating Film Noir,* the Oulipian project outlined in *The Maltese Touch of Evil* testifies to the potential of new interactive media: "In the age of the World Wide Web, this *ouvroir* ['workshop'] has literally stitched together a global noir community—one that seems to have bridged the academic/fan divide."[38]

Not so incidentally, *The Maltese Touch of Evil* also indexes a dramatic shift in the periodization of the genre post Borde and Chaumeton. To wit, when did *Touch of Evil* displace *Kiss Me Deadly* as the end point, however "dirty," of the classical era? One source—a usual suspect, this—is Paul Schrader's "Notes on Film Noir" (1972), in which the author, having conceded that classic noir comprises an "extremely unwieldy period," proposes that it stretches "at its outer limits from *The Maltese Falcon* to *Touch of Evil*."[39] Later in the same essay, Schrader subdivides the genre into "three broad phases"—the wartime period (1941–46), the postwar realistic interlude (1945–49), and the final phase of "psychotic action and suicidal impulse" (1949–53)—before designating *Kiss Me Deadly* as the "masterpiece" of classic noir and *Touch of Evil* as its "epitaph."[40]

Schrader would appear to be adverting to Borde and Chaumeton's designation of *The Maltese Falcon* as *the* inaugural film noir. At the same time, the discrepancy between Schrader's demarcation of the end of the final phase of film noir in 1953 and its epitaph in 1958 betrays a certain ambivalence on his part, as if he was torn between Borde and Chaumeton's periodization of noir in *Panorama du film noir américain* (the original version of which he cites at the end of his essay) and his own recognition of the French New Wave, which, with a film like Godard's *Breathless* (1959) and its gestural invocation of Bogie, signifies a new, postclassical era.

What is clear for Schrader is that, by the "middle fifties," catalyzed by television and suburbanization, McCarthyism and color photography, a "new style of crime film had become popular": "[T]he criminal put on a grey-flannel suit, and the foot-sore cop was replaced by the 'mobile unit' careening down the expressway. [Think criminal syndicates à la Murder Inc. and *Highway Patrol* with Broderick Crawford.] Any attempt at social criticism had to be cloaked in ludicrous affirmations of the American way of life."[41] For Schrader, the transition from *film gris* to the spanking new, populist school of crime is exemplified by Sam Fuller's *Pickup on South Street* (1953), in which the "black look" of the waterfront scenes devolves to the anti-Red action of the climactic subway sequence.

Schrader is wrong, I think, about the politics and aesthetics of *Pickup on South Street*,[42] but his staggered history of the demise of classic noir (1953, 1955, 1958) suggests that the genre, like radioactivity, has a definite half-life, a "nuclear" conceit that has real pertinence in the context of the "death" of the genre. In *Pickup on South Street*, the apparently un-American protagonist Skip McCoy (played to snarling perfection by Richard Widmark) has snatched some classified microfilm from the purse of an unwitting Commie courier named Candy (the underrated Jean Peters). After Skip shows up at police headquarters, Zara, the "big thumb" Fed who was tailing a "top Red agent" when Skip "broke up the ball game," barks, "That girl was carrying TNT, and it's gonna blow up right in your face." Skip protests he's "just a guy with his hands in his pockets," at which point a desperate Zara tries to appeal to his patriotic instincts: "If you refuse to cooperate, you'll be as guilty as the traitors that gave Stalin the A-bomb."

The apocalyptic dénouement of *Kiss Me Deadly* detonates the atomic subtext of *Pickup on South Street*. In the addendum to his 1975 essay on *Kiss Me Deadly*, "Evidence of a Style," Alain Silver rehearses the critical debate about the "mushroom cloud-over-Malibu" conclusion of Aldrich's film, in particular scenes 305 and 307, which were missing from earlier sixteen-millimeter prints and VHS versions of the film. Here, in the form of the screenplay, is the evidence:

305 BEACH—VELDA AND MIKE
Velda helps Mike and they run through the darkness which is stabbed by sharp flickers of light. Now, as they COME CLOSER TO CAMERA, there is a tremendous explosion.
Light gushes fiercely upon them[,] and they stop, turn.

306 ON BEACH COTTAGE

It is a boiling ball of fire.

307 ON BEACH—VELDA AND MIKE

As he holds her, to protect her from the sight[,] debris from the shattered house falls hissing into the sea behind them.[43]

In an interview, Aldrich insisted that he had "never seen a print without, repeat, without Hammer and Velda stumbling in the surf. That's the way it was shot, that's the way it was released."[44]

The original, "Let's go fission" conclusion of *Kiss Me Deadly* appears made to order as the bangup end of classic noir, but it's worth remembering—to reiterate one of the motifs of Aldrich's film (see Christina's [Cloris Leachman] dying invocation of Christina Rossetti's "Remember")—that just as "*Kiss Me Deadly* concludes with an explosion, *Touch of Evil* famously begins with one."[45] Unsurprisingly, the explosive opening of Welles's film, which features a spectacular three-minute-and-twenty-second mobile crane shot, has been read as a metacommentary on the previous history of film noir. This is "noireme 007" in *The Maltese Touch of Evil*: "It does not seem too much of a stretch to argue that [the opening shot] is intended to blow up the conventions of noir filmmaking, and that this film is often considered the last film of the classical period because it is so self-conscious . . . that it ultimately explodes any possibility from this point forward of making a[n] un-self-conscious noir film."[46] In the Oulipian spirit of *The Maltese Touch of Evil,* would it be too much of a stretch to propose that the noiremes that constitute the body of Clute and Edwards's book are so many "bits" of debris from the explosion generated by *Touch of Evil*? (I can't resist adding that the number "007" echoes the globally popular James Bond series, the early films of which, starring Sean Connery, have been adduced—by, inter alia, Borde and Chaumeton—as evidence of the end of classic noir.)[47]

The accent on filmmaking in Clute and Edwards's exegesis of *Touch of Evil* is a forceful reminder of the vagaries of postproduction and historical spectatorship. Just as the finale of *Kiss Me Deadly* has been the subject of extensive commentary, so too has the beginning of Welles's last Hollywood picture show. As with Welles's *The Lady from Shanghai, Touch of Evil* was taken out of the director's hands and reedited by the studio suits: Universal not only put the credits over the opening sequence but scored it with Henry Mancini's cool jazz/Afro-Cuban theme.[48] Later, in 1998, a team supervised by the film/sound editor Walter Murch restored *Touch of Evil* on the basis of Welles's famous 1957 fifty-eight-page memo.[49] Still, it's obvious from the previous two studio versions that the opening sequence, concluding as it does with a kiss and a bang, is a *coup de maître*: "The famous tracking shot at the beginning of the film ends with a kiss . . . between Vargas [Charlton Heston] and his wife and the simultaneous explosion of Linnekar's automobile, which starts the film's central investigation."[50]

While a similar dynamic between violence and sexuality informs *Kiss Me Deadly* (see, for instance, the scene where Velda says to Mike as they're standing in front of the picture window of his apartment, "Stay away from the window, somebody might blow you a kiss"), *Touch of Evil* represents a substantial departure from Aldrich's film. Whereas *Kiss Me Deadly* is set in Los Angeles (Westwood, Bunker Hill, Beverly Hills), *Touch of Evil* is set in the fictional town of Los Robles and the adjacent borderlands. (The real locations were two California locales—Venice for Los Robles, and Palmdale for the Bates-like motel.) In his hallucinatory tour of this *frontera*, William Nericcio concludes that *Touch of Evil* is a "true border text" and, in its baroque exploration of the figure of *el mestizo* or "half-breed," a "quintessential example of Tex(t)-Mex."[51] In other words, *Touch of Evil* signifies "not so much the end of film noir as . . . the beginning of a new kind of border film."[52]

"Terror Lurks in Every Shadow": Mexican lobby card for *Touch of Evil* (1958), with insert photo of Miguel "Mike" Vargas (Charlton Heston) after his wife Suzy (Janet Leigh), pictured upper right, has been terrorized in their "honeymoon hotel." Note the figure of the bull ("Los Robles"), which is associated in the film with Hank Quinlan (Orson Welles), who dominates the lower right quadrant of the card.

In fact, *Touch of Evil* is coterminous for Nericcio with the rise of film theory as well as a privileged site for Chicano cultural studies. The critical locus classicus is Stephen Heath's monumental reading of *Touch of Evil*, "Film and System," which appeared in *Screen* in 1975.[53] Although Heath's reading has become something of a lost text, if recent noir-oriented readings of Welles's film are any indication,[54] "Film and System" references, like *Touch of Evil*, the elective affinity between classic noir and film theory. Thus, discussing the "production of histories of film noir," Fay and Nieland point out that E. Ann Kaplan's "foundational" collection, *Women in Film Noir* (1978), "marks the beginning of a productive marriage between feminist film theory and film noir that continues to this day."[55]

Moreover, one of the central political and intellectual conditions of possibility for *Women in Film Noir* was screen theory, a discursive formation that comprises Heath's "Film and System" and another foundational essay, Laura Mulvey's "Visual Pleasure" (1975).[56] As Kaplan recounts in the introduction to the 1998 edition of *Women in Film Noir*, "[M]any of the essays built on prior Screen film theories in their (then) innovative critique of classical Hollywood 'realism'": "Film noir, precisely because of its potential for subversion of dominant American values and gender-myths, provided an ideal group of films through which to make feminist uses of classical-text arguments."[57]

If the critical reception of *Touch of Evil* is coincident with the birth of border studies and Anglo-American feminist film theory, Welles's film also blurs the borders between genres—between, for example, melodrama and film noir. So, in *Noir Anxiety* (2002), Kelly Oliver and Benigno Trigo argue that the dirty little secret that propels the "didactic melodrama" of *Touch of Evil* is not the "explosive mixing of races but the contact with an evil that transcends race."[58] In a nutshell, behind every bad man—here, the "exposed white American cop," Hank Quinlan (Orson Welles)—is a woman, or the real source of evil ("Cherchez la femme!"), Suzy Vargas (Janet Leigh).[59] I will return to Oliver and Trigo's determination to delimit the "intended or unwitting ambiguity of *Touch of Evil* in particular and film noir in general,"[60] but suffice it to say that Welles's film demonstrates what Elizabeth Cowie calls the "melodramatic *in* noir."[61]

To be sure, hardcore noir critics can get a bit touchy when other critics start invoking the "m" word, as in "melodrama." For example, responding to Edward Gallafent's reading of *Kiss Me Deadly* in the addendum to "Evidence of a Style," Silver contends that the author "tries to make the entire narrative revolve around sexual frustration" (and here's the kicker) "complete with obscure allusions to Douglas Sirk."[62] I'm not sure what's so "obscure" about Gallafent's allusions to *Written on the Wind* (1955)—Sirk's film appeared the same year as Aldrich's and, like *Kiss Me Deadly*, broaches the intimate relation between masculinity and (homo-) sexuality.[63] As Robert Porfirio recounts in "No Way Out," "[I]f one looks at the description of [private eye, mystery, or crime films] in the trade journals of the period or speaks with some of the people involved in their production, one discovers that the term *film noir* was unknown in America and the closest equivalent was 'psychological melodrama.'"[64]

The gist of Porfirio's argument is that film noir, perhaps more so than any other "genre," is a composite, hybrid one. While the generic heterogeneity of classic noir is only one reason why delineating its parameters is such a fraught enterprise, a little history—all due deference to Sam Cooke—is instructive. In 1976, in the aftermath of Schrader's "Notes on Film Noir," Porfirio observed apropos of classic noir that it "lasted no longer than twenty years from 1940 (*Stranger on the Third Floor*) roughly to 1960 (*Odds against Tomorrow*)."[65] Porfirio's revision of Schrader's periodization of classic noir—from *The Maltese Falcon* and *Touch of Evil* to *Stranger on the Third Floor* and *Odds against Tomorrow*—is, as we shall see, a slight but significant one.

Intermission: *Stranger on the Third Floor*

Elaborating on his periodization of classic noir in "No Way Out," Porfirio writes in his entry on the film for Silver and Ward's encyclopedia that "*Stranger on the Third Floor* is the first true noir."[66] This estimation has recently been taken up by critics such as Sheri Chinen Biesen, who, in *Blackout: World War II and the Origins of Film Noir* (2005), remarks that *Stranger on the Third Floor* "first anticipated film noir," and Geoff Mayer, who, in *Encyclopedia of Film Noir* (2007), states that it is the "most fully developed film noir prior to the surge in noir films after 1944."[67]

There are numerous reasons why *Stranger on the Third Floor* is now perceived as a better candidate than *The Maltese Falcon* for the title of "first true [American] noir."[68] One is that Ingster's film predates *The Maltese Falcon* and *Citizen Kane* (1941). Another is that, unlike both *Citizen Kane* and *The Maltese Falcon*, *Stranger on the Third Floor* was a B film, albeit a premiere one, and presages the constitutive relation between program pictures and classic noir. As Arthur Lyons recounts in *Death on the Cheap: The Lost B Movies of Film Noir* (2000), the noir cycle may have been "kick-started by the success of . . . higher-budget productions" like *The Maltese Falcon*, but "it actually has its roots in the B movie."[69] Indeed, Lyons, citing the invention of the paperback, argues that 1939 was the "year that inaugurated the film noir with the release of three prototypical films: *Let Us Live, Rio,* and *Blind Alley*."[70]

While Lyons's argument about the origination of American film noir is suggestive, the decisive issue here is the "genius of the system": *Blind Alley* was made at Universal and *Rio* and *Let Us Live* at Columbia, and neither studio is as integral to the history of classic noir as RKO. In other words, it may be difficult to make the case for Boris Ingster, the director of *Stranger on the Third Floor*, as an auteur (if only because he helmed so few films), but it's easy to appreciate, at least from the perspective of *Citizen Kane,* the collective brilliance of the creative personnel surrounding him, including cinematography (Nicholas Musuraca), art direction (Van Nest Polglase), music (Roy Webb), and, last but by no means least, sound recording (Bailey Fesler).

Not only is RKO's "house sound" distinctly audible in *Stranger on the Third Floor* (in, for example, the film's pervasive recourse to an echo chamber), but Michael Ward's (John McGuire) interior monologue is a precedent for one of the defining features of classic noir, first-person voiceover narration, a device that Frank and Chartier remark upon in their 1946 reviews.[71] All of which is to say, as Auerbach does, that the "charged condensing of sight and sound" in *Stranger on the Third Floor* is "unprecedented in the history of American cinema."[72] The moment that Ward starts questioning himself ("What's the matter with me?") is absolutely singular: "[W]e have entered noir territory—and for the first time in history."[73]

It's no coincidence, I think, that this seminal moment is associated with Ward's first glimpse of the eponymous Stranger played by Peter Lorre. Lorre is a critical figure in early American noir. In addition to acting as a conduit between Weimar cinema and appearing in *Stranger on the Third Floor* and

Courtship: U.S. lobby card for *Stranger on the Third Floor* (1940) with Jane (Margaret Tallichet) and Michael Ward (John McGuire). Note the disembodied head of The Stranger (Peter Lorre).

The Maltese Falcon, the difference between Lorre's characters in these films highlights the strangeness of Ingster's B vis-à-vis Huston's A picture. While Joel Cairo in *The Maltese Falcon* is the stereotypically queer, cosmopolitan double of Kasper Gutman (Sidney Greenstreet), the Stranger, notwithstanding his multifaceted symbolic function in *Stranger on the Third Floor,*[74] retains a certain "foreign" (read: Jewish) element, a "hitherto unknown moral and epistemological ambiguity" that resists the assimilative logic of the American private-detective film.[75]

The most striking difference between *Stranger on the Third Floor* and *The Maltese Falcon,* however, may well be the films' respective figuration of femininity. Whereas Brigid O'Shaughnessy (Mary Astor) in *The Maltese Falcon* is a classic femme fatale (the first, 1932 adaptation of Hammett's novel was titled *Dangerous Female*), so much so that whatever redemptive qualities accrue in the end to Sam Spade (Humphrey Bogart) derive almost entirely from his knightlike renunciation of her, Jane (Margaret Tallichet) in *Stranger on the Third Floor* anticipates the female sleuths in *Phantom Lady* (1944), *Black Angel* (1946), *The Dark Corner* (1946), and *I Wouldn't Be in Your Shoes* (1948), intrepid women who actively assume the private-investigative mantle in order to come to the rescue of their distressed *male* partners.[76]

In their critique of noir studies in *The Maltese Touch of Evil,* Clute and Edwards call for a return to the "films themselves," which "seem to have lost their ability to surprise after having been viewed for so long through certain critical lenses."[77] But the potential use-value of seriously entertaining *Stranger on the Third Floor* as the first American film noir in light of its generic complexion, production history, or representation of femininity is that it "makes strange" the conventional historiography encapsulated in the title of Clute and Edwards's inventive book.

Omega: *Odds against Tomorrow*

To return to the issue of the end or omega of classic noir—indexed in Clute and Edwards's study as *Touch of Evil*—neither Borde and Chaumeton in *A Panorama of American Film Noir* nor Schrader in "Notes on Film Noir" mentions *Odds against Tomorrow,* although in the original 1979 edition of Silver and Ward's encyclopedia Blake Lucas states that Wise's film "may well qualify as the last film of the noir cycle."[78] Lucas's claim for *Odds against Tomorrow* turns on the film's "visual style" and its generic connection to the "caper film series inaugurated by *The Asphalt Jungle*" (1950).[79] Oliver and Trigo, by contrast, invoke the standard historiography ("in 1959, just one year after what is considered to be the last film noir, *Touch of Evil*") and classify *Odds against Tomorrow* as a "neo-noir."[80] Focusing on the "plot theme" of racism, the authors situate Wise's film with respect to a trio of popular "Negro problem" films—*Pinky* (1949), *Home of the Brave* (1949), *Intruder in the Dust* (1949)—and Sirk's *Imitation of Life* (1959).

Lucas's and Oliver and Trigo's differing takes on *Odds against Tomorrow* italicize its mixed generic makeup and "borderline" historical status. In the 2011 edition of Silver and Ward's encyclopedia, Porfirio elaborates on the transitive character of Wise's film: "It looks backward to the classic era in terms of its action (e.g., *White Heat, Asphalt Jungle*) and its visual style (Venetian blinds; dark, wet streets; lowered ceilings; deep focus; etc.). But it also looks forward to the contemporary era in terms of its subject matter (racism, homosexuality), its cool jazz score . . . and, most significantly for an A-budget film, the absence of a definable studio look."[81]

I have discussed *Kiss Me Deadly* and *Touch of Evil* in terms of the 1950s discourse about "the Bomb," so it's notable that the convulsive conclusion of *Odds against Tomorrow* references the ending of *White Heat* (1949) in the form of a "nuclear explosion . . . in which everything is charred and dead."[82] *Odds against Tomorrow* can also be said to look backward in that it was Wise's "last [black-and-white] film . . . and the culmination of the grittily realistic style with which he had become so closely identified since the late forties."[83] Indeed, Wise's proto- and classic noirs—*Curse of the Cat People* (1944), *Born to Kill* (1947), *Blood on the Moon* (1948), *The Set-Up* (1949), *The House on Telegraph Hill* (1951), *The Captive City* (1952), and *I Want to Live!* (1958)— range over virtually the entire classical period of the genre and vividly illustrate noir's generic mutability (horror, Western, melodrama, etc.).

The most pronounced way in which *Odds against Tomorrow* can be said to look backward to 1940s noir, however, is its screenplay, which was written by Abe Polonsky, the author of a number of classic noirs such as *Body and Soul* (1947) and, with Ira Wolfert, *Force of Evil* (1948). The circumstances surrounding the script for *Odds against Tomorrow* have acquired a mystery-like aura over the years and reflect the film's distinction as at once an end-of-the-line and proto-neo-noir. The credited writers were Nelson Giddings and John Oliver Killens,[84] but Killens and Giddings were essentially "fronts" for Polonsky, who was still blacklisted at the time.[85]

One of the ironies of this collective "subterfuge" was that precisely because of Killens's "view of art as a medium of social protest, his affirmation of black manhood and the resistance to white intimidation, his advocacy of black violence as a response to white violence, [and] his indictment of Hollywood's traditional portrayal of blacks," he was the "perfect front."[86] Although Killens's contribution to the film, despite his ardent desire to be more actively involved in the production, was ultimately negligible, *Odds against Tomorrow* was produced by Harry Belafonte, who had acquired the rights to William P. McGivern's novel and "was the only African American [acting] in this capacity at the time."[87] Hence the screen credit: HarBel Productions.

If the necessity of a front for Polonsky, not to mention an African American one, conjures the blacklist and the bad old days of the 1950s, Belafonte's production company nevertheless exemplifies the rise of independent production or "package-unit system" in the same decade, a mutation that has been linked to the "End of an Era."[88] Belafonte's star persona was a sign of the times as well. On the plus side, his role as a producer was predicated on his successful career as the "King of Calypso" and black matinee idol who, with his trademark shades and turtleneck sweater, was the very incarnation of cool. On the minus side, as Belafonte discovered while shooting *The World, the Flesh, and the Devil* (1959), a postapocalyptic film where two of the three survivors of a nuclear holocaust are a black man and white woman: "in the late 1950s the figure of the black man [was] emasculated. I could not have a relationship with a white woman."[89] In other words, brotherhood wins out at the end of *The World, the Flesh, and the Devil*, but at the direct expense of a richer, less impoverished representation of the black brother.

I have rehearsed the preproduction and historical context of *Odds against Tomorrow* in some detail because it has become fashionable for critics to dismiss the film. For example, Eric Lott, in his pathbreaking essay "The Whiteness of Film Noir" (1997), opines that *Odds against Tomorrow* is "politically interesting but cinematically dull."[90] (The fact that one can just as easily reverse this claim testifes to the film's oddity.) And Oliver and Trigo, explicating the film's "nuclear" conclusion, assert, "Racial hatred is the true danger that ignites the deadly explosion. Yet in the end, the film equates Earle's [Robert Ryan] racism with Johnny's [Harry Belafonte] anger in the face of it."[91]

To fully appreciate the unusual historical status of *Odds against Tomorrow*, though, it's imperative to attend to both its film noir *and* "evolutionary racial motifs."[92] Consider, for instance, the film's depiction of Johnny's ex-wife Ruth (Kim Hamilton) interacting at home with a PTA steering committee, about which depiction *Variety* wrote in 1959: "The home life of Belafonte's estranged wife is a unique view (for films) of a normal, middle-class Negro home—with an integrated Parent-Teachers Assn. meeting going on."[93] (The parenthetical qualification—"for films"—speaks volumes about the moribund state of Hollywood at the time vis-à-vis the reality of the African American experience.)

This scene, like the later one of Johnny traveling by bus to Melton, a small town north of New York City on the Hudson, is pregnant with meaning. In the South, Rosa Parks and the Montgomery bus boycott of 1955–56 were potent symbols of the fight for civil rights, as were the volatile events circa 1957 surrounding Orval Faubus and school desegregation at Little Rock Central High School. But Johnny is used to sporting around the city in a white Alfa Romeo, so he's not about to ride on a bus. As for the sort of integration

represented by the PTA and its "mix of liberal whites and young black professionals,"[94] Johnny has nothing but scorn, as becomes clear in a post-PTA
spat between Ruth and him:

> INGRAM: You're tough.
> RUTH: Not tough enough to change you.
> INGRAM (with searing bitterness): For what? To hold hands with those
>   ofay friends of yours.
> RUTH (flaring): I'm trying to make a world fit for Eadie to live in. It's a cinch
>   you're not going to do it with a deck of cards.
> INGRAM: But you are, huh? You and your big white brothers. Drink enough tea
>   with 'em and stay out of the watermelon patch and maybe our little colored
>   girl will grow up to be Miss America, is that it?

Not unlike the pre-Mecca Malcolm X, for whom the white man was the devil,
Johnny violently rejects the assimilationist impulse associated with Martin
Luther King. In an unauthorized biography of Belafonte contemporary with
Odds against Tomorrow, Arnold Shaw observed, "The Negro that bullets
from the screen is . . . proud, belligerent, defiant, unyielding, and attractively
hostile."[95] And Belafonte himself has remarked about the role of Ingram as
written by Polonsky, "He walked in and he demanded his equality *just by his
presence.*"[96]

None of this belies the fact that Johnny, like the classic noir antihero,
is trapped. The difference is that Ingram's imprisonment has a specifically
black dimension. Belafonte again: "In the way that Ingram was written, it
became evident that the way he was 'heroic' is based upon the very way he
was trapped in his skin and trapped in his environment."[97] Polonsky plays
on this "colored" angle when, at the beginning of the film, Johnny visits the
"mastermind" of the heist, Dave Burke (Ed Begley), at his apartment near
Riverside Drive. Burke is an ex-cop who's already spent a year in prison for
refusing to talk to the State Crime Commission. (The allusion to Polonsky, as
Mark Osteen notes in his essay on the 1950s noir heist film in this volume, is
tacit.) Burke has the idea for a "one-time job," and he wants to hire Johnny,
who has amassed substantial gambling debts playing the ponies, because—in
Belafonte's words—"he needs a black deliveryman for his scheme."[98]

The gang has assembled in Burke's apartment to review his plans for the
heist. While Slater takes stock of their weapons ("We have four police specials
that have no history and a couple of shotguns"), Johnny is busy thinking about
how best to solve the problem of the chain on the bank's door. But as Slater
sees it, Johnny's role is perfunctory; all he has to do is be himself—which is
to say, act the part of a stereotype—since the "plan itself is founded on the
alleged inability of whites to tell two dissimilar black men apart":[99]

SLATER: Don't worry about it, boy, we'll be right there with you. All you
  got to do is carry the sandwiches. In a white monkey jacket. And give a big
  smile. And say yessir. You don't have to worry and you don't have to think.
  We'll take care of you.

Ingram's face is suffused with rage.

INGRAM: Then you'll have to start right now.

BURKE (fiercely): Don't beat out that Civil War jazz, Slater.

"Civil War jazz" is a remarkably poetic phrase, splicing together the an-
tiquated nature of Slater's racism (he's still fighting a lost cause) and the
film's progressive jazz score, which Belafonte commissioned John Lewis to
compose.

As can be seen in the script's notations for the first sequence set in New
York City on a "cross street in the Nineties," Belafonte was following Polonsky's lead in his instructions for the film's music: "It is in a modern, moody,
sometimes progressive jazz vein, carrying an overture of premonition, of
tragedy—of people in trouble and doomed. The music will be a continuing
and highly expressive voice in the story."[100] In the late 1950s, Lewis was
already an established figure in the world of jazz, having been present at the
"Birth of the Cool," the memorable 1949 and 1950 recording sessions featuring Miles Davis, Gil Evans, John Lewis, and Gerry Mulligan.[101] When Belafonte approached Lewis, Lewis was a "member of the famed Modern Jazz
Quartet and the principal architect for the group's style and sound," which,
post-bebop, appealed to both whites and blacks.[102] Lewis was therefore an
inspired choice on Belafonte's part: just as the Modern Jazz Quartet sought
to integrate jazz and classical music, so too Wise and Belafonte sought to
mix film noir and social commentary.

Integration, however, is not quite as harmonious in *Odds against Tomorrow*
as it is in the Modern Jazz Quartet because the relationship between Johnny
and Slater is a shotgun marriage that's a product, in turn, of the characters'
vexed relationship with women. (Johnny is divorced from his wife and bitter about having to make alimony payments, while Slater is economically
dependent on Lorry [Shelley Winters] and completely emasculated.) The
film's dynamic contradictions are brilliantly realized in the driving sequence,
where Slater, testing the getaway car, opens it up en route to Melton:

EXT. HIGHWAY.
Car winding up and hurtling at CAMERA with a roar. The speedometer reads
112 mph.
INT. STATION WAGON.
Slater's face is almost exultant, enjoying the sense of power he gets from the
speed, the roar of the supercharged motor and the roar of the wind against the car.

Stereo: Jazz Noir

Right speaker. John Lewis's score for *Odds against Tomorrow* is not the "first fully fledged jazz score."[1] That honor goes to Miles Davis's music for Louis Malle's 1957 *Ascenseur pour l'échafaud* ("Lift" or "Elevator to the Scaffold"). The back story, as always with Miles, is fascinating. As Malle, who had been listening to a lot of Davis at the time, recalls, "When I was shooting the film it seemed inconceivable to me that I could have a score by Miles Davis."[2] Later, when Malle was editing *Ascenseur pour l'échafaud,* Davis just happened to be playing in Paris, so the director contacted him via Boris Vian. (Vian, fellow trumpet player, translator of Raymond Chandler, and author—under the nom du plume of Vernon Sullivan—of the notorious and fabulously titled 1947 novel, *I Spit on Your Graves* [*J'irai cracher sur vos tombes*], was the jazz director at Philips, Davis's record company.)[3] In the Poste Parisien recording studio on the Champs-Elysées and over the course of the only December night that Davis had off from the Club St. Germain where he was playing, Malle screened the passages that the two had singled out for music, and the score was effectively improvised on the spot by Davis and the other members of the quintet: Barney Wilen on tenor saxophone, René Urtreger on piano, Pierre Michelot on bass, and Kenny Clarke on drums. The score's "flavor" is modal, the tonality notional, and the music moves between "limpid beauty" and "fierce abstraction," summoning "fugitive images of rain-washed Parisian streets at dawn, of empty night clubs, of lonely figures prowling the shadows."[4]

Left speaker. On August 25, 1959—between the completion of principal photography for *Odds against Tomorrow* in May and the film's release in October—Miles Davis suffered what the black newspaper *Amsterdam News* called, referencing the beatings that civil rights activists received in the Deep South during the Jim Crow era, a "Georgia head whipping."[5] Davis was playing at Birdland with his sextet. After completing a recording for the Armed Forces Radio Service, he escorted a young white woman named Judy to a taxi, then stood smoking on the sidewalk when a policeman told him to move. Miles refused: "Go ahead, lock me up."[6] When the policeman told him, "You're under arrest," a scuffle ensued, and Miles ended up being beaten about the head "like a tom-tom" by a plainclothes detective.[7] The policeman and detective justified the brutality on the grounds that, as Arnold Shaw recounts in "Stereo," Davis had "refused to move when ordered and allegedly grabbed the patrolman's nightstick."[8] "If I had taken his club from him," Miles later, sensibly queried, "would I have these head wounds?"[9] *Touché.*

Notes

1. David Butler, *Jazz Noir: Listening to Music from* Phantom Lady *to* The Last Seduction (Westport, Conn.: Praeger, 2002), 12. A little context: In "Jazz: Classic French Film Noir and Transatlantic Exchange," Alistair Rolls and Deborah Walker note that American jazz was not only associated with classic American noir but was a vehicle, like noir itself, of social critique: "Jazz and film noir—and the predominance of jazz in the musical scores of French film noir—enabled the French to . . . position themselves firmly on the side of the 'good'"—that is to say, against the racism of American culture (*French and American Noir: Dark Crossings* [London: Palgrave Macmillan, 2009], 118). On jazz in French film noir, see also Robin Buss, "Jazz," in *French Film Noir* (London: Marion Boyars, 1994), 50–69. For a critical appraisal of the French enthusiasm for black American jazz, see Elizabeth Vihlen, "Jammin' on the Champs-Elysées: Jazz, France, and the 1950s," in *Here, There, and Everywhere: The Foreign Politics of American Popular Culture,* ed. Reinhold Wagnleitner and Elaine Tyler May (Hanover, N.H.: University Press of New England, 2000), 149–162.

2. Louis Malle, *Malle on Malle*, ed. Philip French (London: Faber and Faber, 1993), 18–19.

3. For Vian's own translation with Milton Rosenthal of *J'irai cracher sur vos tombes,* see *I Spit on Your Graves* (Edinburgh: Canongate, 2001).

4. Ian Carr, *Miles Davis: The Definitive Biography* (New York: Thunder's Mouth Press, 1998), 119; Brian Morton, *Miles Davis* (London: Haus, 2005), 55; Richard Williams, *The Man in the Green Shirt* (New York: Henry Holt, 1953), 93.

5. Amiri Baraka, "Homage to Miles Davis," in *The Miles Davis Companion: Four Decades of Commentary,* ed. Gary Carner (London: Omnibus, 1996), 48. See also Carr, *Miles Davis,* 55.

6. Miles Davis qtd. in John Szwed, *So What: The Life of Miles Davis* (New York: Simon and Shuster, 2002), 179. As Szwed recounts, a "group of musicians was rehearsing at the Music Unlimited Studio" across the street. When they saw what was happening, "they shoved a microphone out on a boom to record it" (as transcribed by the *Journal-American*): "Take him to the precinct, that _____. Don't let him get away free. Get that _____ outta here" (180).

7. The fact that Miles titled a 1985 Columbia recording *You're under Arrest* testifies to the impact that the Birdland incident had on his life. For Miles's "tom-tom" metaphor, see Carr, *Miles Davis,* 155.

8. Arnold Shaw, *Belafonte* (Philadelphia: Chilton, 1960), 264.

9. Ibid.

To enhance this scene in which Earle's momentarily inflated sense of masculinity is bound up with the car's "supercharged" performance, John Lewis composed a "four-note rhythmic ostinato" that becomes a pretext for Milt Jackson to "take an extended vibes solo for almost sixty seconds."[103] The result is a "genuinely subversive moment in terms of crossing the racial divide," what David Butler calls "audiovisual miscegenation": "Slater, a white racist, has his moment of emotional freedom accompanied by an improvised jazz solo played on the instrument diegetically associated with his colleague, Johnny, the black jazz musician."[104]

Face Off: Earle Slater (Robert Ryan) and Johnny Ingram (Harry Belafonte) in *Odds against Tomorrow* (1959), with Ingram wearing a white deliveryman hat.

Slater's euphoria is, needless to say, ephemeral. The dialectical forces that drive *Odds against Tomorrow* ensure that Johnny and Earle will not end up cradled in each other's arms, as in the hopeful conclusion to *Edge of the City* (1957) and *The Defiant Ones* (1958). Instead, the robbery botched and Burke left for dead from a self-inflicted gunshot wound to the head, the keys to the getaway car now forever out of reach on the sidewalk, Johnny chases Earle down to a series of gas-storage tanks where, facing off against each other, they ignite a "Niagara of gorgeous sparks cascading into the night."

Coda: "Thrillers of Tomorrow"

The final image of *Odds against Tomorrow*—STOP DEAD END—appears to represent a point of no return, but in its fusion of film noir and social consciousness, Wise's film looks forward to "noirs by noirs" like Carl Franklin's *One False Move* (1992) and *Devil in a Blue Dress* (1995).[105] As a "thriller of tomorrow," *Odds against Tomorrow* also anticipates a certain trend or tendency in transnational (neo-) noir, a legacy that is most apparent in the work of Jean-Pierre Melville.

In its exorbitant negations, Jean-Pierre Mockey's mockery of Melville attests to his fellow French filmmaker's extraordinary—dare one say, Tarantinian?—enthusiasm for Wise's heist film: "I am not Melville; I do not watch *Odds against Tomorrow* hundreds of times; I am not anaesthetized to the point of remaking entire scenes from American movies."[106] Melville is an especially evocative figure in the context of *Odds against Tomorrow* because his *Le Samouraï* (1967)—itself based on *This Gun for Hire* (1942), a "key film in the French definition of the film noir canon" established by Borde and Chaumeton—has influenced neo-noirs as diverse as John Woo's *The Killer*

(1989), Quentin Tarantino's *Reservoir Dogs* (1992), and Jim Jarmusch's *Ghost Dog: The Way of the Samurai* (1999).[107]

The issue of influence—whether understood as citationality or para-phrase[108]—is always a complicated one. In an interview in *Outlaw Masters of Japanese Film* (2005), Chris Desjardins submits to the Japanese "New Wave" director Masahiro Shinoda, "People have compared *Pale Flower* to the films of J.-P. Melville."[109] Shinoda acknowledges the influence—"I often watch film noir. Isn't *Le Samouraï* by Jean-Pierre Melville?"—although he goes on to say that when he made *Pale Flower* (1964), he "had not seen any of [Melville's] movies."[110] Instead, Shinoda recalls: "The American movie, *Odds against Tomorrow,* by Robert Wise has a scene with gangsters gathered before their big heist. They have to kill time until the appointed hour, and they're doing nothing but hanging out at a place by the riverside. I was moved by that scene. . . . [T]hat feeling was one of the big motivations for creating *Pale Flower.*"[111] Shinoda's exchange with Desjardins beautifully captures the peculiar, effluvial history of film noir. From *Stranger on the Third Floor* to *Odds against Tomorrow* to *Pale Flower* and beyond, this history is as strange as the films—whether "meller" or whodunit, série noire or yakuza-eiga—that comprise it. In the end (if one can even speak of endings), classic noir is ultimately less a straightforward tale of alphas and omegas, origins and epilogues, than a rich structure of feeling that continues to bloom, like some fragrant *fleur du mal*, in odd moments and places.

Notes

1. Although a properly transnational history of film noir is beyond the scope of this essay, such a history—to mention only the origins of the genre—would minimally involve accounting for French, British, and German (proto-) noir. On French noir, see, for example, Alistair Rolls and Deborah Walker, *French and American Noir: Dark Crossings* (London: Palgrave Macmillan, 2009); Robin Buss, *French Film Noir* (London: Marion Boyars, 1994); and Ginette Vincendeau, "French Film Noir," in *European Film Noir,* ed. Andrew Spicer (Manchester: Manchester University Press, 2007), 23–54. On British film noir, see Laurence Miller, "Evidence for a British Film Noir Cycle," in *Re-Viewing British Cinema, 1900–1952,* ed. Wheeler Winston Dixon (Albany: State University of New York Press, 1994), 155–64; Tony Williams, "British Film Noir," in *Film Noir Reader 2,* ed. Alain Silver and James Ursini (New York: Limelight, 1999), 243–70; and Robert Murphy, "British Film Noir," in *European Film Noir,* 84–111. On German film noir, see Thomas Elsaesser, "Caligari's Legacy—Film Noir as Film History's German Imaginary," in *Weimar Cinema and After: Germany's Historical Imaginary* (London: Routledge, 2000), 420–44; Tim Bergfelder, "German Cinema and Film Noir," in *European Film Noir,* 138–63; and Jennifer Fay and Justus Nieland, "Occupation Noir and the Shadow of Weimar," in *Film Noir: Hard-Boiled Modernity and the Cultures of Globalization* (New York: Routledge, 2010), 42–50. For an excellent example of the sort of synthesizing history of film noir I have in mind, see Jennifer Fay and Justus

Nieland, "Dislocating James M. Cain's *The Postman Always Rings Twice*," in *Film Noir,* 2–28.

2. "Thriller of tomorrow" is Claude Chabrol's capsule description of Robert Aldrich's *Kiss Me Deadly*. See Claude Chabrol, "Evolution of the Thriller," trans. Liz Heron, in *Cahiers du cinéma*, vol. 1, *The 1950s: Neo-Realism, Hollywood, New Wave*, ed. Jim Hillier (New York: Routledge, 2001), 163.

3. Raymond Borde and Étienne Chaumeton, *A Panorama of American Film Noir, 1941–1953*, trans. Paul Hammond (San Francisco: City Lights, 2002), 5.

4. Ibid.

5. Ibid., 1.

6. Ibid., 155.

7. Ibid., 15.

8. James Naremore, "A Season in Hell or the Snows of Yesteryear," in *A Panorama of American Film Noir,* by Raymond Borde and Étienne Chaumeton (San Francisco: City Lights, 2002), ix.

9. Charles O'Brien, "Film Noir in France: Before the Liberation," *Iris* 21 (Spring 1996): 10.

10. Borde and Chaumeton, *Panorama of American Film Noir,* 8–9.

11. O'Brien, "Film Noir in France," 16.

12. Marc Vernet, "*Film Noir* on the Edge of Doom," trans. J. Swenson, in *Shades of Noir,* ed. Joan Copjec (London: Verso, 1993), 4.

13. Ibid., 27 n. 11. On French film audiences in the wake of the Blum-Byrnes accord, see, for example, Jill Forbes, "The Série Noire," in *France and the Mass Media*, ed. Brian Rigby and Nicholas Hewitt (London: Macmillan, 1991), 85–97; and Richard Kuisel, "The Fernandel Factor: The Rivalry between the French and American Cinema in the 1950s," *Yale French Studies,* ed. Susan Weiner 98 (2000): 119–34.

14. Ibid., 5.

15. See Richard F. Kuisel, "Yankee Go Home: The Left, Coca-Cola, and the Cold War," in *Seducing the French: The Dilemma of Americanization* (Berkeley: University of California Press, 1993), 37–69.

16. Henri-François Rey, "Hollywood Makes Myths Like Ford Makes Cars," trans. R. Barton Palmer, in *Perspectives on Film Noir,* ed. R. Barton Palmer (New York: G. K. Hall, 1996), 28–29.

17. Louis Aragon, "Victor Hugo," *Les Lettres françaises,* June 28, 1951, cited in Kuisel, *Seducing the French,* 41.

18. Emilie Bickerton, *A Short History of Cahiers du Cinéma* (London: Verso, 2009), 10.

19. Fay and Nieland, *Film Noir,* 37.

20. Jean-Pierre Chartier, "The Americans Are Making Dark Films Too," trans. R. Barton Palmer, *Perspectives on Film Noir,* ed. R. Barton Palmer (New York: G. K. Hall, 1996), 27.

21. Ibid., 27.

22. Borde and Chaumeton, *Panorama of American Film Noir,* 155.

23. Naremore, "Season in Hell," xviii.

24. Jonathan Auerbach, *Dark Borders: Film Noir and American Citizenship* (Durham, N.C.: Duke University Press, 2011), 197.

25. Ibid., 195. On cars as commodities in *Kiss Me Deadly,* see Mark Osteen, "Bombing Around," in *Nightmare Alley: Film Noir and the American Dream* (Baltimore: Johns Hopkins University Press, 2013), 150–52.

26. Roger Tailleur, "The Advent of Robert Aldrich," in *Positif: 50 Years*, ed. Michel Ciment and Laurence Kardish (New York: Museum of Modern Art, 2002), 38.

27. Peter Stanfield, *Maximum Movies and Pulp Fictions: Film Culture and the Worlds of Samuel Fuller, Mickey Spillane, and Jim Thompson* (New Brunswick, N.J.: Rutgers University Press, 2011), 76.

28. Chabrol, "Evolution of the Thriller," 163.

29. François Truffaut, "Robert Aldrich: *Kiss Me Deadly,*" in *The Films in My Life*, trans. Leonard Mayhew (New York: Da Capo Press, 1994), 93; Stanfield, *Maximum Movies*, 78.

30. Auerbach, *Dark Borders*, 193 and 197.

31. Fay and Nieland, *Film Noir*, xiv.

32. Borde and Chaumeton, *Panorama of American Film Noir*, 13.

33. Auerbach, *Dark Borders*, 4.

34. Ibid., 16 and 198.

35. Shannon Scott Clute and Richard L. Edwards, *The Maltese Touch of Evil: Film Noir and Potential Criticism* (Hanover, N.H.: Dartmouth College Press, 2011), 32. See also my review of *The Maltese Touch of Evil* in *Film and History: An Interdisciplinary Journal of Film and Television* 43.2 (Fall 2013): 80–83.

36. Clute and Edwards, *Maltese Touch of Evil*, 10.

37. It is worth noting, to reference surrealism, that Marcel Duhamel, who conceived and edited Gallimard's Série noire as well as wrote the introduction to Borde and Chaumeton's *Panorama of American Film Noir*, "assisted in the development of the 'Exquisite Corpse' game in 1925." James Naremore, *More than Night: Film Noir in Its Contexts* (Berkeley: University of California Press, 1998), 17. On the "exquisite cadaver," see, for example, Mark Nelson and Sarah Hudson Bayliss, *Exquisite Corpse: Surrealism and the Black Dahlia Murder* (New York: Bulfinch, 2006).

38. Clute and Edwards, *Maltese Touch of Evil*, xvii.

39. Paul Schrader, "Notes on Film Noir," in *Perspectives on Film Noir*, ed. R. Barton Palmer (New York: G. K. Hall, 1996), 100.

40. Ibid., 107.

41. Ibid.

42. On the history of the critical reception of *Pickup on South Street*, see Peter Stanfield, "American Primitive: Samuel Fuller's Pulp Politics," in *Maximum Movies and Pulp Fictions: Film Culture and the Worlds of Samuel Fuller, Mickey Spillane, and Jim Thompson* (New Brunswick, N.J.: Rutgers University Press, 2011), 112–51. For an example of a reading that problematizes Schrader's position on *Pickup on South Street*, see Michael Rogin, "*Kiss Me Deadly*: Communism, Motherhood, and Cold War Movies," in *Ronald Reagan, the Movie and Other Episodes in Political Demonology* (Berkeley: University of California Press, 1987), 236–71.

43. Alain Silver, "*Kiss Me Deadly*: Evidence of a Style," in *Film Noir Reader*, ed. Alain Silver and James Ursini (New York: Limelight, 2005), 234.

44. Robert Aldrich qtd. in ibid., 229–30.

45. Auerbach, *Dark Borders*, 200.

46. Clute and Edwards, *Maltese Touch of Evil*, 63.

47. See, for example, the "Postface" to *A Panorama of American Film Noir*, where Borde and Chaumeton write: "[Audiences] gave a huge welcome to the spy stories the success of James Bond has brought into fashion" (155).

48. But for a spirited and sympathetic defense of Mancini's score, see Jill Leeper, "Crossing Musical Borders: The Soundtrack for *Touch of Evil*," in *Soundtrack Available:*

Essays on Film and Popular Music, ed. Pamela Robertson Wojcik and Arthur Knight (Durham, N.C.: Duke University Press, 2001), 226–43.

49. On the restoration of *Touch of Evil,* see Jonathan Rosenbaum, *"Touch of Evil* Retouched," in *Discovering Orson Welles* (Berkeley: University of California Press, 2007), 248–57.

50. Kelly Oliver and Benigno Trigo, *Noir Anxiety* (Minneapolis: University of Minnesota Press, 2003), 123.

51. William Anthony Nericcio, *Tex(t)-Mex: Seductive Hallucinations of the "Mexican" in America* (Austin: University of Texas Press, 2007), 80.

52. Oliver and Trigo, *Noir Anxiety,* 115.

53. See Stephen Heath, "Film Noir and System: Terms of Analysis," *Screen* 16.1 (Spring 1975): 7–77; Stephen Heath, "Film Noir and System: Terms of Analysis," *Screen* 16.2 (Summer 1975): 91–113; and Stephen Heath, *"Touch of Evil*—The Long Version," *Screen* 17.1 (Spring 1976): 115–17.

54. Heath's essay is not cited, for example, in Fay and Nieland's *Film Noir,* Auerbach's *Dark Borders,* or Clute and Edwards's *Maltese Touch of Evil.*

55. Fay and Nieland, *Film Noir,* 134.

56. For example, Mulvey's "Visual Pleasure and Narrative Cinema" recruits Hitchcock's *Vertigo* to illustrate the investigative sadism that is the corollary of scopophilic fetishism. Laura Mulvey, *Visual and Other Pleasures* (London: Macmillan, 1989), 23–24.

57. E. Ann Kaplan, "Introduction to New Edition," *Women in Film Noir,* ed. E. Ann Kaplan (London: British Film Institute, 1998), 3.

58. Oliver and Trigo, *Noir Anxiety,* 115.

59. Ibid.

60. Ibid.

61. Elizabeth Cowie, *"Film Noir* and Women," in *Shades of Noir,* ed. Joan Copjec (London: Verso, 1993), 125.

62. Silver, "Evidence of a Style," 233.

63. On homosexuality in *Kiss Me Deadly,* see Robin Wood, "Creativity and Evaluation: Two Film Noirs of the Fifties," in *Personal Views* (Detroit: Wayne State University Press, 2006), 84, and 385–86; and Robert Lang, "Looking for the 'Great Whatsit': *Kiss Me Deadly* and Film Noir," in *Masculine Interests: Homoerotics in Hollywood Film* (New York: Columbia University Press, 2002), 121–39.

64. Robert Porfirio, "No Way Out," in *Perspectives on Film Noir,* ed. R. Barton Palmer (New York: G. K. Hall, 1996), 116.

65. Ibid.

66. Porfirio, *"Stranger on the Third Floor,"* in *Film Noir: An Encyclopedic Reference to the American Style,* ed. Alain Silver and Elizabeth Ward (Woodstock, N.Y.: Overlook, 2002), 269.

67. Sheri Chinen Biesen, *Blackout: World War II and the Origins of Film Noir* (Baltimore: Johns Hopkins University Press, 2005), 22; Geoff Mayer, *"Stranger on the Third Floor,"* in Geoff Mayer and Brian McDonnell, *Encyclopedia of Film Noir* (Westport, Conn.: Greenwood, 2007), 394.

68. See, for example, Tony Williams, who argues that "British film noir begins a few years earlier than its American counterpart with such examples as *The Green Cockatoo* (1937), *They Drive by Night* (1938), *I Met a Murderer* and *The Night of the Fire* (both 1939) predating Boris Ingster's *Stranger on the Third Floor."* Williams, "British Film Noir," 245.

69. Arthur Lyons, *Death on the Cheap: The Lost B Movies of Film Noir* (New York: Da Capo, 2000), 3.

70. Ibid., 35.

71. See Robert Miklitsch, "House Sound: Reverb, Offscreen Sound, and Voice-Over Narration in Early RKO Noir," in *Siren City: Sound and Source Music in Classic American Noir* (New Brunswick, N.J.: Rutgers University Press, 2011), 24–52. On Frank and Chartier's isolation of voiceover narration, see, respectively, "The Crime Adventure Story: A New Kind of Detective Film" and "Americans Are Making Dark Films Too," in *Perspectives on Film Noir*, ed. R. Barton Palmer (New York: G. K. Hall, 1996), 23 and 26.

72. Auerbach, *Dark Borders*, 42.

73. Ibid.

74. On the Stranger as a double of Ward, the murder suspect Briggs (Elisha Cook Jr.), and Ward's neighbor Meng, see ibid., 52.

75. On the transformation of Peter Lorre's persona from *M* (1931) to *Stranger on the Third Floor*, see Gerd Gemünden, "From 'Mr. M' to 'Mr. Murder': Peter Lorre and the Actor in Exile," in *Light Motives: German Popular Film in Perspective*, ed. Randall Halle and Margaret McCarthy (Detroit: Wayne State University Press, 2003), 85–107.

76. On the female investigator, see, for example, Helen Hanson, "At the Margins of *Film Noir*: Genre, Range and Female Representation," in *Hollywood Heroines: Women in Film Noir and the Female Gothic* (London: I. B. Tauris, 2007), 1–32; and Philippa Gates, "In Name Only: The Transformation of the Female Detective in the 1940s" and "The Maritorious Melodrama: The Female Detective in 1940s Film Noir," in *Detecting Women: Gender and the Hollywood Detective Film* (Albany: State University of New York Press, 2011), 135–62 and 163–88.

77. Clute and Edwards, *Maltese Touch of Evil*, xvi.

78. Blake Lucas, "*Odds against Tomorrow*," in *Film Noir: An Encyclopedic Reference to the American Style*, ed. Alain Silver and Elizabeth Ward (Woodstock, N.Y.: Overlook, 2002), 216.

79. Ibid.

80. Oliver and Trigo, *Noir Anxiety*, 10.

81. Porfirio, "*Odds against Tomorrow*," in *Film Noir: The Encyclopedia*, ed. Alain Silver, Elizabeth Ward, James Ursini, and Robert Porfirio (New York: Overlook Duckworth, 2010), 217.

82. Oliver and Trigo, *Noir Anxiety*, 10.

83. Sergio Leeman, *Robert Wise on His Films* (Los Angeles: Silman-James, 1995), 40.

84. Abraham Polonsky, cited in *Odds against Tomorrow: The Critical Edition*, ed. John Schultheiss (Northridge: California State University Center for Telecommunication Studies, 1999), 241.

85. The noir icon Sterling Hayden—in an act that he would later rue—named Polonsky in 1951 as a Communist in a session of the House Un-American Activities Committee. Polonsky was also named by Meta Reis Rosenberg and Richard Collins. See Paul Buhle and Dave Wagner, *A Very Dangerous Citizen: Abraham Lincoln Polonsky and the Hollywood Left* (Berkeley: University of California Press, 2001), 11.

86. John Schultheiss, "*Odds against Tomorrow*: Film Noir without Linguistic Irony," in *Odds against Tomorrow: The Critical Edition*, ed. John Schultheiss (Northridge: California State University Center for Telecommunication Studies, 1999), 241.

87. Ibid., 165. Keith Gilyard argues that Killens "reportedly acknowledged he contributed little to *Odds against Tomorrow*, but that he contributed any less than Nelson Giddings . . . is doubtful." Keith Gilyard, *John Oliver Killens: A Life of Literary Activism* (Athens: University of Georgia Press, 2010), 144.

88. Leonard Spinrad, "End of an Era," (1956), cited by Blair Davis, *The Battle for the Bs: 1950s Hollywood and the Rebirth of Low-Budget Cinema* (New Brunswick, N.J.: Rutgers University Press, 2012), 27.

89. Harry Belafonte qtd. in Schultheiss, *"Odds against Tomorrow,"* 235–36.

90. Eric Lott, "The Whiteness of Film Noir," *American Literary History* 9.3 (Autumn 1997): 561.

91. Oliver and Trigo, *Noir Anxiety,* 9.

92. Schultheiss, *"Odds against Tomorrow,"* 169.

93. Belafonte qtd. in ibid., 243.

94. Ibid., 200.

95. Arnold Shaw, *Belafonte: An Unauthorized Biography* (Philadelphia: Chilton, 1960), 316.

96. Belafonte qtd, in Schultheiss, *"Odds against Tomorrow,"* 252.

97. Belafonte qtd. in ibid., 169.

98. Harry Belafonte with Michael Shnayerson, *My Song* (New York: Knopf, 2011), 206.

99. Osteen, *Nightmare Alley,* 172.

100. Polonsky qtd. in *Odds against Tomorrow,* 14.

101. The "workshop" for Davis's "Birth of the Cool" was Gil Evans's Fifty-fifth Street basement apartment in New York. Frank Tirro, *Birth of the Cool of Miles Davis and His Associates* (Hillsdale, N.Y.: Pendragon, 2009), 67.

102. Martin Myrick, "John Lewis and the Film Score for *Odds against Tomorrow,"* in *Odds against Tomorrow: The Critical Edition,* ed. John Schultheiss (Northridge: California State University Center for Telecommunication Studies, 1999), 299.

103. David Butler, "'No Brotherly Love': Hollywood Jazz, Racial Prejudice, and John Lewis' Score for *Odds against Tomorrow,"* in *Thriving on a Riff: Jazz and Blues Influences in African American Literature and Film,* ed. Graham Lock and David Murray (New York: Oxford University Press, 2009), 230.

104. Ibid., 231, 230.

105. See, for example, Manthia Diawara, "Noir by Noirs: Toward a New Realism in Black Cinema," in *Shades of Noir,* ed. Joan Copjec (London: Verso, 1993), 261–78; and Dan Flory, *Philosophy, Black Film, Film Noir* (University Park: Penn State University Press, 2008).

106. Jean-Pierre Mockey cited in Ginette Vincendeau, "Transnational Aesthetics in Melville's Série Noire Films," in *Jean-Pierre Melville: "An American in Paris"* (London: British Film Institute, 2003), 169.

107. Ibid., 185. For the link between Wise, Melville, and Shinoda, I'm indebted to Fay and Nieland; see their *Film Noir,* 212.

108. On the notion of "paraphrase," see ibid., 218.

109. Chris Desjardins, *Outlaw Masters of Japanese Film* (London: I. B. Tauris, 2005), 122.

110. Ibid.

111. Ibid.

Classic Noir on the Net

All Things Noir (www.noircast.net): "Website dedicated to criticism and creative works inspired by film noir, mystery/crime writing, and hard-boiled literature," "intended to bring noir fans, critics, writers and filmmakers into meaningful dialogue and debate." Archived podcasts on classic and neo-noir ("Out of the Past: Investigating Film Noir," "Behind the Black Mask: Mystery Writers Revealed").

American Film Noir (www.americanfilmnoir.com): Articles on classic film noir: "Top Ten," "Noir People (The Actors)," "Femme Fatales (Women in Noir)," "Los Angeles (Backdrop of Noir)," "The Red Menace (Film Noir and the Cold War)."

Classic Noir: The Hardboiled World of Film Noir (www.classicnoir.com): "Committed to reviewing the work of the Classic Noir era."

Crimeculture (www.crimeculture.com): Essays on "crime fiction, crime films, and representations of criminality." Aims to "explore different critical approaches to the study of crime literature/film, and to be as entertaining and wide-ranging as possible."

Dark City: Film Noir and Fiction (www.eskimo.com/~noir): Web site that provides an in-depth examination ("images, memorable lines, plot summaries, and reviews") of film and roman noir.

Film Noir: An Oasis of Noir in a Desert of Banality (www.filmsnoir.net): Portal comprised of news, reviews (for example, *Christmas Holiday* [1944]: Never Mind the Melodrama"), articles, and creative work on film noir. Focus: "Classic Film Noir cycle of the 1940's and 1950's."

Film Noir File (www.filmnoirfile.com): Dossier that "challenges standard interpretations of film noir" as they have been "presented in the mass media and academic literature." Includes articles such as "Against the Hardboiled Paradigm," "What

Explains the Visual Style of Film Noir?" and "Internationalism of Film Noir, 1923–1963."

Film Noir—Films (www.filmsite.org/filmnoir.html): "Descriptions of various subgenres" and synopses of exemplary films. Composed of five parts, with additional sections on "examples" ("Greatest Early and Classic Film Noir," "Greatest Modern Film Noir [Post-Noir or Neo Noir]").

Film Noir Foundation (www.filmnoirfoundation.org/): "Educational resource for regarding the cultural, historical, and artistic significance of film noir as an original American cinematic movement." Resources: noir-related video archive; forum, "Back Alley Noir"; quarterly electronic magazine, *Noir City*; and information on Blu-Ray and DVD releases of classic and neo-noir.

Film Noir of the Week (www.noiroftheweek.com): Weekly, in-depth reviews of classic and neo-noirs from *Stranger on the Third Floor* (1940) to *Drive* (2011).

Film Noir Studies (www.filmnoirstudies.com): Focuses on the classic noir films of the 1940s and 1950s. Features timeline, glossary, and essays ("Outer Limits of Film Noir," "No Place for a Woman: The Family in *Film Noir*"). For film students and professors, critics and film buffs.

Film Noir: They Shot Dark Pictures, Didn't They? (www.theyshootpictures. com/noir.htm): Entries on "250 Quintessential Noir Films (1940–1964)," "50 Key Noir Filmmakers," "Non-American Noir Films from 1940 to 1964," "Noir Precursors (Pre-1940)," "Neo-Noir/Modern Noir (Post-1964)." Quintessential list includes recommendations.

Noir Nation: International Crime Fiction (www.noirnation.com): "Discussion platform for all things noir" ("crime fiction, film noir, and tattoos"): "crime fiction writers and film noir bloggers . . . share news and opinion from their respective national and artistic communities."

Sidney's Film Noir Page (www.gaskcadd.com/ssk_pix/FilmNoir.htm): List, compiled from more than ten sources, of "1,449 film titles for the years 1940–1965." Also included: list of "647 neo-noir/retro noir titles" from 1966 to 2010.

Critical Literature on Film Noir

Reference Guides

Robert Ottoson, *A Reference Guide to the American Film Noir* (1981).
Alain Silver and Elizabeth Ward, eds., *Film Noir: An Encyclopedic Reference to the American Style* (1992).
Karen Burroughs Hannsberry, *Femme Noir: Bad Girls of Film Noir* (1998).
Karen Burroughs Hannsberry, *Bad Boys: The Actors of Film Noir* (2003).
Michael F. Keaney, *Film Noir Guide* (2003).
Alexander Ballinger and Danny Graydon, *The Rough Guide to Film Noir* (2007).
Geoff Mayer and Brian McDonnell, *Encyclopedia of Film Noir* (2007).
Michael F. Keaney, *British Film Noir Guide* (2008).
Alastair Phillips and Jim Hillier, *100 Film Noirs* (2009).
Alain Silver, Elizabeth Ward, James Ursini, and Robert Porfirio, *The Film Noir Encyclopedia* (2010).
Andrew Spicer, *Historical Dictionary of Film Noir* (2010).
Paul Duncan, *100 All-Time Favorite Film Noirs* (2013).
John Grant, *A Comprehensive Encyclopedia of Film Noir: The Essential Reference Guide* (2013).
Andrew Spicer and Helen Hanson, *A Companion to Film Noir* (2013).

Collections

E. Ann Kaplan, ed., *Women in Film Noir* (1978 [1998]).
Ian Cameron, ed., *The Book of Film Noir* (1993).
Joan Copjec, ed., *Shades of Noir* (1993).
R. Barton Palmer, ed., *Perspectives on Film Noir* (1996).
Alain Silver and James Ursini, eds., *Film Noir Reader* (1996).

Lee Server, Ed Gorman, and Martin H. Greenberg, eds., *The Big Book of Noir* (1998).

Alain Silver and James Ursini, eds., *Film Noir Reader 2* (1999).

Robert Porfirio, Alain Silver, and James Ursini, eds., *Film Noir Reader 3: Interviews with Filmmakers of the Classic Period* (2002).

Alain Silver and James Ursini, eds., *Film Noir Reader 4: The Crucial Films and Themes* (2004).

Mark Conard, ed., *The Philosophy of Film Noir* (2006).

Andrew Spicer, ed., *European Film Noir* (2007).

Chi-Yun Shin and Mark Gallagher, *East Asian Film Noir: Transnational Encounters and Intercultural Dialogue* (2013).

Studies

Raymond Borde and Étienne Chaumeton, *A Panorama of American Film Noir, 1941–1953*. Trans. Paul Hammond (1955 [2002]).

Charles Higham and Joel Greenberg, *Hollywood in the Forties* (1968).

Foster Hirsch, *The Dark Side of the Screen: Film Noir* (1981).

Bruce Crowther, *Film Noir: Reflections in a Dark Mirror* (1983).

Spencer Selby, *Dark City: The Film Noir* (1984).

Jon Tuska, *Dark Cinema: American Film Noir in Cultural Perspective* (1984).

J. P. Telotte, *Voices in the Dark: The Narrative Patterns of Film Noir* (1989).

Frank Krutnik, *In a Lonely Street: Film Noir, Genre, Masculinity* (1991).

Carl Richardson, *Autopsy: An Element of Realism in Film Noir* (1992).

Robin Buss, *French Film Noir* (1994).

R. Barton Palmer, *Hollywood's Dark Cinema: The American Film Noir* (1994).

James F. Maxfield, *Fatal Woman: Sources of Male Anxiety in American Film Noir, 1941–1991* (1996).

Nicholas Christopher, *Somewhere in the Night: Film Noir and the American City* (1997).

Eddie Muller, *Dark City: The Lost World of Film Noir* (1998).

James Naremore, *More than Night: Film Noir in Its Contexts* (1998).

Alain Silver and James Ursini, *The Noir Style* (1999).

Jans B. Wager, *Dangerous Dames: Women and Representation in the Weimar Street Film* (1999).

Arthur Lyons, *Death on the Cheap: The Lost B Movies of Film Noir* (2000).

Barry Gifford, *Out of the Past: Adventures in Film Noir* (2001).

Eddie Muller, *Dark City Dames: The Wicked Women of Film Noir* (2001).

Ronald Schwartz, *Noir, Now and Then: Film Noir Originals and Remakes, 1944–1999* (2001).

Megan Abbott, *The Street Was Mine: White Masculinity in Hardboiled Fiction and Film Noir* (2002).

David Butler, *Jazz Noir: Listening to Music from* Phantom Lady *to* The Last Seduction (2002).

Andrew Dickos, *Street with No Name: A History of the Classic American Film Noir* (2002).

Paula Rabinowitz, *Black and White and Noir: America's Pulp Modernism* (2002).

Andrew Spicer, *Film Noir* (2002).

William Hare, *Early Film Noir: Greed, Lust and Murder Hollywood Style* (2003).

Kelly Oliver and Benigno Trigo, *Noir Anxiety* (2003).

Edward Dimendberg, *Film Noir and the Spaces of Modernity* (2004).

William Hare, *L.A. Noir: Nine Dark Visions of the City of Angels* (2004).

Alain Silver, James Ursini, and Paul Duncan, *Film Noir* (2004).

Sheri Chinen Biesen, *Blackout: World War II and the Origins of Film Noir* (2005).

Mark Bould, *Film Noir: From Berlin to Sin City* (2005).

Nathaniel Rich, *San Francisco Noir: The City in Noir from 1940 to the Present* (2005).

Eddie Robson, *Film Noir* (2005).

Alain Silver and James Ursini, *L.A. Noir: The City as Character* (2005).

Jans B. Wager, *Dames in the Driver's Seat: Rereading Film Noir* (2005).

Philippa Gates, *Detecting Men: Masculinity and the Hollywood Detective Film* (2006).

John T. Irwin, *Unless the Threat of Death Is Behind Them: Hard-Boiled Fiction and Film Noir* (2006).

Helen Hanson, *Hollywood Heroines: Women in Film Noir and the Female Gothic Film* (2007).

Dan Flory, *Philosophy, Black Film, Film Noir* (2008).

Paul Meehan, *Tech-Noir: The Fusion of Science Fiction and Film Noir* (2008).

Dennis Broe, *Film Noir, American Workers, and Postwar Hollywood* (2009).

Vincent Brook, *Driven to Darkness: Jewish Émigré Directors and the Rise of Film Noir* (2009).

Jennifer Fay and Justus Nieland, *Film Noir: Hard-Boiled Modernity and the Cultures of Globalization* (2009).

Alistair Rolls and Deborah Walker, *French and American Noir: Dark Crossings* (2009).

Wheeler Winston Dixon, *Film Noir and the Cinema of Paranoia* (2010).

Julie Grossman, *Rethinking the Femme Fatale in Film Noir: Ready for Her Close-Up* (2010).

Marlisa Santos, *The Dark Mirror: Psychiatry and Film Noir* (2010).

Jonathan Auerbach, *Dark Borders: Film Noir and American Citizenship* (2011).

Shannon Scott Clute and Richard L. Edwards, *The Maltese Touch of Evil: Film Noir and Potential Criticism* (2011).

Phillipa Gates, *Detecting Women: Gender and the Hollywood Detective Film* (2011).

David Greven, *Representations of Femininity in American Genre Cinema: The Woman's Film, Film Noir, and Modern Horror* (2011).

Paul Meehan, *Horror Noir: Where Cinema's Dark Sisters Meet* (2011).

Robert Miklitsch, *Siren City: Sound and Source Music in Classic American Noir* (2011).

Ronald Charles Nesbitt, *The Femme Fatale and Male Anxiety in Twentieth-Century American Literature, "Hard-Boiled" Crime Fiction, and Film Noir* (2011).

William Park, *What Is Film Noir?* (2011).

Gene D. Phillips, *Out of the Shadows: Expanding the Canon of Classic Film Noir* (2011).
Imogen Sara Smith, *In Lonely Places: Film Noir beyond the City* (2011).
William Hare, *Pulp Fiction to Film Noir: The Great Depression and the Development of a Genre* (2012).
William Luhr, *Film Noir* (2012).
Robert B. Pippin, *Fatalism in American Film Noir: Some Cinematic Philosophy* (2012).
Thomas C. Renzi, *Screwball Comedy and Film Noir: Unexpected Connections* (2012).
Erik Dussere, *America Is Elsewhere: The Noir Tradition in the Age of Consumer Culture* (2013).
Brian Nicol, *The Private Eye: Detectives in the Movies* (2013).
Mark Osteen, *Nightmare Alley: Film Noir and the American Dream* (2013).
Ronald Schwartz, *Houses of Noir: Dark Visions from Thirteen Studios* (2013).

BFI Volumes

Colin McArthur, *The Big Heat* (1992).
Richard Schickel, *Double Indemnity* (1992).
Dana Polan, *In a Lonely Place* (1993).
Jim Kitses, *Gun Crazy* (1996).
David Thomson, *The Big Sleep* (1997).
Kim Newman, *Cat People* (1999).
Simon Callow, *The Night of the Hunter* (2001).
Charles Barr, *Vertigo* (2002).
Ernest Lawson, *The Usual Suspects* (2002).
Rob White, *The Third Man* (2003).
Noah Isenberg, *Detour* (2008).
Amelie Hastie, *The Bigamist* (2009).
James Naremore, *Sweet Smell of Success* (2010).
Andrew Pulver, *Night and the City* (2010).
Melvyn Stokes, *Gilda* (2010).

Contributors

KRIN GABBARD is a professor of comparative literary and cultural studies at Stony Brook University. He is the author of *Jammin' at the Margins: Jazz and the American Cinema* (1996), *Black Magic: White Hollywood and African American Culture* (2004), and *Hotter than That: The Trumpet, Jazz, and American Culture* (2008). He is also the editor of *Representing Jazz* (1995) and *Jazz among the Discourses* (1995) and coeditor of *Screening Genders* (2008). His essays have appeared in numerous collections, including *Music and Cinema* (2000), *Soundtrack Available: Essays on Film and Popular Music* (2001), *Riffs and Choruses: A New Jazz Anthology* (2001), *The Cambridge Companion to Jazz* (2003), *Movie Music, The Film Reader* (2003), *Uptown Conversation: The New Jazz Studies* (2004), *Beyond the Soundtrack: Representing Music in Cinema* (2007), and *Thriving on a Riff: Jazz and Blues Influences in African American Literature and Film* (2009).

PHILIPPA GATES is a professor of film studies at Wilfrid Laurier University, Canada. She is the author of *Detecting Men: Masculinity and the Hollywood Detective Film* (2006) and *Detecting Women: Gender and the Hollywood Detective Film* (2011), as well as coeditor of *The Devil Himself: Villainy in Detective Fiction and Film* (2002) and *Transnational Asian Identities in Pan-Pacific Cinemas: The Reel Asian Exchange* (2011). Her articles on gender and crime films have appeared in *Framework,* the *Journal of Film and Video,* the *Journal of Popular Culture,* the *Journal of Popular Film and Television, Post Script,* and the *Quarterly Review of Film and Video.* She is also a frequent contributor to the online journal *Crimeculture* and the online database Crime Fiction Canada.

JULIE GROSSMAN is a professor in the Departments of English and Communication and Film Studies at Le Moyne College. She is coauthor of *A Due Voci: The Photography of Rita Hammond* (2003) and author of *Rethinking the Femme Fatale: Ready for Her Close-Up* (2012). Her essay on desire, domesticity, and the femme fatale appeared in *The Femme Fatale: Images, Histories, Contexts* (2010), and other work has been published in *Criticism, desistfilm, English Literary History, Henry James Review,* the *Journal of Popular Culture, La Furia Umana, Popular Culture Review,* the *Quarterly Review of Film and Video,* and the *Review of Communication.* She is presently writing a book on film adaptation and a monograph (with Therese Grisham) on the directing work of Ida Lupino.

ROBERT MIKLITSCH is a professor in the Department of English Language and Literature at Ohio University. His work on film and television has appeared in *Camera Obscura, Film Quarterly,* the *Journal of Film and Video,* the *Journal of Popular Film and Television, New Review of Film and Television Studies,* and *Screen.* His essays have appeared in numerous collections, including *Cultural Materialism* (1995), *Education and Cultural Studies* (1997), *Roland Barthes* (2003), *Traversing the Fantasy: Critical Essays on Slavoj Zizek* (2005), *Lowering the Boom* (2008), and *Neo-Noir* (2009). He is the editor of *Psycho-Marxism* (1998) and the author of *From Hegel to Madonna: Towards a General Economy of "Commodity Fetishism"* (1998), *Roll Over Adorno: Critical Theory, Popular Culture, Audiovisual Media* (2006), and *Siren City: Sound and Source Music in Classic American Noir* (2011). He is currently writing a book on film noir in the "atomic age."

ROBERT MURPHY is Emeritus Professor in Film Studies at De Montfort University, Leicester. He has contributed essays to a variety of collections, written several entries for the *Oxford Dictionary of National Biography,* and published articles in *Screen,* the *Journal of British Cinema and Television, Sight and Sound, Senses of Cinema, Film International,* and the *Historical Journal of Film, Radio and Television.* His books include *Realism and Tinsel: Cinema and Society in Britain 1939–49* (1989), *Sixties British Cinema* (1992), *Smash and Grab: Gangsters in the London Underworld 1920–60* (1993), *British Cinema and the Second World War* (2000), and, as editor, *British Cinema of the 90s* (2000), *Directors in British and Irish Cinema* (2006), *The British Cinema Book* (3rd ed., 2009), and *British Cinema* (2014). He is currently writing a book about British film noir and researching early British sound feature films.

MARK OSTEEN is a professor and Chair of the Department of English and Founding Director of Film Studies at Loyola University Maryland. He is the author of *The Economy of Ulysses: Making Both Ends Meet* (1995), *American*

Magic and Dread: Don DeLillo's Dialogue with Culture (2000), and *One of Us: A Family's Life with Autism* (2010). He is the editor of *White Noise* (1998), *The Question of the Gift* (2002), *Autism and Representation* (2008), and coeditor of *The New Economic Criticism* (1999) and *Music at the Crossroads* (2010). His articles have appeared in *Gender and Joyce* (1997), *Joycean Cultures/Culturing Joyce* (1998), *The Cambridge Companion to Don DeLillo* (2008), and *Modernism and Copyright* (2010). His essays on film have appeared in the *Journal of Film and Video,* the *Journal of Popular Film and Television, Literature/Film Quarterly,* and the *Quarterly Review of Film and Video.* His most recent book is *Nightmare Alley: Film Noir and the American Dream* (2013).

VIVIAN SOBCHACK is Professor Emerita in the Department of Film, Television, and Digital Media at the University of California, Los Angeles. She is the author of numerous books, including *Screening Space: The American Science Fiction Film* (1997 [1987]), *The Address of the Eye: A Phenomenology of Film Experience* (1992), and *Carnal Thoughts: Embodiment and Moving Image Culture* (2004), and editor of *The Persistence of History: Cinema, Television, and the Modern Event* (1996) and *Meta-Morphing: Visual Transformation and the Culture of Quick-Change* (2000). Her articles—in addition to the seminal essay, "'Lounge Time': Postwar Crises and the Chronotope of Film Noir" (*Refiguring American Film Genres* [1998])—have appeared in numerous collections, including *Screening Violence* (2000), *Reading Digital Culture* (2001), *Reality Squared* (2002), *Technological Visions* (2004), *Postphenomenology* (2006), *The Prosthetic Impulse* (2006), *Dynamics and Performativity of Imagination* (2009), *New Takes in Film-Philosophy* (2011), *Media Archaeology* (2011), *Releasing the Image* (2011), and *Carnal Aesthetics* (2013). She has also been a participant on numerous noir and gangster DVD documentaries, including *Double Indemnity* (2006) and *His Kind of Woman* (2006).

ANDREW SPICER is Professor of Cultural Production and Director of Research in the Faculty of Arts, Creative Industries, and Education at the University of the West of England. He is the author of *An Ambivalent Archetype: Masculinity, Performance, and the New Zealand Films of Bruno Lawrence* (2000), *Typical Men: The Representation of Masculinity in Popular British Cinema* (2001), *Film Noir* (2002), *Sydney Box* (2006), the *Historical Dictionary of Film Noir* (2010), and, with A. T. McKenna, *The Man Who Got Carter: Michael Klinger, Independent Production, and the British Film Industry, 1960–1980* (2013). He is editor of *The Lion That Lost Its Way* (2005), *European Film Noir* (2007), and, with Helen Hanson, *A Companion to Film Noir* (2013). His articles have appeared in numerous collections, including *British Crime Films* (1999), *The Trouble with Men* (2004), *The Unsilvered Screen* (2007), *Don't Look Now: British Cinema in the 1970s* (2009), *Analysing the Screenplay* (2010), and *Crime Cultures* (2010).

J. P. TELOTTE is a professor in the School of Literature, Media, and Communication at the Georgia Institute of Technology. He is the author of numerous books, including *Dreams of Darkness: Fantasy and the Films of Val Lewton* (1985), *Voices in the Dark: Narrative Patterns of Film Noir* (1989), *Replications* (1995), *A Distant Technology: Science Fiction Film and the Machine Age* (1999), *Science Fiction Film* (2001), *Disney TV* (2004), *The Mouse Machine* (2008), and *Animating Space: From Mickey to* Wall-E (2010). He is the editor of *The Cult Film Experience* (1991) and *The Essential Science Fiction Television Reader* (2008), and coeditor of *Science Fiction Film, Television, and Adaptation: Across the Screens* (2012). His essays have appeared in numerous collections, including *Full of Secrets: Critical Approaches to* Twin Peaks (1995), *Post-War Cinema and Modernity* (2001), *Dark Alleys of Noir* (2002), *Enfant Terrible! Jerry Lewis in American Film* (2002), *Dark Thoughts* (2003), *Nothing That Is* (2004), *The Essential Cult TV Reader* (2010), and *Westerns* (2012).

NEIL VERMA is Harper-Schmidt Fellow in the Society of Fellows in the Liberal Arts, affiliated with the Department of Cinema and Media Studies, and Collegiate Assistant Professor in the Humanities at the University of Chicago. He is the author of *Theater of the Mind: Imagination, Aesthetics, and American Radio Drama* (2012), which won the 2013 Best First Book Award from the Society for Cinema and Media Studies. He serves on the Advisory Board for *Sounding Out! The Sound Studies Blog,* and his work has appeared in the *Journal of American Studies.*

Index

Index

The University of Illinois Press
is a founding member of the
Association of American University Presses.

Composed in 10/13 Cantoria MT Std
with Proxima Nova Condensed display
by Lisa Connery
at the University of Illinois Press
Manufactured by Sheridan Books, Inc.

University of Illinois Press
1325 South Oak Street
Champaign, IL 61820–6903
www.press.uillinois.edu